The Contemporary Ensemble

Interviews with theatre-makers

Edited by
Duška Radosavljević

 Routledge
Taylor & Francis Group

LONDON AND NEW YORK

First published 2013
by Routledge
2 Park Square, Milton Park, Abingdon, Oxon OX14 4RN

Simultaneously published in the USA and Canada
by Routledge
711 Third Avenue, New York, NY 10017

*Routledge is an imprint of the Taylor & Francis Group, an informa
business*

© 2013 Duška Radosavljević

British Library Cataloguing in Publication Data A catalogue record
for this book is available from the British Library

Library of Congress Cataloguing in Publication Data
A catalog record for this book has been requested

ISBN: 978-0-415-53528-1 (hbk)
ISBN: 978-0-415-53530-4 (pbk)
ISBN: 978-0-203-11270-0 (ebk)

Typeset in Goudy
by Book Now Ltd, London

The Contemporary Ensemble

Inte

Questions of ensemble – what it is, how it works – are both inherent to a variety of Western theatre traditions, and re-emerging and evolving in striking new ways in the twenty-first century. *The Contemporary Ensemble* draws together an unprecedented range of original interviews with world-renowned theatre-makers in order to directly address both the former and latter concerns. Reflecting on 'the ensemble way of working' within this major new resource are figures including:

Michael Boyd, Yuri Butusov, Lyn Gardner, Elizabeth LeCompte, Phelim McDermott, Emma Rice, Adriano Shaplin, Max Stafford-Clark, and Hermann Wündrich;

representing companies including:

The Berliner Ensemble, Kneehigh Theatre, The Neo-Futurists, Ontroerend Goed, Out of Joint, The Riot Group, The RSC, The Satirikon Theatre, Shadow Casters, Song of the Goat, and The Wooster Group.

All twenty-two interviews were conducted especially for the collection, and draw upon the author's rich background working as scholar, educator and dramaturg with a variety of ensembles. The resulting compendium radically re-situates the ensemble in the context of globalisation, higher education and simplistic understandings of 'text-based' and 'devised' theatre practice, and traces a compelling new line through the contemporary theatre landscape.

Duška Radosavljević is a Lecturer in Drama and Theatre Studies at the University of Kent, UK. She has previously worked as the Dramaturg at Northern Stage, education practitioner at the Royal Shakespeare Company and theatre critic for *The Stage* newspaper.

Contents

Acknowledgements

My thanks are due to all the individuals who agreed to be interviewed for this project and to their various collaborators and assistants who helped to set up the meetings and, in some cases, proof the transcripts. In addition to the interviewees, I'd like to thank Charlotte Bond (Kneehigh), Jane Tassell (RSC), Barney Norris and Stella Feehly (Out of Joint), Jason Gray Platt (The Wooster Group), Anastasia Razumovskaya and Polina Zhezhenova (MHAT School), the Edinburgh International Festival Press Office and the Interferences International Theatre Festival Cluj; David Barnett (University of Sussex) for facilitating contact with the Berliner Ensemble, and John Britton (Duende) for making me part of his own ensemble project; Anastasia Razumovskaya and Martin Schnabl for their help with translation, as well as to Thomas Colley for his transcription services. Special thanks to Dr George Rodosthenous for all his support in many different ways, as well as Professor Paul Allain, Dr Bryce Lease and Miloš Jakovljević for close reading and editorial suggestions on selected sections of the book. My work has also benefited from Nick Awde's eagle eye whose own project *Solo Show: The Creation of the One-Person Play in British Theatre* (London: Desert Hearts, 2013) is a cousin of this book through the Edinburgh family line.

Due to various circumstances, some of the interviews did not take place or just never made it to the final draft of the book, but I am grateful to Joseph Alford (Theatre O), Anne Bogart (SITI Theatre), Erica Daniels and Paul Miller (Steppenwolf Theatre Company), Lin Hixon (ex-Goat Island; Every House Has a Door), movement director Natalia Fedorova (ex-MHAT), writer and actor Tim Crouch and producer Michael Redington for their time, preliminary discussions and correspondence on the subject.

I was very lucky to have been able to gain access to various performances discussed in this volume with thanks to: Phelim McDermott for a memorable evening at the Metropolitan Opera House; Gabor Tompa for inviting me to the Interferences Festival Cluj 2010; Patrice Pavis for letting me have his ticket to Shadow Casters' sold out performance of *Vacation from History*; Jonathan Meth and members of The Fence for introducing me to various wonders of European theatre; Paul Miller for a ticket to *The March* at Steppenwolf; Ivona Ataljević and her family for their hospitality in Chicago; Suzanne Worthington for countless discounted RSC tickets, cups of tea and inspiring conversations; David Bauwens for ensuring entry into various Ontorerend Goed performances; Rachel Chavkin (TEAM), Adriano Shaplin and Dan Rothenberg for letting me see recordings of their work; the Edinburgh International Festival Press Office and The Fringe Press Office for their help; and to *The Stage* newspaper for the privilege of bearing its press accreditation.

Special thanks to the editors of the *Journal of Adaptation in Film and Performance* Katja Krebs and Richard Hand for their support and collaboration in publishing some of this research and allowing me to reprint the interview with Emma Rice.

I owe the initial inspiration for this book to Alan Lyddiard and Michael Boyd, both of whose respective ensemble ways of working are in their own ways always coupled with extraordinary humanity and generosity of spirit. In addition, I would like to thank my colleagues at *The Stage* and the University of Kent for insightful exchanges over the years. Many thanks to Talia Rodgers for her enthusiasm and suggestions, for the editorial support of her team at Routledge and of Richard Cook at Book Now. The Routledge readers' reports from Gareth White, Jackie Smart, Sara Jane Bailes, Jane Goodall, David Roesner and Kate Craddock have been particularly helpful in the development of this project and I am grateful to them too.

Elements of this work have been supported by research funding at the University of Kent, Professor Paul Allain's Leverhulme-funded 'Tradition and Innovation: Britain/Russia Training for Performance' project, and, crucially, by an AHRC Fellowship, for which I am also indebted to various anonymous readers and panellists whose enthusiasm has made this possible.

Finally thank you to the ensemble of all my close friends and relatives, and especially to 'the Dragons', without whom, I wouldn't even be here.

Postscript

As this book goes into print, two of its chapters have also been made available in audio-visual form in the Routledge Performance Archive (RPA): an audio recording of the interview with Mike Alfreds and a video recording of the interview with Adriano Shaplin. Please see www.routledgeperformancearchive.com for more information.

Preface

It may seem inappropriate for a book about ensembles to open with a personal statement about the editor's singular aims and her particular circumstances that lead her into this research. However, I feel compelled to outline how this book has emerged from very real problems, ideas and challenges I have encountered in my interactions with various theatre-makers, critics, teachers and students of theatre, ever since my own student days in the UK in the mid-1990s.

Of partial significance here is my own cultural background as a person who was brought up in a collectivist atmosphere of a former socialist country – Yugoslavia – a place that was, thanks to its liberal form of socialism during the Cold War, often defined as 'the best of both worlds'. The *Cambridge Guide to World Theatre* (Cambridge University Press, 1988, p. 1093) pointed out the significance of the Belgrade International Theatre Festival (BITEF) 'which has since 1967 featured the most important avant-garde works from all over the world'. Nevertheless, the country's own theatre production carried an emphasis on the so-called 'dramatic theatre' and was heavily influenced by the German and Russian repertory theatre models which customarily included resident ensembles.

My first degree in Theatre Studies at the University of Huddersfield featured a healthy mix of Grotowski-influenced physical theatre, performance studies, drama and theatre history without an explicit acknowledgement of any tensions that might have historically existed between various paradigms of the study of theatre and performance, thus indicating that by the mid-1990s those battles might have been laid to rest, ushering in a more layered understanding of the field, whatever its name might be. As an example of this, I recall that in our first year we were taken to see Forced Entertainment, Trestle Theatre, the Wrestling School and the multi-award winning TV actor Warren Mitchell as King Lear, as part of one and the same course.

Changes were afoot within the theatre sector itself. By the time I joined *The Stage* newspaper's Edinburgh Reviewing team in 1998, a new category of the annual Acting Excellence Awards was being added to the already-existing Best Actor and Best Actress – the Best Ensemble Award. Incidentally, Howard Goorney of the Theatre Workshop was one of the members of the Stage Awards judging panel in those years. Since 1998, nominees in this category have included Steven Berkoff's East Productions, Grid Iron, Trestle Theatre, Kaos, Theatre O, the Riot Group, but also more recently Traverse Theatre, National Theatre of Scotland, Song of the Goat and Ontroerend Goed – indicating an increasingly diversified understanding of the term 'ensemble'. Our award-judging discussions in this category have often revolved around two questions: 'Are all of the individual performances in the ensemble of award-winning quality?' and 'To what extent is the whole greater than the sum of its parts?'. As it happens, I have been dealing with these and a number of other questions concerning ensemble throughout most of the rest of my career.

From 2002 to 2005 I was employed as the Dramaturg at Northern Stage in Newcastle-upon-Tyne which, under the leadership of Alan Lyddiard, had been trying desperately to survive as a regional ensemble company ever since 1998. A lot of my time and energy was invested in promoting the values of the ensemble way of working, without always fully understanding the odds which were stacked against it and just how out of place – culturally and locally – this mode of working had been. It was the Equity and the Directors' Guild of Great Britain (DGGB) Conference on Ensemble Theatre at the Barbican on 24 November 2004 that opened my eyes to this. In a characteristically inspiring keynote speech, Michael Boyd, the then newly appointed Artistic Director of the Royal Shakespeare Company, outlined his vision for the company as an ensemble. This proved to be enough to lure me into the RSC, when Alan Lyddiard abruptly resigned from his position at the helm of Northern Stage in January 2005. For a year – which also saw a year-long Complete Works Festival – I had an opportunity to witness from the inside the complexities associated with imbuing a world-renowned national institution with the spirit of togetherness, experimentation and community.

Having finally returned to academia, I find myself asking these questions: What is meant by the 'ensemble way of working' in the twenty-first century? What advantages and problems are entailed therein? How does the contemporary ensemble fit with the heritage of the twentieth century, and how does it proceed forward?

Both as a practitioner and researcher, I am interested in how the ensemble way of working alters the theatre-making process by comparison to the process that exists between a number of otherwise-assembled freelance artists working on a project for five to eight weeks – including the run – and then going their separate ways. In addition, as a pedagogue,

I am confronted with an increasing trend of groups of young people graduating from drama and theatre courses together and going on to become successful ensemble companies, rather than seeking out individual careers. This requires recognition in terms of how we work as educators, but also in terms of how it has changed and continues to change the current theatre landscape.

Following the end of Michael Boyd's artistic directorship of the RSC in 2012, this book may come out in the aftermath of one significant ensemble project in the UK. However, I hope that this collection, featuring an ensemble of distinct international voices testifying to the virtues of collaborative ways of working, will continue to inspire new similar ventures. It is therefore dedicated to the ensembles of the future.

Duška Radosavljević
Canterbury, April 2012

Introduction

I also get very upset when I see a production where the only pulse beating is that of the director, whereas the other thirty people who are on the stage may also have a beating pulse, and these pulses united are not just thirty pulses, they are much, much more. It's like the notion of critical mass in physics, where this mass comes to a certain point and there is an explosion.

(Lev Dodin in Delgado and Heritage 1996: 74)

You can't push everyone to be, you know, magnesium sulphate. There will never be two of the same element – so the fusion is unique. [...] Sometimes you get explosions!

(Lloyd Newson in Tushingham 1994:51)

On face value, one may struggle to find much aesthetic common ground between the London-based dance theatre company DV8 and the Maly Theatre from St Petersburg, renowned for its meticulous renditions of famous literary classics. The way that their respective leaders, Lloyd Newson and Lev Dodin, both serendipitously resort to the scientific analogy of an increase and sudden release of considerable energy is, however, indicative of a commitment that each of those directors has to a particular way of working – namely, a group of individuals working together. Although these two companies are sadly not featured in this collection, their underlying ethos is – as well as the wide-reaching capacity of the term 'ensemble', illustrated by the synergy provided between the two quotes above.

Part of the purpose of this introduction is to engage with a definition of terms, their historical development, and the choice of vocabulary for this particular volume. It is worth briefly foregrounding here the online Oxford Dictionary's designation of the term 'ensemble' as originating from the Middle English adverb (via French and Latin) meaning 'at the same time'. The adverbial aspect of this usage emphasises a process rather than a fixed state, making it particularly applicable in the context of theatre-making. In addition, the primary meaning of the noun 'ensemble' as we use it today – to mean 'a group of musicians, actors or dancers who perform together' – is augmented by a more conceptual use: 'a group of items viewed as a whole, rather than individually'.[1] As suggested by Dodin above, advocates of the ensemble way of working very often emphasise the notion of the whole being greater than the sum of its parts.

The following discussion is therefore intended to contextualise the collection of interviews presented in the volume in four specific ways. First, it will provide some historical and theoretical frameworks within which to begin engaging with potential taxonomies, methodologies and types of ensembles. This will serve to raise particular questions and problems that the concluding analysis of the empirical research will seek to address to some extent, while also framing the enclosed interviews. Second, it will define the key terms chosen for the title of this book: 'contemporary', 'ensemble' and 'theatre-maker'. Further it will explain the criteria for selection of the subjects of these interviews, the resulting formats of the conversations, and the overarching organisational principles of their layout. Wishing to leave enough space for the reader's own conclusions, the final section will tease out some preliminary areas of insight gained through the field research, in response to the initial questions raised concerning the definition of the ensemble way of working in the twenty-first century.

Histories, issues and taxonomies

Combing through histories of Western theatre, one might come across the use of the term 'ensemble' in relation to theatre only as late as the nineteenth century, and specifically the Meiningen Ensemble. Having toured Europe extensively between 1874 and 1890, the Meiningen Ensemble is often hailed as a precursor to and an influence on both André Antoine's Théâtre Libre (1887–1896) and Konstantin Stanislavsky's Moscow Art Theatre (1897 to present). Prior to the nineteenth century, groups of actors working together are often referred to as companies (e.g. King's Men) or troupes (e.g. commedia dell' arte). The semantic choice of denominators by various writers is probably unconscious, but this is what Michael Booth highlights as the distinguishing characteristic of the Duke Saxe-Meiningen's aesthetic approach:

> Georg laid great stress on ensemble; he was opposed to the star system and required leading actors in one production to take minor roles and even walk on in another, if necessary. Lengthy rehearsal periods also

ensured perfection of the crowd scenes, which much impressed
European reviewers and theatre people.

(Booth 1997: 336)

The use of the term ensemble in this context seems to imply a lack of the
hierarchy that is perhaps inherent to acting companies led by actor managers in the nineteenth century and the allocation of roles on the basis of
seniority. Thus the organising structure of the ensemble implies that the
actor's contribution is closer to that of a musician – which is also where
the term ensemble is found more frequently.

In addition to the principle of equal attention being extended to all
minor parts in a play or towards individuals within crowd scenes, as illustrated by the Meiningen Ensemble, Stanislavsky's embracing of the
ensemble way of working is also understood to be linked to his interest
in training as an indispensable part of the actor's life in theatre. In
Chapter 10 of *An Actor Prepares*, for example, Stanislavsky outlines the
importance of 'communion' between actors, or 'a sincere effort to
exchange living human feelings with [each] other' (Stanislavski 2006
[1937]: 205). Stanislavsky's contemporary, the director Theodore
Komisarjevsky, described the achievement of this kind of quality in performance as ground-breaking, and in Magarshack's quotation below, the
term 'ensemble' – which thus acquires another level of meaning – is used
to denote it:

It is the method of the formulation of an inner ensemble, based on
inner communication, that was Stanislavsky's greatest discovery, and
in the Moscow Art Theatre we saw and felt such an ensemble for the
first time.

(Komisarjevsky quoted in Magarshack 1973 [1950]: 84)

Simon Shepherd traces the first calls for ensemble in Britain back to 1904
and the early plans for the National Theatre which would 'establish a
company of performers for at least three years' (Shepherd 2009: 65).
Proponents of this project over the next 60 years, and those in Britain
who believed in the art rather than the business model of theatre which
had dominated the British stage in the nineteenth century,[2] repeatedly
looked to Europe for inspiration and for evidence to support their arguments for greater subsidy. Of particular impact was the visit in 1935 of
Michel Saint-Denis with his Compagnie des Quinze, which Gielgud
described as one of 'the most perfect examples of teamwork ever presented
in London' (in Shepherd 2009: 68). This subsequently led to Saint-Denis'
ensemble-oriented pedagogical experiments in London with George

Devine through the London Theatre Studio in the 1930s and Bristol Old Vic after World War Two.

Meanwhile in New York, in his account of the formation in 1931 of the Group Theatre collective, Harold Clurman describes a situation that may not have been dissimilar to the one that took place in Moscow in 1897, when Nemirovich-Danchenko and Konstantin Stanislavsky founded the Moscow Art Theatre. Two men, Clurman and Lee Strasberg – later joined by the producer Cheryl Crawford – with distinct but compatible sets of skills and a shared passion for raising quality standards, arrived at a decisive conclusion: continued collaboration and growth of a group of artists together, relieved of the pressures of the market economy, was a required necessity. Having produced such artists as Elia Kazan, Stella Adler, Clifford Odets, Sanford Meisner and Morris Carnovsky, the Group Theatre could be seen to have eventually contributed more to the film industry than to the reinvention of the American theatre scene. The reasons for the limited influence of its collective model of working on other theatre artists in the United States before the 1960s might be sought in the nature of US arts funding, and historical factors including World War Two and, later, Senator McCarthy's anti-communism. However, by the 1960s, this had changed radically, with the growing prominence of experimental companies such as the Living Theatre (which had started in 1947), the Open Theatre and the Performance Group.

The term 'ensemble' as a mode of theatre-making probably began to catch on in the English-speaking world as a result of another influential guest appearance in London – that of the Berliner Ensemble in 1956. According to Michael Billington, this event was one of the two in the 'pivotal year' (Billington 2007: 93) that had a long-term effect on British Theatre as a whole.[3] The other was the opening of the English Stage Company at the Royal Court with the premiere of *Look Back in Anger* by John Osborne. Its founder, George Devine, and the founder of the Royal Shakespeare Company, Peter Hall, did fall under the spell of Brecht's company, but they were not the only ones. Joan Littlewood, aligned with Brecht ideologically as well as aesthetically, was the first in England to actually direct and star in a professional production of Brecht's play *Mother Courage*, also in 1956.

Littlewood is another name often invoked in relation to the ensemble way of working, particularly in the British context. According to Nadine Holdsworth, throughout her career, which spanned 1945–1975, Littlewood 'maintained faith in the centrality of a permanent creative ensemble, the "composite mind" engaged in a cooperative sharing of ideas, skills and creativity' (Holdsworth 2006: 49). This was rooted in Littlewood's working class allegiances, her interest in agit-prop before World War Two, and active engagement with popular forms of entertainment as well as the classics. Holdsworth highlights the problem of the evolving 'cult of Joan' (2006: 24) which ensued with her growing success in the mid-to-late 1950s. In addition, in 1955, her life partner and Theatre Workshop member Gerry Raffles got enough money to acquire their base, the Theatre Royal Stratford East, which shifted the organisational structure from a collective of equal individuals to an entity with a defined leadership – Raffles as business manager and Littlewood as an artistic director who made repertoire-related decisions.

This notion of a prominent leader being associated with an ensemble was by no means exclusive to Theatre Workshop as a company. In fact, it is a story that repeats case after case throughout the twentieth century: Jerzy Grotowski's Teatr Laboratorium, Ariane Mnouchkine's Théâtre du Soleil, Eugenio Barba's Odin Teatret, Richard Schechner's Performance Group, Max Stafford-Clark's Joint Stock, Anne Bogart's SITI Company.[4] In contrast to this, however, various directors have been eager to acknowledge their ensemble members as co-authors. In an unpublished handout in English, believed to have been distributed during the Theatre Laboratorium's visit to New York in 1969, Jerzy Grotowski stated:

> Without in any way wishing to give an impression of mock modesty, I must stress that in the end I am not **the** author of our productions, or at any rate, not the only one. I am not somebody who has devised the whole show by himself, set up all the roles in advance, planned the décor, arranged the lighting and designed the costumes. "Grotowski" is not a one-man band. [...] My name is, in fact, only there as a symbol of a group and its work in which are fused all the efforts of my associates. And these efforts are not a matter of collaboration pure and simple: they amount to **creation**.
>
> (Grotowski n.d., original emphasis)[5]

In the Delgado and Rebellato's 2010 volume on *Contemporary European Theatre Directors*, both Stephen Knapper and Lourdes Orozco seem to identify a move from collective creation to director-led decision making as a more recent development. Orozco provides the example of La Carnicería Teatro, which even got renamed to include the director's name, and thus became 'the more hierarchical La Carnicería-Rodrigo Garcia' (in Delgado and Rebellato 2010: 309). Interestingly, both Knapper and Orozco cite Complicite as an example of a similar move from collectivity towards a singular directorial leadership,[6] even though Helen Freshwater has highlighted Complicite's ongoing self-professed emphasis on collaboration as an essential working methodology (in Holdsworth and Luckhurst 2008: 177). Prompted by Grotowski's quote above, and in the context of this research project, one might also do well to ask: What is the difference between 'collaboration pure and simple' and collective creation?

As this section is intended to raise questions and frame the issues that will be addressed later on the basis of empirical research, it is also worth adding some nuance to the problem already mentioned of ensemble leadership. Despite Orozco's observation of 'a shift towards director-led theatre at the expense of collective creative structures' (Orozco 2010: 309), there is ample historical evidence that a dominant leader has often been associated with ensemble, especially if training and group development formed part of the picture.

In *Environmental Theater*, Richard Schechner (1994 [1973]) rather openly shares his experience of dealing with the power struggles within the Performance Group just at the time when the group outwardly seemed to be at its peak. He notes that *Dionysus in 69* gave an impression of group cohesion which was extremely attractive to the audience but at the same time entirely unrepresentative of the company's inner dynamics. Even though Schechner confesses that his motives in forming the group with his students were rooted in a desire to create a sense of community and a kind of 'family' (1994 [1973]: 255), he observes that the life of the group took its own course, turning him from a loved guru to a figure of hate. This was apparently a common feature of organised groups according to Philip Slater's 1966 classic on group psychology, *Microcosm*, cited by Schechner in his discussion. Eventually, Schechner observes the importance of delegating power, noting that Stanislavsky had avoided a loss of authority by forming studio theatres and appointing his students to run them (1994 [1973]: 284).

'Should groups break up every few years so that routinization does not encase them in their own discoveries?' (1994 [1973]: 283) asks the closing section of Schechner's analysis. Interestingly, psychologist Bruce Tuckman (1965) found that certain patterns in group dynamics do exist, and his more reassuring model – amended in 1977 and still used by social psychologists today – features a sequence of five stages:

1   Forming – a group comes together around a common goal.
2   Storming – conflicts and disagreements arise.
3   Norming – the group resolves conflicts and arrives at shared norms and standards of behaviour.
4   Performing – the group effectively pursues its goal.
5   Adjourning – following the completion of the task, group members loosen their ties to each other until the next task.[7]

It is clearly the stage of 'storming' that highlights the issues of inner politics of the group and potentially produces a leader in the 'norming' stage. This model applies well to theatre groups as it follows the natural rhythm of creating, performing and temporarily adjourning activity; however, it can also be applied to an overview of a company's lifespan, potentially accounting for phases of initial success followed by a 'storming' period involving funding issues or pressures entailed in the individual members' work-life balance. The sequence is cyclical, regularly returning to the 'storming stage'.

There is another pertinent similarity to be observed between many – though not all – of the ensembles mentioned above. The initial stages of the ensembles formed by Stanislavsky, Schechner, Mnouchkine, Littlewood and Barba were all marked by a transition from 'amateurism' (Schechner 1994 [1973]: 257; Singleton on Mnouchkine in Delgado and Rebellato 2010: 31) to professionalism. The early dependence on the leader and the subsequent desire for emancipation would arguably be greater in such cases than in cases where ensemble members come together as more equal partners. This and other distinctions might provide us with possibilities for looking at nuances of the relationship between the leader and the ensemble, but also at the ways in which pedagogical practices in and around ensemble have changed by the twenty-first century. It may be interesting to add here that Mermikides and Smart have more recently identified a model of ensemble in the UK comprised of a core group of two people as a means of achieving collaboration, resisting directorial authority and dealing with economic pressures (Mermikides and Smart 2010: 16–17). This represents more a model of ensemble leadership than a model of ensemble company per se, but not surprisingly the model is represented in this collection too.

Although the ensemble way of working can be encountered in various cultural contexts, it will be subject to specific differences associated with distinct political histories, cultural attitudes towards the arts and mechanisms of arts funding, or even cultural propensity for collaborative ways of working. Cultural psychologist Harry Triandis has even proposed an empirical set of criteria by which to measure cultural predisposition for group behaviour, for example.[8] More significantly, in the second half of the twentieth century, an important differentiating factor existed between the Eastern and the Western European countries due to their respective political-economic systems of organisation. Despite its many faults, the communist East was graced with generous arts funding which made it a norm for theatres to employ permanent resident ensembles and enjoy long rehearsal periods – a luxury which many theatre artists in Eastern Europe find difficult to relinquish today. On the other hand, from a British perspective where a standard rehearsal period is five weeks, most of European theatre is seen as heavily subsidised, in fact. Lichtenfels and Hunter provide an interesting estimate that 'the cities of Munich and Hamburg each give more to their civic arts programmes than the Arts Council gives to the whole of theatre in England' (in Delgado and Svich 2002: 43). In the early twenty-first century process of globalisation, one might ask what implications does this have on any attempts at cross-cultural ensembles?

In trying to understand the nature of internal relations within an ensemble, it also is important to acknowledge the existence of a number of types of ensemble, which have emerged not simply as a result of training, but as a result of funding and employment structures (Northern Stage, Dundee Rep, RSC and many Continental European ensembles) or shared political or aesthetic values (Welfare State International, Kneehigh, The Neo-Futurists, Forced Entertainment).

Additionally, in her analysis of Forced Entertainment's creative methodology, Alex Mermikides distinguishes between the 'system model' and the 'ensemble model' of collective theatre-making whereby the former refers to companies working together under the banner of a particular methodology as opposed to the latter model where the ensemble is assembled around a charismatic leader (in Harvie and Lavender 2010: 106). Although I admire this incisive classification, I would query the applied terminology, opting for a broader understanding of the term 'ensemble', as this volume will testify. Nevertheless, Mermikides's proposition makes a very helpful contribution to the discussion of ensemble leadership by distinguishing between the post-war type of 'director' and the role that Tim Etchells assumed within Forced Entertainment. The key departure taken by the company is a rejection of the Romantic idea of an artist having total control over the artwork – an attitude held by the 'post-war director'. The company therefore disassociated itself from 'calculated intentionality, individual authorship and the display of artistic virtuosity – trappings of cultural elitism and hierarchy' (2010: 105). However:

> At the same time, recognition of the power of the individual director's vision in creating innovative theatre, as well as the practical advantages of leadership in making both administrative and creative decisions, ensure that the *auteur*-director never really goes away.
>
> (Harvie and Lavender 2010: 105)

In other words, it is indeed possible for a director within an ensemble to choose to be a benevolent or a non-authoritative presence, rather than conforming to previously-held preconceptions representing a threat to the creative and political life of the group. Effectively, Mermikides's analysis points to another issue which underlies this volume – the issue of authority and the changing attitudes of contemporary theatre-makers towards it.

Finally, before proceeding with a definition of key terms deployed by this book, it is useful to conclude the historical overview by considering Simon Shepherd's taxonomy of group organisation in British theatre, arranged in a vaguely chronological order by the time of their emergence: repertory, ensemble, collective and collaboration. Shepherd associates repertory theatres with the first half of the twentieth century in Britain, seeing them as a step between the Victorian entrepreneurial model of theatre-making and an artistic ensemble, and highlights their key value as being a greater empowerment for the actors and their increased connection with the community. Ensembles are understood by reference to the continental influences described above and seen as emerging mid-twentieth century. Shepherd cites an interesting example of Joint Stock under Max Stafford-Clark starting off as an ensemble but in the course of the rehearsals of David Hare's highly political piece *Fanshen* in 1974 arriving at a crossroads between an ensemble and a collective. The distinction between the two is drawn on the basis of how the principles of political organisation and aesthetic effect are prioritised in relation to each other, with the latter prioritising political over the artistic concerns.[9]

In the aftermath of 1968 in Europe, the notion of political organisation of artists was clearly becoming paramount, and this is illustrated by the example of Mnouchkine's work in France (Singleton 2010), as well as the rise of fringe companies following the end of theatre censorship in Britain. Sandy Craig credits this particular year with the emergence of what he calls 'alternative theatre' in Britain, encompassing political theatre, community theatre, theatre-in-education, performance art and companies presenting plays with a different agenda from the mainstream literary theatre (Craig 1980: 20). From this temporal distance, one has to recognise that such developments, including the formation of an increasing number of collectives at the time, were clearly linked to their political context of Great Britain during the Cold War, and often motivated by a strong left wing ideology which, although it was losing popular support (paving the way for Margaret Thatcher's victory in 1979), had found fertile ground among the artists. This resulted in significant and highly influential examples of collectives defined by their socialist (Red Ladder), gender (Monstrous Regiment) or sexual (Gay Sweatshop) politics.

The 1970s are marked not only by the proliferation of fringe companies and collectives, but also by the emergence of a new theatre-making process. According to Jen Harvie (2005), through the abolition of the Lord Chamberlain, British theatre was no longer bound by the notion of a pre-written text.[10] This process which gives the ensemble members an authorship role in the making of a piece has variously been referred to as: improvisation (in the Stanislavskian tradition); authorial work ('autor-skirad RAD', 'autorsko divadlo' in East European contexts where fine art or scenography exerted greater influence than dramatic text on theatre-makers); collective creation (in the French context); workshopping (by Joan Littlewood); creative collaboration (in the US); and devising (more broadly in the UK).

The term 'devising' appears to have entered the theatre-making vocabulary in the UK via the very specific practice of theatre-in-education (TIE), which often involved groups of artists devising educational 'programmes' rather than solely 'plays'. The term emerged between the inception of the Belgrade Theatre Coventry in 1964 (as an institution which pioneered TIE work) and 1980 when the first written record of it appeared in Dave Pammenter's contribution to Tony Jackson's book on TIE *Learning Through Theatre*. Nevertheless, 'devising' has since grown to become synonymous with an entire field of non-dramatic theatre and performance in the UK, and progressively in the rest of the English-speaking world.[11]

It is interesting that Shepherd recognises a fourth type of a theatre-making group of artists which he denotes using the American term 'collaboration', but under which he clearly refers to a type of collective which has left its political drives behind in the interest of art, interdisciplinarity and public engagement. This type of ensemble is popularly associated with devising as a methodology; however, Shepherd's choice of term appears to be determined also by the Arts Council's emphasis on 'collaboration' as a desired quality of fundable work at the turn of the twenty-first century.[12] 'Collaboration', he concludes, 'slides from being an organizational issue into being a funding category' (Shepherd 2009: 79), thus polarising even further away from the notion of collective 'creation'.

However, the attempt at a departure from the term 'devising' may well be wise, not least because of the fact that its apparent inflation in the UK has led to a number of misconceptions. First, its implied binary opposition to text-based theatre tends to create confusion in Continental Europe, as work on any pre-written text in many European mainstream theatres customarily involves a collective and an improvisational approach in the process of rehearsal. Attending Eugenio Barba's 2005 International School of Theatre Anthropology in Wroclaw on the topic of Improvisation, I was repeatedly struck by the amount of devising we were involved in under the name of 'improvisation'; my Anglo-Saxon understanding of the term 'improvisation' had led me to anticipate a focus on 'extemporaneous performance'. More importantly for this project, the overuse of the term in the British context has also led to a conflation of the terms 'devising' and 'ensemble', where it is implied that ensembles typically devise and only exceptionally work with plays and playwrights. I am keen to redress this balance as part of this project, and to recognise the increasing and undeniably healthy interplay between actors and writers in the contemporary ensemble (e.g. Frantic Assembly, Kneehigh, The Riot Group, Third Angel).

Definitions of key terms

The historical overview above has highlighted potential uses of the term 'ensemble' as applying to an anti-hierarchical – art rather than business-oriented – model of working which emphasises inner interconnectedness between individual members and is often characterised by a commitment to training. The 'ensemble', as suggested by Shepherd (2009), could be specifically perceived as being the result of a mid-twentieth century Continental European influence which was outgrown in the UK by 'devising' collectives in the 1970s, and counterpointed in the US by groups engaged in 'creative collaboration'. Different conceptions and manifestations of the ensemble way of working in different cultural contexts must therefore be understood in relation to their own specific genealogies, if meaningful cross-cultural collaboration is to take place in an increasingly globalised world. The twenty-first century ensemble takes into consideration different funding structures, different attitudes to tradition and innovation, changing conceptions of leadership and authority, and varying artistic vocabularies.

More specifically, the understanding of the term 'ensemble' in this volume is culturally broad enough to include manifestations of collective theatre-making that comply with and depart from notions of twentieth century divisions of labour (actors, directors, playwrights, designers, composers); various models of organisation (from state-funded residential ensembles to peripatetic associations of like-minded individuals, to abstracted notions of ensemble in the absence of continuous funding); and various models of artistic practice (text-based, movement-based, inter-disciplinary, conceptually-driven). The main criterion is that the subjects represented here are speaking not only on behalf of themselves as individuals, but on behalf of an artistic entity which depends upon the contribution of other – often long-term – collaborators as constituent parts of that entity.

'The ensemble way of working' is understood to represent a work ethos which is collective, creative and collaborative – whether by means of individual members making the same kind of contribution (devising) or making distinct kinds of contribution towards the same artistic outcome (writing, directing, composing, designing, performing). Both devising and playwriting are therefore understood as potentially ensemble-based activities. This book may even go as far as to suggest that the ensemble way of working is a default methodology for theatre-making as it is discernable even among practitioners who do not work under the banner of an ensemble, such as director Katie Mitchell, but may work with the same individuals repeatedly.[13]

This may also be true of individuals, such as the director Mike Alfreds, whose work is contingent on an ensemble methodology and on audience participation in the creation of meaning, as he will reveal in his interview. These examples may well raise the question of the economic context within which this kind of work is being made. As will be pointed out by Michael Boyd, the notion of 'the ensemble way of working' and the inherently collaborative nature of theatre-making is in practice more difficult to achieve in a free market economy than it is in the heavily subsidised context of a Central European country in which it is simply standard practice.

The term 'contemporary' is used to disassociate the notion of 'ensemble' from any previously held conceptions of either the political or the aesthetic nature of the ensembles represented here. In most cases, the featured ensembles are still active, and if they are not, they have been chosen for inclusion because of the ways in which they have been ahead of their time and have precipitated changes that we are witnessing today in relation to theatre authorship and its relationship with the audience. The contemporary – early twenty-first century – ensemble is often characterised by shared authority, multi-ethnicity, cultural mobility, multilingualism, inter-disciplinarity and a broad understanding of theatre and performance. The contemporary ensemble deploys collaboration as a strategy, not for purely political or pragmatic reasons, but as an indication of a system of artistic values.

And finally a word about 'theatre-making' – a term which is increasingly gaining currency in the twenty-first century. In 2010, in the process of writing a case study of Alan Lyddiard's Northern Stage (1998–2005) and its debt to Lev Dodin for Jonathan Pitches' volume *Russians in Britain*, I interviewed the Guardian critic Lyn Gardner, a one-time advocate of Lyddiard's work. Talking more broadly about ensemble work during this interview, Gardner made a useful and inspiring distinction between actors and 'theatre-makers' in British theatre. The implication seemed to be that – contrary to the drama school graduates, customarily bound by the strategising of their agents – the latter type of performer would be associated with devised work and the kind of organic ensembles that have emerged from universities. Interestingly, the term is also deployed by Harvie and Lavender in their 2010 volume on international theatre-making processes, where in the summation of the project as a whole, it is closely linked to the notion of postdramatic theatre practices.[14] Needless to say, the book encompasses theatre-makers who work both with playtexts and the creative methodologies that might be called 'devising'. These theatre-makers are also not simply directors, actors, designers or writers, but often combine a number of different kinds of labour into one role. My recourse to the term 'theatre-making' is intended to register a certain change of climate. Even when live art is brought into this book's frame of reference, it is with the understanding that its use is integrated within a working process that is ultimately theatre-based – and my understanding of this is that it presupposes the presence of an audience in a singular time and space (however complex this notion might have become in a mediatised society) and an act of communi(cati)on with them. This is by no means intended to discredit the efforts of live and performance artists, but on the contrary to acknowledge their achievement in bringing theatre back in touch with its heritage of live performance and visual art in those contexts where literary standards might have predominated.

There are no catchphrases – the terms used here are existing terms being imbued with new meanings through changing times. The ambition of this book is therefore not to radically break with the past, but to observe the possibility that theatre may change organically, leaving behind some of its old concerns – such as psychological realism, particular divisions of labour, notions of professionalism and amateurism, forms of authorship and authority, political and ideological drives, aesthetic preferences, established relationships with the audience. Its ability to move with and reflect the changing times is precisely its defining characteristic, and this book is an attempt to keep a finger on the pulse of the time.

Selection criteria

Being a compilation of primary research, this volume provides an opportunity for many of the previously unheard voices to share information about their practice and their way of working. The questions posed to them are often open questions, driven by a genuine curiosity, and by a desire to connect with and understand my interlocutors. A reader might feel that there are potential issues emerging within some of the interviews that are not made sufficiently explicit through questioning, or that certain questions are evaded. As an interviewer, I found it important to ensure the interviewees' trust by avoiding undue confrontation or challenging issues. Prior to publication, all of the interviews were sent to the interviewees for comments, in the process of which some were edited. Most of them have also been slightly condensed by me in order to sharpen the focus on the issues under examination. The kind of material made available here should certainly be open to the reader's interpretation and critical analysis, rather than forming any kind of gospel truth. As a means of summarising my findings, I offer a brief overview at the end of this chapter. Some of these findings will have subsequently informed an examination of the modes of authorship in contemporary theatre – and specifically the interplay between text and performance – in a separate book project entitled *Theatre-Making* (Palgrave 2013), which partly explores the thesis that the ensemble way of working has effected notable changes in this domain.

As implied above, one of the main criteria in selecting subjects for this volume has been inclusivity – although of course the limited space of this volume will inevitably raise questions about certain exclusions. I wanted to have a variety of voices ranging from performers to directors, writers and dramaturgs. (Ideally, I wanted some composers, designers and choreographers as well, but these kinds of professionals often tend to work as freelancers rather than as permanent ensemble members). I also wanted a variety of cultural backgrounds, although for reasons of my own geographical location, almost half of the selected subjects are UK-based. However, rather than aiming to have particular cultural groups and ethnicities represented in the selection (Asian and African representatives are conspicuous by their absence here), I was more interested in examples of cross-cultural ensembles which have achieved international recognition (Not Yet It's Difficult, Song of the Goat, Ontroerend Goed). In most cases, the ensembles represented are at least 10 years old; they have therefore already survived potential moments of 'storming' in their career and acquired certain wisdom worth sharing in this context. And finally, I wanted a variety of ensemble models – from big state-funded residential companies such as the Royal Shakespeare Company and the Berliner Ensemble, to those that have gone through various phases of development (Kneehigh, Pig Iron), and those that are experimental in their structure (Shadow Casters, Ontroerend Goed). Sometimes, the chosen subjects have had the experience of working with more than one kind of ensemble, such as Joanna Holden (Northern Stage, Kneehigh, Cirque du Soleil), or they may have more than one hat or cultural base, such as Gabor Tompa. In one case, the representatives of two different ensembles Alexander Kelly (Third Angel) and Chris Thorpe (Unlimited) are interviewed about their ongoing collaboration.

I was also highly motivated by a desire to include some of the voices that are not usually heard in this context (dramaturg Hanna Slättne – Tinderbox, producer Richard Jordan), and conversely, despite my own desire to hear the voices of Frantic Assembly, Simon McBurney and Forced Entertainment, I refrained from including these companies as they have recently received analysis in some of the titles cited above. Rare exceptions to this are Elizabeth LeCompte and Max Stafford-Clark, where I was motivated to draw further insights in addition to those already available in recent publications, and actually elicit their own accounts of the initial emergence of their companies and their working methods.

Each interview features a short contextual statement about the company/artists being represented in it and a brief bibliography (where available). Typically, the subject's background and formative influences are covered, as well as any characteristic working methodologies and individual examples of work. Most of the interviews were recorded live and transcribed, with the exception of Ian Morgan where the interview took place in writing. Both of these methodologies have their advantages and disadvantages – spontaneity on the one hand, as opposed to depth of insight on the other – and I opted to have both represented in this collection. Live interviews provided an opportunity to respond to the moment, and I allowed each interviewee to drive the conversation in the direction they wanted, as long as this was within the parameters of my enquiry: Shaplin, Shadow Casters and Ontroerend Goed were clearly motivated by a desire to record a certain chronology of their ensemble works as part of the interviews; Holden wanted to offer details from rehearsals; and Tompa had strong feelings on the comparative advantages and disadvantages of working in distinct cultural contexts. In terms of length, the interviews range from 2,500 to 7,500 words, becoming longer towards the end of the volume as more contemporary or innovative practices are brought into the mix, requiring more detailed contextualisation.

The material collected so far has yielded insights falling into three broad categories:

1 *Redefinitions of ensemble.* For example, the term 'family' as a metaphor divides the subjects: Boyd and Rice are against it, while some subjects, like Pejović and Bakal (Shadow Casters), literally do have families together.[15] Admittedly, the notion of 'ensemble as family' does seem to belong to an age of political idealism which has long been replaced by other realities, although other kinds of personal idealism are still in evidence. Boyd's project is motivated by a desire to overcome the pervading culture of individualism and isolation in

contemporary society. LeCompte, on the other hand, has defined her ensemble by reference to a space which has kept the company together ever since its inception. Adassinsky and Shaplin tend to use musical analogies when discussing their creative processes. Most interestingly, Ontroerend Goed define themselves as a group with 'mutual compatibilities' – which, according to some theorists of business organisation (Amabile 1998), is a highly positive model.

2   *Redefinitions of the roles and processes within the ensemble.* As noted above, the twentieth century notions of professionalisation in theatre are being challenged by contemporary ensemble practices, both in terms of the power relations within the ensembles (e.g. notions of leadership) and the kinds of expertise carried by individual ensemble members. This is partly a result of the new theatre-makers' training backgrounds. In the English-speaking world we are witnessing a pro-liferation of university drama graduates who, by the nature of the pedagogical processes they are exposed to and due to the sheer numbers of those wishing to study the subject in the 2000s, are increasingly conditioned to work in groups. Most notable additions to this trend include Little Bulb (University of Kent), Belt Up (University of York), Paper Birds (University of Leeds) and Rash Dash (University of Hull). However, they have predecessors in Unlimited Theatre (University of Leeds), Third Angel (University of Lancaster), The Riot Group (Sarah Lawrence College), Ontroerend Goed (Ghent University) and Frantic Assembly (Swansea Univer-sity), none of whom have had formal theatre training, and in the case of the latter three, little or no exposure to drama/theatre/performance as a university subject. What each of these companies has encoun-tered is a certain necessity to defend or justify their entitlement to practice theatre-making, which brings to mind the guild-like exclu-sivity of the theatre establishments in various cultures. However, their success is by all means good news for the contemporary ensem-ble, as each one of these examples has brought in a new perspective on the craft itself and the notions of authority and authorship. This is also true of some companies which did not graduate together, such as The Neo-Futurists, founded by Greg Allen to include specifically writer-performers.

3   *Redefinitions of the relationship with the audience.* One of the most nota-ble of my recent theatre-going experiences has been the encounter with Ontroerend Goed in their one-to-one exploration of contem-porary relationships *Internal* (2009). This piece, which turned audience members into protagonists of sorts, soon proved to be no isolated case, as a whole range of one-to-one performances got

presented by the Battersea Arts Centre for two years running in 2010 and 2011. Simultaneously, the Croatian troupe Shadow Casters has over the years developed a series of interactive performances, at times designed to empower audience members to take action in the changing political world of what was once Eastern Europe. Both Schechner (1994 [1973]) and Shepherd (2009) have pointed out that what is particularly appealing about ensembles is the opportunity for the audience to witness and hypothetically partake of a certain kind of collectivity: 'What is performed is a possible way of working together in the world' (Shepherd 2009: 71). Bert O. States uses the term 'collaborative mode' to define the default relationship between the actor and the audience in most dramatic theatre (in Zarrilli 1995: 29), while Simon Murray quotes an interesting instance of Theatre de Complicite expressing the Lecoqian principle of 'the pleasure of play' by defining their communication mode as a 'collusion of cele-brants' in the programme note for *The Three Lives of Lucy Chabrol* (Murray 2003: 71). Claire Bishop has noted a paradigmatic move in the UK towards a more active engagement of the audience across the arts (Bishop 2006, 2012) while an increasing number of scholars have turned to the study of spectatorship (Grehan 2009; Kennedy 2009; Fensham 2009). Examples such as Ontroerend Goed and Shadow Casters clearly highlight the possibility of audience members becoming part of the contemporary ensemble. The fact that these three examples point to a simultaneous pursuit of similar goals, in what might have previously been seen as Eastern and Western Europe, is also a good sign in my view. One advantage of a globalised world in the twenty-first century might be the possibility that we intuitively understand each other better.

These trends of redefinition have been used to group the interviews into the three parts *Redefinitions of ensemble, Working processes* and *Ensemble and the audience*, although these themes – as well as a number of other resonant themes – run throughout the whole collection. Additional reso-nances include redefinitions of leadership, training and education, ensem-ble economics, and cross-cultural collaboration. Some of the artists represented will have worked together – Joanna Holden and Gabor Tompa at Northern Stage; Michael Boyd and Adriano Shaplin at the RSC; the RSC and The Wooster Group – testifying to a certain like-mindedness shared by those companies. More interestingly, however, some of the examples show striking similarities in method and outlook even if they have never met – especially the artists featured in the final part of the volume.

Preliminary conclusions

Representing an ensemble of distinct but harmonious voices, this collection should ideally serve only as a potential starting point for consideration of other examples whose absence may be noted here, or which are yet to emerge. The user of this book is encouraged to make personal observations about the particular nature of ensemble work or any other emerging ideas concerning the twenty-first century ensemble. By way of conclusion to this introduction, I offer some of the observations I have arrived at in the process of collecting these testimonies in the last three years.

Artistic and methodological values, inherent in collaborative ways of working associated with the creative practices of the latter half of the twentieth century in the West, are in fact to be found in many text-based and playwright-centred ensemble models. The ensemble way of working therefore spans the previously-perceived binary between text-based and devised theatre in the English-speaking world.

Text-oriented ensembles, as opposed to temporary casts of actors, appear to have a deeper, more sophisticated approach to their treatment of plays or the stories used as their departure point. Even the reservations about logistical and artistic drawbacks of institutionalised ensembles in Eastern Europe, voiced by directors such as Tompa and Butusov, are easily outweighed by the benefits of the ensemble way of working. Ensembles of long-term collaborators tend to be interested in foregrounding a shared performance vocabulary which may range from 'actor's jargon' as noted by Stanislavsky (Pitches 2006: 6)[16] to notions of visual vocabulary layered together with textual content described by Tompa, and the kinds of physical vocabulary described by Peter Eckersall or Dan Rothenberg. In addition, intuition is often identified as an underlying principle of the processes unfolding within ensembles, as in the work of The Wooster Group, Derevo or Improbable. This may be the case even when the ensemble ethos is being shared by these practitioners with first-time or one-off collaborators, as is sometimes the case with Phelim McDermott or Mike Alfreds' freelance projects. In some cases, the ensemble processes are understood as being analogous to orchestral or musical performance, even when the ensemble, such as The Riot Group, is centred around a playwright. This is not a recent development. According to Govan, Nicholson and Normington, this musical sensibility in ensemble theatre-making is traceable back to Joan Littlewood's Theatre Workshop and Julian Beck's Living Theatre, both of whose working processes were likened to jazz improvisation (Govan *et al.* 2007: 49).

Ensembles are ultimately geared towards acknowledging the centrality of the actor/performer's contribution to the process of theatre-making

(Alfreds, McDermott, Adassinsky). Even when some of the respondents, such as Stafford-Clark, allow for the possibility of having a star ensemble, they are adamant about nurturing and protecting the star quality from within, and resisting commercial casting pressures coming from the outside. Similarly, Michael Boyd in his keynote speech at the Equity and DGGB Ensemble Conference in November 2004 said that the ensemble should be about 'making stars, not chasing them'. And it is also interesting to note that many of the ensemble leaders represented here are (or once were) performers themselves (e.g. Rice, Shaplin, Kelly, Allen, McDermott).

Specific key terms appear to be resonating throughout the collection: transformation, liveness, connectedness, openness and the 'here and now'[17] are performance qualities valued by a range of companies, including Derevo, Song of the Goat, Improbable and Pig Iron, as well as practitioners oriented towards including the audience in the 'ensemble work' such as Mike Alfreds, Shadow Casters and Ontroerend Goed. The removal of the fourth wall is perhaps indicative of a desire to dispense with previously-held hierarchies and models of authority in theatre too.

Despite observations made about the nature of ensemble leadership in the twentieth century, it is increasingly evident that the nature of artistic directorship in contemporary ensembles is changing too. As noted above, companies such as Third Angel, Shadow Casters and Song of the Goat are distinguished by having tandems at the helm. The founder of The Neo-Futurists, Greg Allen, has temporarily shared the Artistic Directorship of the Chicago company with ensemble member Jay Torrence, while the New York Neo-Futurists has its own leadership.[18] Meanwhile Improbable and Pig Iron have each had a triumvirate of artistic directors. Allen and McDermott have both expressed an interest in group self-determination – Allen's route has been through consensus voting, which he has found to be better for the creative process than for organisational governance (Love 2008: 31), while McDermott has opted for Open Space conferencing and process-oriented psychology as a means of facilitating ensemble dynamics. The interviews that follow reveal that ensemble leaders in fact rarely relish the leadership role: Anton Adassinsky prefers performing to directing, and The Riot Group doesn't even have a 'director'; Mike Alfreds is noted as behaving more as a 'coach'; Phelim McDermott 'puts [himself] out of a job'; and Elizabeth LeCompte sees herself as a 'director in a group' rather than 'director of a group'.[19]

My recent interview with Erica Daniels, the Associate Artistic Director of Chicago's Steppenwolf Theatre Company (which unfortunately did not make the final draft of the book), highlights that Martha Lavey, Artistic Director of the company since 1995, 'doesn't ever really lead from the place of "This is what I want"'. Instead, her leadership style is a matter of a 'delicate balance' of maintaining the founding principles of the company and articulating the present strengths of 'ensemble, innovation and citizenship'.[20] Daniels notes that the entire company, including administrative staff, are treated as an ensemble. This has also been the nature of Michael Boyd's vision for the Royal Shakespeare Company during his artistic directorship 2002–2012. In the 2010 Demos report on the company, Hewison and colleagues conclude from analysing the RSC example that:

> when it comes to applying the term more broadly to organisational development, ensemble should be thought of not only as a way of doing or as a management tool, but as a way of being, based on a set of moral principles that guide leadership decisions and administrative actions.
>
> (Hewison *et al.* 2010: 46)

Even though companies on this scale are often seen to be in an economically privileged position by comparison to ensembles which are primarily held together by their members' moral investment, it should not be underestimated how challenging for a leader it must be to maintain an artistic vision which aims to imbue 600–700 employees with the same work ethos.[21] Part of the aim of this book is to recognise the commitment to the ensemble way of working on all levels, regardless of scale, in the hope that this might facilitate a more supportive cultural environment for emerging ensembles.[22]

Another important aspect of the ensemble way of working is its interrelation with training and education. Pig Iron, The Riot Group, Third Angel, Unlimited Theatre and Ontroerend Goed all acknowledge that they owe their origins to shared training or educational environment, which facilitated their initial encounter. Some of the interviewees, such as Dan Rothenberg and Emma Rice, also note the ways in which they developed their individual ensemble methodologies by responding to and even reacting against the particular training practices they had previously absorbed. Thus both Rice and Tompa are suspicious of 'fidelity' in theatre: Tompa encourages 'sacred unfaithfulness',[23] while Ian Morgan reports that Grotowski encouraged 'excellent rebellion'. As they mature, ensembles such as Derevo, Improbable, Pig Iron and Steppenwolf proceed to develop support networks, mentoring and even accredited training programmes for younger artists, while The Neo-Futurists constantly regenerate the ensemble through frequent auditions. Both Steppenwolf and the RSC also have very healthy and busy education departments intended to connect with school audiences. Sometimes, as in the case of Shadow Casters, the process of mutual learning and development between the artists and the audience becomes intertwined with the company's aesthetic and work ethic.

Finally, as noted by Morgan, Eckersall and Jordan, increased mobility and technological development is opening up possibilities for some fascinating exchange and cross-cultural ensemble initiatives, thus creating scope for further learning and internationalisation.

Despite these extraordinary achievements of ensemble theatre-makers, one major problem remains: how to survive periods of 'storming' and to defend to funding bodies a model of working which involves long rehearsal periods and, in some cases, a number of people on payroll? Some self-made ensembles, like Derevo, Kneehigh, The Neo-Futurists, The Wooster Group and Pig Iron, are lucky to have acquired their own spaces in which to make work, but in many cases the struggle is still on to gain recognition and proper support for the values inherent in working together long-term. This book is a small contribution to that struggle.

Notes

1 Oxford Dictionaries: http://oxforddictionaries.com/definition/ensemble?q=ensemble.
2 For the business model of theatre in Britain, see Davis (2000). Early proponents of the National Theatre model included William Archer, Harley Granville-Barker and George Bernard Shaw.
3 John Bull has however argued that 'Brecht's direct influence on the theatre of the 1950s in Britain was fairly negligible, and chiefly concerned with a new understanding of the use of stage space'. Although he concedes that the aesthetic influence was evidenced in the work of William Gaskill at the Royal Court, for example, he blames the general anti-intellectualism of British theatre artists for a partial appropriation of Brechtian influence overall. See Bull (1994).
4 Deirdre Heddon and Jane Milling have also raised concerns over this model of ensemble, acknowledging some more extreme interpretations of such ways of working. Arnold Aronson sardonically noted that:

> most groups functioned more on the model of the totalitarian phase of communism: there was a collective of actors, but the groups tended to have autocratic, even dictatorial, leaders in the form of visionary directors, who, in essence, replaced the playwright as the creative fount for texts.
>
> (Heddon and Milling 2006: 61)

5 Many thanks to Paul Allain who found this document in the Wroclaw Grotowski archive and made it available for reference here.

6 Stephen Knapper notes in relation to Complicite:

> In common with many other European companies – Théâtre du Soleil and Els Joglars, for example – the initial emphasis on collective creation and decision-making gave way to a more director-led operation in such ground-breaking productions as Dürrenmatt's *The Visit* (1989), where McBurney directed alongside fellow company co-founder Annabel Arden.
>
> (in Delgado and Rebellato 2010: 234)

7 The fifth stage, added in 1977, is attributed jointly to Tuckman and Mary Ann Jensen.

8 According to this structure, cultural values are measured in relation to the horizontal and vertical individualism-collectivism scale, whereby a horizontal disposition is more inclined towards equality and social cohesion, while a vertical disposition is more inclined towards hierarchy and the notions of deference and sacrifice for the group. Various studies have interestingly contrasted the US as a – presumably typical – example of a Vertical Individualist culture to either the Vertical Collectivist cultures of the East (e.g. Turkey in Cukur *et al.* 2004) or the Horizontal Individualist cultures of the West (Denmark in Shavitt *et al.* 2006), though the former study was admittedly more interested in dispelling the notion of cultural stereotyping and focusing on the correlation of 'universal' values instead. What this provides for our research into ensembles is a potential set of criteria when analysing the attitudes of the individual ensemble members towards their ensemble and their way of working. These criteria might include power, achievement, benevolence, self-direction and security (as was the case in Cukur *et al.*'s experiment), and they may provide templates for various models of leadership designed to foster either performance quality or group cohesion or both. Ultimately, however, what these structures provide is the possibility of examining more objectively perceived power relations within an ensemble and dispelling the myth that groups with leaders necessarily imply oppression. Even if this kind of enquiry cannot be addressed within the scope of the current study, it would certainly create a good basis for a further empirical research project.

9 Interestingly, Anne Fliotsos notes a brief existence in the US of director-less collectives, where authority was devolved among company members, but she explains their failure to survive by the fact that the model was ignored by the educational system (Fliotsos 2004: 78).

10 Jen Harvie notes that, in the UK, 'censorship legally enhanced the primacy of the written script and made devised and improvised theatre nearly impossible to stage' (Harvie 2005:116).

11 In July 2011, I conducted an informal survey on the Standing Conference of University Drama Departments (SCUDD) mailbase – at the time comprising 1,400 predominantly British subscribers – seeking references to the potential first use of the term 'devising' before Alison Oddey's seminal 1994 work *Devising Theatre*. Kathleen McCreery, Tony Coult and Paul Kleiman all independently suggested that the use of the term 'devising' was linked specifically to the theatre-in-education (TIE) work.

12 Collaboration has stayed on the agenda since, and as of 2010 it has manifested itself through an emphasis on interdisciplinarity and the so-called 'Combined Arts' agenda associated with the Grants for the Arts scheme

(http://www.artscouncil.org.uk/funding/funded-projects/case-studies/grants-for-arts-combined-arts/).

13 In his recent article on Mitchell, Rebellato specifies that Mitchell's involvement with regular collaborators is driven by the interests of the artwork rather than the 'collaborative working [as] an end in itself, a political or ethical rehearsal for the revolution' (Rebellato 2010: 329), but he also offers a useful quote of Mitchell's views on the matter:

> I don't like new relationships because you have to waste a lot of energy shaping the relationship and you can't work so easily because you are learning the person. My relationship with an actor should be equivalent to my relationship with my creative team: it's another exceptional adult I'm in partnership with and we're going to make something together.
> (Rebellato 2010: 329)

14 In her introductory chapter, Harvie dissects Lehmann's term to imply, in a more layered sense, that contemporary theatre, which has surpassed not only the concerns of dramatic but also of postmodern theatre, is to be understood as a 'communicative art' which uses a broad set of means, a 'communicative act' which addresses a broad set of themes and 'an industry embedded in globalization, commodity culture and economic markets' (Harvie 2010: 13).

15 In contrast to Boyd, Peter Hall believes that 'family' and 'ensemble' are interchangeable. According to Hewison *et al.*, Hall also '[does] not believe that it is possible to run a family, a tribe, or a collective, or whatever, without there being a boss' (Hewison *et al.* 2010: 56) – an attitude perhaps more typical of the 'post-war director' as defined by Mermikides.

16 'Language, then, is a crucial aspect in the formulation of groups, acting at one and the same time to facilitate communication within the group and as a vehicle for defining the boundaries of that group. Stanislavsky was appealing to the same logic in the preface to *An Actor's Work on Himself*, defining the community of System actors by their 'actors' jargon' (Pitches 2006: 6). In this collection, Mike Alfreds notes that even a shared jargon can no longer be relied on in contemporary theatre.

17 Małgorzata Sugiara has noted that this move from the Stanislavskian 'as if' to the 'here and now' is a characteristic of postdramatic theatre: 'The basic "as if" convention, upheld in theatre (as well as in the drama written for this theatre), has gradually been replaced by theatre's *differentia specifica*: its 'here and now' quality and the temporal immediacy of its media' (Sugiara 2004).

18 In an interview with Bret Love, Allen has explained how this model of leadership is in keeping with the founding principles of the company based on egalitarianism (Love 2008).

19 Similarly, according to Freshwater '[Simon] McBurney takes every opportunity to shift critical attention away from issues of his own achievements as a director and towards the creative input of the performers' (in Holdsworth and Luckhurst 2008: 186).

20 Interview with Erica Daniels, 29 April 2012, Chicago.

21 The figure is given by the RSC website as the total number of employees 'including actors, permanent and casual members of staff and freelancers' (http://www.rsc.org.uk/about-us/our-work/whos-who.aspx).

22 Currently in the UK, the National Theatre and the Young Vic do have schemes intended to nurture and support young directors, while similar schemes at the same level are as yet unavailable for ensembles.
23 Admittedly, Rice and Tompa were both referring to issues of 'fidelity' in relation to the original text being used for their productions rather than specifically a training heritage; however the attitude is indicative of the necessity to rely on one's own performance idiom rather than following blindly in the footsteps of others.

Bibliography

Amabile, Teresa (1998) 'How to kill creativity', *Harvard Business Review*, 76(5): 76–87.

Banham, Martin (1988) *The Cambridge Guide to World Theatre*, Cambridge: Cambridge University Press.

Billington, Michael (2007) *State of the Nation: British Theatre Since 1945*, London: Faber and Faber.

Bishop, Claire (2006) *Participation: Documents of Contemporary Art*, London: Whitechapel Gallery, Cambridge, MA: MIT Press.

Bishop, Claire (2012) *Artificial Hells: Participatory Art and the Politics of Spectatorship*, London: Verso.

Booth, Michael R. (1997) 'Nineteenth Century Theatre', in John Russell Brown (ed.) *The Oxford Illustrated History of Theatre*, Oxford: Oxford University Press.

Boyd, Michael (2004) Keynote Speech at The Equity and DGGB Conference on Ensemble Theatre, Barbican, The Pit, 24 November 2004 (personal notes from the event).

Bull, John (1994) *Stage Right: Crisis and Recovery in British Contemporary Mainstream Theatre*, Basingstoke: Macmillan, pp. 43–4.

Carron, Albert V., Widmeyer, W. N. and Brawley, Lawrence R. (1985) 'The development of an instrument to assess cohesion in sport teams: the Group Environment Questionnaire', *Journal of Sport Psychology*, 7: 244–66.

Clurman, Harold (1983 [1941]) *The Fervent Years: The Group Theatre and the Thirties*, New York: Da Capo Press.

Craig, Sandy (ed.) (1980) *Dreams and Deconstructions: Alternative Theatre in Britain*, Ambergate: Amber Lane Press.

Cukur, Cem Safak, de Guzman, Maria Rosario and Carlo, Gustavo (2004) 'Religiosity, values, and horizontal and vertical individualism-collectivism: a study of Turkey, the United States and the Philippines', *The Journal of Social Psychology*, 144(6): 613–34.

Davis, Tracy C. (2000) *The Economics of the British Stage 1800–1914*, Cambridge: Cambridge University Press.

Delgado, Maria M. and Heritage, Paul (1996) *In Contact with the Gods?: Directors Talk Theatre*, Manchester: Manchester University Press.

Delgado, Maria and Svich, Caridad (2002) (eds) *Theatre in Crisis?: Performance Manifestos for a New Century*, Manchester: Manchester University Press.

Delgado, Maria M. and Rebellato, Dan (eds) (2010) *Contemporary European Theatre Directors*, Abingdon, Oxon: Routledge.

Fensham, Rachel (2009) *To Watch Theatre: Essays on Genre and Corporeality*, Brussels: Peter Lang.

Fliotsos, Anne L. (2004) 'The Pedagogy of Directing, 1920–1990: Seventy Years of Teaching the Unteachable', in Anne L. Fliotsos and Gail S. Medford (eds) *Teaching Theatre Today: Pedagogical Views of Theatre in Higher Education*, New York: Palgrave Macmillan.

Govan, Emma, Nicholson, Helen and Normington, Katie (2007) *Making a Performance: Devising Histories and Contemporary Practices*, London: Routledge.

Grehan, Helena (2009) *Performance, Ethics and Spectatorship in a Global Age*, Basingstoke: Palgrave.

Grotowski (n.d.). Photocopy of a typewritten pamphlet in English, signed by Jerzy Grotowski and held in the Grotowski Archive, Wrocław.

Harvie, Jen (2005) *Staging the UK*, Manchester: Manchester University Press.

Harvie, Jen (2010) 'Introduction: Contemporary Theatre in the Making', in Jen Harvie and Andy Lavender (eds) *Making Contemporary Theatre: International Rehearsal Processes*, Manchester: Manchester University Press.

Harvie, Jen and Lavender, Andy (eds) (2010) *Making Contemporary Theatre: International Rehearsal Processes*, Manchester: Manchester University Press.

Heddon, Deirdre and Milling, Jane (2006) *Devising Performance: A Critical History*, Basingstoke: Palgrave Macmillan.

Hewison, Robert, Holden, John and Jones, Samuel (2010) *All Together: A Creative Approach to Organisational Change*, London: Demos.

Holdsworth, Nadine (2006) *Joan Littlewood*, London: Routledge.

Holdsworth, Nadine and Luckhurst, Mary (eds) (2008) *A Concise Companion to Contemporary British and Irish Drama*, Malden, MA: Blackwell.

Kennedy, Dennis (2009) *The Spectator and the Spectacle: Audiences in Modernity and Postmodernity*, Cambridge: Cambridge University Press.

Knapper, Stephen (2010) 'Simon McBurney: Shifting Under/Soaring Over the Boundaries of Europe', in Maria M. Delgado and Dan Rebellato (eds) *Contemporary European Theatre Directors*, Abingdon: Routledge.

Lichtenfels, Peter and Hunter, Lynnete (2002) 'Seeing Through the National and Global Stereotypes: British Theatre in Crisis', in Maria Delgado and Caridad Svich (eds) *Theatre in Crisis?: Performance Manifestos for a New Century*, Manchester: Manchester University Press.

Love, Bret (2008) 'New visions in artistic direction', *Stage Directions*, 21(5): 30–1.

Magarshack, David (1973 [1950]) *Stanislavsky and the Art of the Stage*, London: Faber and Faber.

Małgorzata, Sugiera (2004) 'Beyond drama: writing for postdramatic theatre', *Theatre Research International*, 29(1): 16–28 and 25.

Mermikides, Alex (2010) 'Forced Entertainment – The Travels (2002) – The Anti-Theatrical Director', in Jen Harvie and Andy Lavender (eds) *Making Contemporary Theatre: International Rehearsal Processes*, Manchester: Manchester University Press.

Mermikides, Alex and Smart, Jackie (eds) (2010) *Devising in Process*, Basingstoke: Palgrave Macmillan.

Murray, Simon (2003) *Jacques Lecoq*, London: Routledge.

Orozco, Lourdes (2010) 'Rodrigo García and La Carnicería Teatro: From the Collective to the Director', in Maria M. Delgado and Dan Rebellato (eds) *Contemporary European Theatre Directors*, Abingdon: Routledge.

Pitches, Jonathan (2006) *Science and the Stanislavsky Tradition of Acting*, London: Routledge.

Platt, Steve (2009) 'Epic Drama', http://www.redpepper.org.uk/Epic-drama/ (accessed 19 December 2012).

Rebellato, Dan (2010) 'Katie Mitchell: Learning from Europe', in Maria M. Delgado and Dan Rebellato (eds) *Contemporary European Theatre Directors*, Abingdon, Oxon: Routledge.

Schechner, Richard (1994 [1973]) *Environmental Theater*, New York: Applause Theatre and Cinema Books.

Shavitt, Sharon, Zhang, Jing, Torelli, Carlos J. and Lalawani, Ashok K. (2006) 'Reflections on the meaning and structure of the horizontal/vertical distinction', *Journal of Consumer Psychology*, 16(4): 357–62.

Shepherd, Simon (2009) *Cambridge Introduction to Modern British Theatre*, Cambridge: Cambridge University Press.

Singleton, Brian (2010) 'Ariane Mnouchkine: Activism, Formalism, Cosmpolitanism', in Maria M. Delgado and Dan Rebellato (eds) *Contemporary European Theatre Directors*, Abingdon, Oxon: Routledge.

Stanislavski, Constantin (2006 [1937]) *An Actor Prepares*, London: Methuen Drama.

Tuckman, Bruce (1965) 'Developmental sequence in small groups', *Psychological Bulletin*, 63(6): 384–99.

Tushingham, David (1994) *Live 1: Food for the Soul: A New Generation of British Theatre Makers*, London: Methuen.

Zarrilli, Philip (ed.) (1995) *Acting (Re)Considered*, London: Routledge.

Themes table

This table is intended to help the reader navigate through the book and its main themes. As indicated in the introduction, the interviews have been organised into three parts – *Redefinitions of ensemble*, *Working processes* and *Ensemble and the audience* – on the basis of each interviewee's overriding preoccupations. Therefore, this division is mostly arbitrary, as many themes run throughout the collection. The overall structure imposed on the material follows two lines of logic:

- one that mirrors theatre production itself: defining a conceptual departure point, pursuing a creative process in rehearsal, and pursuing a relationship with the audience; and
- a loosely chronological one: starting from the ensembles rooted in a repertory tradition, via devising and contemporary performance ensembles and ending with those that engage in experimental and/or increasingly globalised practices.

It is no surprise therefore that Part I is dominated by directors, Part II by actors and performers who have developed authorship roles, and Part III by groundbreaking practitioners.

Most of the companies represented here were founded in the mid-1990s, and by 2001 at the latest. The year of foundation is enclosed in the left-hand column next to the abbreviated name of the company.

I have chosen to trace ten themes across the entire sample of represented companies, and they broadly include questions regarding creative methodology and questions regarding organisational issues. The first five columns trace the incidence of companies working with plays/playwrights, devising, dramaturgical use of music, the figure of the dramaturg and audience interaction. The next five columns focus on the type of theatre-maker involved (whether they are narrowly specialised or not), the incidence of training within the ensemble, outwardly-oriented training, use of contracts (as opposed to personal commitment of ensemble members) and whether or not the ensemble is building-based.

The table clearly shows that there are no set patterns or clear-cut distinctions between individual cases, which would have facilitated a systematic split between, for example, text-based and devised theatre, or between building-based and itinerant ensembles.

The index should be used for more specific in-text references.

	Interviewee(s)	Plays and playwrights	Primarily devising	Music	Dramaturg on board
1	Boyd RSC (1961)	Yes	No	Has music department	Yes
2	Tompa HT of Cluj (1792)	Yes	No	Interest in rhythm	Yes
3	Wündrich Berliner Ensemble (1949)	Yes	No	Use of songs	Yes
4	Butusov	Yes	No	Directing as composing	Not known
5	Stafford-Clark Out of Joint (1993)	Yes	No	No	No
6	LeCompte Wooster Group (1975)	Yes, plays	Yes	Sound design	Not formally
8	Adassinsky & Yarovaya Derevo (1988)	No	Yes	Always crucial	No
9	Rice Kneehigh (1980)	Stories and writers	Yes	Musicians on stage	Not formally
10	Holden	Yes	Yes	N/a	N/a
11	Morgan Song of the Goat (1996)	No	Yes	Singing ensemble	No
12	Rothenberg Pig Iron (1995)	Works with writers	Yes	Occasionally crucial	Not formally
13	Shaplin Riot Group (1997)	Yes	No	Writing as composing	Not formally
14	Slättne Tinderbox (1988)	Yes	Yes	No	Yes
15	Kelly Third Angel (1995)	Works with writer	Yes	Not crucial	Not formally
15	Thorpe Unlimited (1997)	Yes	Yes	Not crucial	Not formally
16	Alfreds	Yes	Yes	Not crucial	No
17	Allen Neo-Futurists (1988)	Yes	Not primarily	Not crucial	Not formally
18	McDermott Improbable (1996)	No	Yes	Occasionally crucial	Not formally
19	Eckersall Not Yet It's Difficult (1995)	No	Yes	Sound design	Yes
20	Pejović & Bakal Shadow Casters (2001)	No	Yes	Not crucial	Yes
21	Bauwens, Devriendt & Smet Ontroerend Goed (2001)	No	Yes	Not crucial	Yes
22	Richard Jordan RJ Productions (1998)	Yes	Yes	Not crucial	N/a

Audience interaction	Multiprofess-ionalisation	Training together	Training others	Contracts or commitment	Building	
Yes	Possible	Yes	Education department	Up to 3-year contract	Yes	1
No	No	N/a	University post	1 year	Yes	2
Yes	No	N/a	No	Long contracts	Yes	3
No	No	N/a	Not known	N/a	N/a	4
No	No	N/a	Outreach	Touring contracts	No	5
Mostly no	Yes	On the job	Yes, offers courses	Commitment, no contracts	Yes	6
Mostly no	No	Yes	Runs a school	N/a	Yes	8
Mostly yes	Actor/directors, actor/writers	Yes	History of teaching	Up to 1 year	Tent	9
N/a	Actor/clown	N/a	No	N/a	N/a	10
No	No	Yes	Offers qualification	N/a	Yes	11
Yes and no	Not crucial	Yes	Runs a school	Commitment, no contracts	Yes	12
No, except eye contact	Writer/actor/ designer/ director	Yes	Shaplin teaches	Commitment	No	13
No	No	N/a	Outreach department	Up to 12 weeks	No	14
Mostly no	Performer/director/ designer/ dramaturg	Shared past training	Outreach	Combined	No	15
Mostly no	Writer/ performer	Shared past training	Outreach	Combined	No	15
Yes	N/a	N/a	Yes	N/a	N/a	16
Yes	Yes, all writer/ performers	On the job	Allen teaches	Commitment	Yes	17
Yes and no	Actor/director	N/a	Yes	Combined	No	18
Yes and no	No	Yes	Yes	Combined	No	19
Yes	Yes, actor/director, dramaturg/ director	N/a	Work is educational	Commitment	No	20
Yes	Yes, most have dual roles	N/a	Not primarily	Commitment	No	21
N/a	N/a	N/a	N/a	Contracts	N/a	22

Part I
Redefinitions of ensemble

1 A 'contingent community' in a free market economy

Michael Boyd (Royal Shakespeare Company)

The Royal Shakespeare Company (RSC) was founded in 1961 at the initiative of Peter Hall who had been running the Shakespeare Memorial Theatre in Stratford since 1 January 1960. Hall is considered to have been inspired by the European art theatre model – the Moscow Art Theatre and the Berliner Ensemble – to embrace the ensemble way of working, but wished to remain cautious about the associated 'institutional drawbacks' of rigidity, tyranny of seniority and complacency (Chambers 2004: 9). He managed to obtain the commitment of prominent actors for his project – such as Peggy Ashcroft who was 'the first to sign on' (Adler 2001: 4) – and launched the first RSC season with a stellar line up.

The RSC thrived throughout the 1960s under Hall and throughout the 1970s under Trevor Nunn, but entered a crisis period from the mid-1980s onwards. A recent Demos report about the company notes that:

> An Arts Council appraisal carried out in 1990 had warned that the management of the RSC was unusually centralised, and that communications within the organisation were poor.
>
> (Hewison *et al.* 2010: 33)

The downward turn culminated with serious economic problems under Adrian Noble (1991–2003) and the company's loss of its London base in 2002. Michael Boyd, who had joined the RSC as Associate Director in 1996, took over as the Artistic Director in 2002/03 and resolved to return the company to its founding principle of ensemble.

Unlike most of his predecessors, Boyd had absorbed influences from the experimental and regional scene, as well as Scottish and European theatre. He attended the University of Edinburgh and trained at the Malaya Bronnaya Theatre in Moscow. His first assistant directing job was at the Belgrade Theatre Coventry in 1979, followed by an Associate Directorship at Sheffield Crucible in 1982. In 1985, he returned to Scotland and founded the Tron Theatre in Glasgow.

The first three-year ensemble company at the RSC was assembled under Boyd in 2006 to coincide with the year-long Complete Works Festival where all of Shakespeare's plays were presented within one year at Stratford through a combination of visiting international companies and RSC productions. Part of the ensemble project was an implementation of the Artist Development Programme, designed to provide ongoing systematic in-house training for the acting companies, directors, designers and members of the education department. With the so-called Histories Company, Boyd directed the monumental cycle consisting of *Henry VI Part 1*, *Part 2* and *Part 3*, *Richard III*, *Richard II*, *Henry IV Parts 1 and 2* and *Henry V*. Simultaneously, part of Boyd's mission was to have the Royal Shakespeare Theatre, originally built in 1932, refurbished in order to create a more inclusive atmosphere in the auditorium. For five years between 2006 and 2011, a temporary theatre – the Courtyard – was rigged up in Stratford to replace the Royal Shakespeare Theatre. The second ensemble company, the 'Long Ensemble', was assembled in 2009. The new, refurbished Royal Shakespeare Theatre opened in 2011, in time for the 50th anniversary of the RSC. The company has also reinstated its annual London season. Despite these successes, Boyd's journey of innovation was not without its struggles.

This interview, which took place in November 2010 – about a year before Michael Boyd and Vikky Heywood announced that they would step down from their respective positions as Artistic and Executive Directors of the RSC – highlights aspects of Boyd's vision that challenge cultural preconceptions, focusing specifically on his ideas of ensemble and the kinaesthetic approach to text.

Interview

RADOSAVLJEVIĆ: You're a strong advocate of the ensemble way of working. I would be interested to know which formative influences have shaped your particular methodology? I'm guessing your Russian experience has been quite significant in that respect?

BOYD: Yes, spending some time with Anatoly Efros' company at the Malaya Bronnaya, witnessing six-week readthroughs, and an integrated approach to mind and body that was possible because of the time spent and because of the mutual understanding already earned over years between the director and the company, was very influential. Seeing mature work at the numerous Young People's Theatres in Moscow and Leningrad, work that stayed in the repertoire for years, and just sensing the depth and the detail and the virtuosity that was possible over that length of time, it all seemed very different from the hurried 'hair 'em scare 'em' approach to preparation that was usual in

British theatre. At that time I was most inspired in the UK by the powerful, visual theatre work of Phillip Prowse at the Citizens Theatre which engaged with a poetry of mise-en-scène that I didn't see in most text-bound British theatre at that time. I was inspired by the clarity and simplicity of Peter Gill's work at the Riverside Studios and the dogged pursuit of talented new playwrights at the Traverse Theatre in Edinburgh, the emergence of a new native voice in Scottish theatre, and by the political activism of 7:84 and their musical theatre offshoot – Wildcat. There was a sense of ensemble amongst them although they put their work together very quickly – both in terms of members of the team who worked together over a decade, informally, but also a strong sense of connection with their audience in community centres and working men's clubs around Scotland and at their height, with civil society – because they were engaging directly with the headlines of the day. But none of these UK models revealed any such depth or rich attention to the work that I witnessed in my time in Moscow. Living in Edinburgh, of course, I was exposed every year to interesting work from abroad. The work of Kantor, for instance, was a revelation. His *Dead Class* coming to Edinburgh offered us a different idea of what narrative might be, a shocking theatrical modernism that was enormously powerful and actually very accessible. Compared with much of contemporary classical music for instance, which had rather lost its traction on audiences at the time, this was a modernist theatre work which was palpably powerful and effective for its audience.

I went to Russia a year after university. And while I was at university I realised that Scottish theatre at its best was still a highly socialised community art form, either through the populist variety tradition or through the overtly political agenda of companies in the 1970s – like 7:84.

RADOSAVLJEVIĆ: How would you define the RSC as an ensemble at this moment in time?

BOYD: We're in the middle of our second sustained experiment with long-term ensemble, which is a reaction to our first experiment with the Histories. We felt that the experience of the Histories, however successful, had been too intense for the actors and had not left enough time for reflection or just rest. One way we have addressed this problem has been to enlarge the company so that one half of the company can play 'opposite' the other and give people nights off and rehearsal periods off. That has been valuable but also tricky because it has split the company. Everyone has worked with everyone else by now but it took much longer for the company to start firing on all cylinders with each other, because for months they had worked in different tribes within the larger tribe. When I first took on the RSC as artistic director, I had an instinctive feeling that the company size should relate to class size in a school, which should not be more than 30, and I think the 44 of our current ensemble is too big. The 90-strong companies that the RSC used to employ were so large that actors tended to disappear, just not being noticed, not being developed. To give the actors in our current company a less exhausting time we expanded the company size. The second company is also the 'difficult second album' because the first company was enormously successful. A lot of actors who would have or did say 'no' to the Histories were saying 'yes' to this, because of the success of the Histories. There's a different expectation from a company of actors who share an understanding of the almost impossibility of the task of the Histories, and from one made up of actors who think the path has been trod, so the task will be easier. Then they're shocked when it's hard. I think we have a larger number of profoundly gifted individuals in this company than we had in the Histories company, because more leading actors were willing to commit. And we perhaps can see a little more self-interest creeping in; there are more people who feel a need for a greater degree of control of their destiny. Managing those different conflicting desires – was very robust on the Histories – but it has been a harder journey on this one.

RADOSAVLJEVIĆ: What struck me during the brief time that I was here was that there was a strong emphasis on training together. The ensemble members, whoever they were and at whatever point in their career, were all training together for that first period of time and that was structured into the rehearsal process. But also there were emphases on particular ideas, such as kinaesthetics and embodiment and experiential learning. And I just wonder – how did these ways of thinking about the work ethos come about? Was this something that you felt was very important in an ensemble?

BOYD: I was inspired by the rigour of Russian training, by the visceral connection between the profession and training in Russia that simply doesn't exist in this country. Practical experience has also taught me that it requires time to develop deep skills, and the more intangible things like rapport, understanding, mutual instinct. With Shakespeare the artists are addressing an alien culture and an unfamiliar seventeenth century form of English that we have to address, because increasingly drama schools are not addressing it. There was a deficit at the RSC of exploiting the actor's full physical potential. Perhaps British theatre has been too text-bound, too discursive and too cerebral. At the RSC it should be possible to grow out from the text, to be both brilliantly lyrical *and* aspire to a stage poetry that was not just about words, where we could celebrate total theatre.

RADOSAVLJEVIĆ: And how did you and the company proceed to develop those skills; what kinds of influences or elements of learning were brought into the company to facilitate that?

BOYD: The work of Liz Ranken was influential in the early period, and her marriage of different physical disciplines and methods that she had acquired over the years working with DV8 and through her dance training, with an almost spiritual approach. There was a greater emphasis on physical fitness. There were specific skills that were required at different times that the new way of working allowed us to learn. There was a genuine rigour, for instance, about the rope work and the trapeze work that we did on the Histories that would have been impossible if we hadn't stayed together for that length of time. We were able to make the demand of accomplished actors that they become strong physical performers as well; we brought artists with skills in physical theatre into the company when previously they had been regarded as a risk because: 'Can they speak verse?'. We have the resources in the company to work on language with physical performers – they work with Cis Berry, Greg Doran, John Barton, Alison Bomber, so they need not be horribly exposed outside their existing expertise. I bumped into a real appetite for language and narrative at places like Circus Space in Hoxton, a desire to sustain an idea beyond the theatrical equivalent of a three-minute pop song. They were yearning to express more, through sustained narrative, to find a larger vessel in which to express the things that they were feeling, that they wanted to say. We were able to offer them a chance to do that, with Shakespeare being the leading offer but not the exclusive one. Other simple explorations of the art of acting that have become more central in recent years: Meisner, Feldenkrais, the work of Michael Chekhov, are regularly explored throughout the life of the company and have been found to be very useful. As well as more left field things. This company spent a week with the Laboratory for the Study of Movement (LEM) – with Pascale (Lecoq) and Krikor (Belekian) from Lecoq. All the actors were doing sculpture and drawing and, through that, they gained fresh insights about their role as performers in space, and about points of view. Most of the company found it really, really useful. Some found it pretentious and nothing to do with 'what I do'. There is a fear on the part of some artists of exploring their art – a fear of demystifying it to themselves, of becoming self-conscious and therefore not so free. One obstacle to an approach that insists on learning and making art at the same time is that scepticism and fear around what's seen as an analytical approach. But there perhaps has to be a certain amount of destructive self-consciousness in order to move on to a new stage. If there's one central ambition for the companies here it's that the artists leave as different artists to the ones who came in. That can be achieved without them breaking down their own artistry, but if they can have courage to look at it square in the face and go 'What is it actually that I do?', they can make larger quantum leaps.

RADOSAVLJEVIĆ: I have found that music has been quite an important element of the ensemble work with some other companies. The RSC has historically had a music department; how much of a role does music play?

BOYD: We have long maintained a small permanent band at the RSC, but one thing that's happened in the last eight years is that there is more in-house composition – the band are getting more engaged in the process of generating music, and that allows for a more intimate relationship between the musician and the rehearsal room. Music is a wonderful way of creeping up behind the actor who is afraid of self-consciousness and taking them to another place of expanded vocabulary. Unconsciously they are responding to the music and escaping the rational, escaping even naturalism, the over-familiar world of post-Freudian, psychological realism. They find themselves lifted by a rhythm or an emotion or whatever, and they can't help but go somewhere unfamiliar but true.

RADOSAVLJEVIĆ: How would you define the rehearsal process of the RSC at the moment, in terms of what happens in rehearsal, how long the rehearsal period is and what your ideal would be?

BOYD: The 'ideal' isn't necessarily all that helpful just now, because we're right in the thick of what is possible. Within the constraints of British pragmatism, our greatest progress has been made through the ability to revisit shows, so by the end of the life of the company those shows have been thoroughly explored. The problem remains that they are still vulnerable at the beginning of their life, the initial rehearsal process is still not enormously long, and there's still a commercial pressure on time; it must be as productive as possible so, for instance, we still do not enjoy the long technical periods that are possible in other cultures.

RADOSAVLJEVIĆ: How long is the rehearsal process at the moment?

BOYD: It depends on the project. We work for twelve weeks shared between two shows on the opening shows in the season, then there's no fixed pattern through the rest of the life of the company. I suppose there have been two rehearsal periods of around that length of time that have been responsible for about eight of the pieces, and then other pieces have usually been generated in about eight weeks whilst people have been performing as well, so in reality it's less than that because of time lost to matinees. The Russian pieces, for instance, *The Grain Store* and *The Drunks* were rehearsed over eight weeks while playing a four-play Shakespeare repertoire. *Matilda* was developed over seven years.

RADOSAVLJEVIĆ: In the talk that you gave at the Central School of Speech and Drama in January 2010 you said that you are still confronting certain attitudes about the ensemble way of working being 'foreign' or 'communist'. Where do those criticisms come from, and how are you dealing with them?

BOYD: They come from a theatre culture that is heavily influenced by the free market economy of the entertainment industry, where actors are encouraged to move like a commodity on the stock market, where any restriction of that degree of nimble flexibility is seen as leaden, and stifling. The English have a special fondness for the eccentric individual. 'Every man's home is his castle', while a collective is a foreign concept, and long-term commitment risks disappointment. Actors are encouraged to use theatre to get themselves visible enough to earn a proper living through film or television, and that is a competitive process. You might lose your competitive edge by playing the leading role one night and then a supporting role the next – you don't want casting directors to see you in the supporting role, it's dangerous for your career quite apart from potentially being humiliating. We worship celebrity more than ever, and the received wisdom is that audiences want to see their favourite star centre stage, in a spotlight. There's a very healthy fear in English culture of conformity, in political terms of Fascism, Communism, Nazism, the French Revolution. The English are proud to consider themselves an exception to such attempts to homogenise society, and an ensemble can be seen by some as an attempt to homogenise under the control of an autocratic European-style director. Two things happened at the time of the foundation of the RSC in 1961 by the politically astute Peter Hall. One was a meeting in a Moscow hotel room with a big brewer from the Flower family to reinstitute Shakespeare in Stratford as an artistic collective, modelled on the Eastern European ensembles. But, running alongside that was the pursuit of both Peggy Ashcroft and a Royal Charter. It's a wonderful paradox, and a very clever bit of riding two horses at the same time to deflect a lot of the potential antipathy towards the idea.

Some of the resistance to the idea of a learning community is simply a lack of humility on the part of some practitioners. A hunger to
learn can be misread as a lack of confidence in your expertise.

RADOSAVLJEVIĆ: There are two more things. I don't know whether you
can weave them together. One is the idea of home and the fact
that the home is a two-base home for the company (Stratford and
London), because what has emerged from this research is that ensemble makers often talk about 'home' and 'family' in relation to their
way of working. And then you have mentioned the notion of the end
of the current company – the company of actors are just there for a
limited period of time. What do you think will happen when the current company comes to an end of their life in terms of whether there
will be another life with the RSC or another life with another
company?

BOYD: It is not insignificant that the RSC's true home is in Stratford,
badly served by public transport. Dundee Rep is one of our Northern-
most theatre companies; Northern Stage is a long way removed from
London; and Kneehigh in Cornwall are equally far removed. All have
successfully pursued ensemble. For some of the most prominent
examples of pursuing the ensemble idea, it seems important to be
away from the centre but nonetheless in a place with sufficient of its
own specific gravity, to make a virtue of making theatre on retreat. I
don't usually talk about the RSC as a family – a Shakespearean
company should be distrustful of the word 'family'. Family is usually
dysfunctional and exploitative in Shakespeare. We're not a family,
we're not related, we're colleagues. I suppose I try to replace the word
'family' with 'community'.

We are a contingent community – there is a contingent community about the very act of theatre every evening. Our ensembles,
whether they're for six months or three years, are contingent communities; everyone knows there is an end. This company will end in the
summer of 2011 at the end of the New York residency. Some shows
may carry on a life, but outside the life of the ensemble. The experience of the Histories company when they left was first of all a nervous
collapse, and then a sense of withdrawal. Re-entry into the more
pluralistic world of the partly subsidised, partly commercial British
theatre scene was painful for some. I think it took 18 months for
them all to start reaping the benefits of that work, and about 18
months to want to come back for more. Between these two long
ensembles there was a gap of about 18 months, and I suspect it will
be a similar gap before there's another big long commitment, but in
the interim we will be experimenting with different approaches to

ensemble: we are already planning one small company, cast and led by the playwright Tarell Alvin McCraney, which will perform a repertoire of two Shakespeares and a new play by Tarell, in Stratford, Miami and New York, and Tarell's ensemble may prove typical of more 'artist-led' projects, each guided by one clear shared vision, and given time to develop its own aesthetics.

Bibliography

Adler, Steven (2001) *Rough Magic: Making Theatre at the Royal Shakespeare Company*, Carbondale and Edwardsville: Southern Illinois University Press.

Billington, Michael (2007) *State of the Nation: British Theatre Since 1945*, Faber and Faber: London.

Chambers, Colin (2004) *Inside the Royal Shakespeare Company*, Abingdon, Oxon: Routledge.

Hewison, Robert, Holden, John and Jones, Samuel (2010) *All Together: A Creative Approach to Organisational Change*, London: Demos, available online at http://www.demos.co.uk/files/All_Together.pdf?1268865772 (accessed 15 August 2011).

Royal Shakespeare Company
http://www.rsc.org.uk/

2   Between the East and the West today

Gabor Tompa (Hungarian Theatre of Cluj)

In a review of Andras Visky's play *Born for Never*, directed by Gabor Tompa and performed by the National Theatre of Cluj at the Avignon Festival in 2009, Patrice Pavis sees the structure of the company and the aesthetic of the production's mise-en-scène as 'typical of the great Central European professional tradition of Art Theatre' (Pavis 2010: 96). This is the kind of work where the main strength of the staging is contained in a choral performance of the cast and 'perfect harmony of all the scenic elements' – the staging is an atmospheric counterpart to the enigmatic language of the piece rather than being its interpretation. Thus it transcends any language barriers:

> For those who don't speak Hungarian, this surgically precise, extremely rigorous visual language might almost be enough to follow the plot; the visual seems to give birth to the spoken.
>
> (Pavis 2010: 96)

Despite his directorial style, or perhaps thanks to it, Gabor Tompa is one of few Eastern European theatre directors who manages to successfully straddle the Eastern and the Western working contexts. As a young theatre director, after graduating from the I.L. Caragiale Theatre and Film Academy in Bucharest in 1981, he was mostly based at the Hungarian Theatre of Cluj. In 1987, Tompa took over the artistic directorship of this regional theatre – founded in 1792 (and based since 1910 at its current site) – and proceeded to combine directing with his pedagogical work at the theatre academy in Targu Mures, and later in Cluj. Since the 1990s he has directed work in Germany, France, Spain and the UK. In 1999, he directed a highly successful production of *Waiting for Godot* at the Lyric Theatre Belfast, and in 2004 he was invited by Alan Lyddiard to work with members of the Northern Stage ensemble on the *The New Tenant* by Ionesco.

As of 2007, Tompa has been running the Directing Programme at the Theatre and Dance Department at the University of California, San Diego, while also maintaining the artistic directorship of his theatre. He complements his international lifestyle by also bringing significant examples of international theatre to a festival in Cluj named Interferences. This interview took place during Interferences in December 2010.

Interview

RADOSAVLJEVIĆ: You are someone who has worked in Eastern Europe, but also in Western Europe and the US. It would be interesting to share your thoughts on what the advantages and disadvantages of working with an ensemble have been in your experience?

TOMPA: I think that both systems have their advantages and disadvantages. The one that we had before – and I think more than 50 per cent of Romanian theatres still have that system although I don't, having changed it in 1991– involves very long-term, life-long contracts, which make the structure of the companies very rigid. So you couldn't remove anyone who is not competent – you couldn't change technicians or the producer or the production manager. The actors' salaries were given according to the years they spent in service and not according to the artistic quality or the number of performances they carried on their shoulders. I know existentially it's difficult to be a freelancer and not to have a company where you belong – but sometimes the productions with the cast chosen through auditions have a very strong focus and energy. So we are trying to mix what's good in both systems. There was a desire of the Romanian state cultural policy to change the old contractual system but they couldn't fulfil it because of a strong resistance from some union members, and especially from the mediocrities who always fear that they will be dismissed, and that they will lose their jobs in which they don't have to do anything. I think a healthy competition is very, very welcome in theatre life because it can keep this necessary – not tension, but the spirit where you as an actor try to stay in good shape and continue training and taking workshops.

I know in the UK it's very difficult because I met actors when I worked there in Glasgow, Belfast and Newcastle. Newcastle was a special situation because Northern Stage was a quasi-permanent ensemble at the time, but in Glasgow I met an actress who played in Brook's *Mahabharata* and then played in my *Hamlet* in the Tramway, and later she was a waitress. So that's dramatic in a way.

Here in the Hungarian Theatre of Cluj – which was 218 years old in 2010 and is the oldest Hungarian theatre – for the past 20 years everyone has been employed on one-year contracts. They expire in a year and are negotiated or renewed every year – or not. Of course no one is crazy to let the best actors, the best forces, go away and change the whole company every year. It would have been absolutely impossible to find this rather good team we now have in our workshops, in the shops, the stage crew, the technicians, the production manager, even the marketing and the artistic secretary, if we had continued to have those lifelong contracts. We couldn't have experimented – with some people for a very short term like a couple of months, or a year, or two seasons – in order to reach this situation.

At the same time, artistically speaking, I think that it is very important that sometimes a team works together for a longer period, not only on one production. I mean the one-off productions can be good because everyone is focused and motivated, while if you are in a long term company it can be very sad. I had very difficult experiences with permanent companies abroad, for instance in Budapest, where the actors consider they are some kind of mercenaries and they do the job for their salaries, but they are not very curious. You go somewhere as a guest, and there's no mutual curiosity to let yourself be touched by the other, and the whole meeting – which is the essential thing in theatre – doesn't happen.

At the same time I don't believe in changing the company every year because I think it's important to do at least four or five projects over a couple of seasons together to get to know each other, because then you can explore more. An actor shouldn't be used one way only or play similar roles, they always need to be challenged to go to the outer edge of their capacities.

I have worked in Canada and the United States and I consider that the Equity rules – I understand them because they are against commercial abuse of the actor – but they are stupid in terms of the method of working. You have to stop speaking about work during a break, and you can't give notes to the actors after the tech rehearsals, which leads to – dead theatre. Because a theatre performance is evolving all the time, and if you want to discuss it after a tech it's in order to improve it, in order to keep it alive. I am teaching at the University of California in San Diego and I kept giving notes to the actors during techs in order to help them improve, as that's a learning process as well, but I heard that someone from the acting department said that 'a performance should be frozen' – that was the exact expression – 'after the tech rehearsals'. So it's 'frozen theatre'.

RADOSAVLJEVIĆ: When we talk about ensemble, we could be talking in terms of the ensemble of actors on a permanent or temporary basis, but also an ensemble way of working that's about working with the same collaborators, such as designers or composers. Do you have any regular creative collaborators?

TOMPA: Yes, I do. I only work with a couple of people as designers; I think that there are no more than six in total, which is a good thing. Collaborating with one person probably works for a period of time, and then you get tired of each other and they need new challenges and provocations. The same with composers. I used to work with two or three choreographers, and one dramaturg because usually I don't work with dramaturgs except in the Hungarian language productions and sometimes the Romanian productions. The dramaturg of our theatre, Andras Visky, is also a playwright. I directed five of his plays, among them *Born For Never* which was very well received in Avignon in 2009. I want to underline that when I do his plays I like it very much that when we start rehearsals, he ceases to be the playwright who is defending his lines; he is the dramaturg of the production where he is totally collaborating, cutting or changing lines for that particular production because he understands the concept, the idea of the production. And maybe for another production of the same play he could act in the same way because he doesn't mix up these two things; he knows that one production is just one version of the text, one interpretation, and the play is never finished in a script form.

RADOSAVLJEVIĆ: In terms of your experience of working increasingly in the States as well as here in Romania, another issue that I am interested in is the relationship to text that's seemingly different in the English-speaking world. How do you approach that problem – is your response to text as a director the same regardless of which cultural context you work in?

TOMPA: There is a very interesting problem, because I hear terms such as 'text-based' theatre or 'text-based production' and 'visual theatre'. They told me in the United States 'your theatre is very visual'. I didn't know what that means – what theatre is not visual? The theatre you don't go to see is not visual. There is a kind of canonic respect for the text in America – even for the new plays – which kind of withholds and inhibits a great part of the theatre experience. Because what is specific to theatre is that you are not narrating a story by the mouths of the actors, you are telling the story by the context, the dramatic context where the text is generated by the situation. You can't say any line just because it is written; you have to investigate what leads the characters to say what they are saying – what is the dramatic situation? In different situations the same line can be very different.

If I say 'good morning' just to greet you, that's not theatre yet, but if I put my hand in your pocket trying to take away your wallet and I say 'good morning' and you don't react to my text, you react to my action, that is a dramatic situation. So I think that the problem is that they think that the story's told by mouths narrating. That's prose, not theatre.

Of course there are lots of possibilities for interpretation of the text, even for a single director they can change, and that's fantastic because the masterpieces of the theatre are always open structures. They change with time as well, and some things that were hidden in one time, can open up in another time because theatre is so connected to the present. In different times different senses are intensified; different things are important in different contexts, different countries, in different situations with different audiences. I think that there is a kind of sacred unfaithfulness to the text – literally to the text. It is rather because of the faithfulness to the spirit of the text that a director tries to wrestle with the text and it is in this wrestling that something very interesting or exciting can be born. Otherwise, it's nothing – it's dead theatre. So, I think the text is important as the dramatic pre-text. I used to say that we directors, and the actors as well, should behave in connection with the text as jealous lovers: 'don't believe a single word of your lover because they can cheat!'

RADOSAVLJEVIĆ: I often tell the anecdote of when you were in Newcastle working on *The New Tenant* and you wanted to quote Beckett in the work, but because of the Beckett estate's strict regulations, the only way in which you could quote Beckett was non-verbal – you found a way of achieving intertextuality through the mise-en-scène rather than the words. I just wonder, were there other kinds of intertextuality that you might have worked with? Have you tried the process of so-called 'devising'?

TOMPA: I think I did with my last project. I did a couple of shows in the United States: *Woyzeck*, and *Tango* by Mrozek, and recently I did a Beckett-inspired work, *Ruins True*, which is a dance performance with older dancers – two women and a man. There is a text, a prose poem by Beckett, which is all recorded, but it is a dance piece and the music is generated from the words. The text as music is used in this because Beckett is very musical, his work has musical structure. Ionesco too is very musical. You can cut lines from Chekhov and lots of lines from Shakespeare without really hurting the structure of the play. Meanwhile, if you take *The Bald Prima Donna*, every line in itself is nonsense, but if you cut a couple of lines it's like cutting some notes from a symphony because it is very, very musically built, and taking away notes gives you false music. So interpretation of Beckett is a different thing. The actor probably has to be very much like an instrument; he has to have the courage to become nobody in order to make the music sound.

RADOSAVLJEVIĆ: Is that linked to the language of the play or does it also work in translation in the same way?

TOMPA: I think it's the same way. I mean of course *Waiting for Godot* sounds best in English and it's interesting because it was written in French but the thoughts are those of an Irishman. I directed *Godot* several times, I directed it in German, in Hungarian, in English a few times, because I did it in Belfast and in Canada as well, and I think that the rhythm, the real rhythm is the English text, and none of the languages can challenge that. When I did it at the Lyric Theatre in Belfast in 1999, we held the auditions in London and Dublin and Belfast and I met these two guys – Sean Campion and Conleth Hill. They didn't have time to prepare the scenes I gave as sides because they were in the production of *Stones in His Pockets*, with which they went to the West End and Broadway later. They asked me to let them read, and as they started to read I realised that these were the guys, because from the very beginning they understood this very particular humour of the text and also the 'clownishness'. I mean, they were really following what Beckett said when he was asked how we should do his plays: 'Fast, precisely and well'.

Bibliography

Meyer-Dinkgräfe, Daniel (ed.) (2002) 'Gabor Tompa', in *Who's Who in Contemporary World Theatre*, 2nd edn, London: Routledge.

Pavis, Patrice (2010) 'Writing at Avignon 2009: Dramatic, Postdramatic, or post-postdramatic', *TheatreForum – International Theatre Journal*, Summer–Fall 2010: 92–100.

Shuttleworth, Ian (1999) 'Belfast Festival 1: R And J/Romeo E Giulietta/Snow White (Biancaneve)/A Clockwork Orange/Waiting For Godot, Various venues, Belfast, November, 1999', available online at http://www.cix.co.uk/~shutters/reviews/99088.htm (accessed 19 December 2012).

Tompa, Gabor (1994) *A Director's Workshop on Hamlet*, video recorded at The Tramway, Glasgow, as part of the International Workshop Festival, available online at http://spa.exeter.ac.uk/drama/research/exeterdigitalarchives/media_browse.php?type=101 (accessed 18 March 2013).

Hungarian Theatre of Cluj
http://www.huntheater.ro/lista.php?soid=1

3 How the Berliner Ensemble changes with time

Hermann Wündrich (Berliner Ensemble)

In 'A Short Organum for the Theatre', Brecht stated that 'the smallest social unit is not the single person but two people' (Brecht 1964: 197). Therefore, he argued further, the actors should learn and develop their characters together – even swapping them in rehearsal in order to strengthen 'the all-decisive social standpoint from which to present [their] character[s]' (1964: 197).

On their return from exile in the United States, Bertolt Brecht and his wife Helene Weigel were successful in obtaining the financial support of the East German authorities to create their own company. They approached a number of former collaborators and founded the Berliner Ensemble in 1949. The theatre was run by Weigel from its inception until her death in 1971.

Laura Bradley notes that the Berliner Ensemble was treated as 'a national status symbol' (Bradley 2006: 98), but despite the growing international reputation of the company in the 1950s and 1960s, internal power struggles concerning the treatment of Brecht's work ensued following his death in 1956. Choreographer and former Deputy Director Ruth Berghaus was considered too artistically innovative when she took over the running of the company between 1971 and 1977. Brecht's former assistant Manfred Wekwerth followed in the role therefore from 1977 until the fall of the Berlin Wall in 1991. Eventually, playwright Heiner Müller was also an artistic director of the company, initially as part of a team, and then on his own just before his death in 1995. Since 2000, the Berliner Ensemble has entered a more stable phase under the directorship of Claus Peymann, although the question of Brecht's legacy inevitably remains.

Dramaturg Hermann Wündrich joined the Berliner Ensemble in 2003, as one of four members of the Dramaturgy Department, a professional sector highly valued by Brecht himself. Born in 1943 in Dresden, Wündrich studied German, Philosophy, Theatre Studies and History of

Art in Cologne. He worked as a dramaturg at several theatres, namely Schauspiel Düsseldorf, Theater der Stadt Köln and Staatstheater Wiesbaden, and as a reader for publishers. Wündrich has lectured at the Universities of Frankfurt, Kassel and Bonn.

This interview took place in October 2011 in Berlin. Sections of the interview spoken in German were translated by Martin Schnabl.

Interview

WÜNDRICH: There have been many changes at the Berliner Ensemble since the death of Bertolt Brecht. It's a long history. The period during the GDR was very difficult. There were many, many hard fights from the very beginning – the topic of Bertolt Brecht wasn't settled very well. Even under Helene Weigel, the Berliner Ensemble faced difficult times, because after Brecht's death she introduced a reform. Her successor, Ruth Berghaus, was too modern for her times, so she was sacked. After that came Manfred Wekwerth, who led the theatre in a very dogmatic way – he was closely associated with the communist party. One of the big turning points in history was the fall of the Berlin Wall, when it all started anew again. It was a big shock when it was revealed that Wekwerth had worked for the Stasi as well. The city of Berlin wanted to close the theatre, but then they changed their mind and asked a group of five famous directors to lead it. However, these directors could not work together, and it all fell apart. Around the year 2000, a new artistic director Claus Peymann came along, and the Berliner Ensemble became functional again. So the house has seen many changes, and the most recent change is one that has led the theatre back to the way that Brecht led it, because Brecht never just staged his own plays, he always had an international repertoire, the same as we do now. The way it was done during the last years of the GDR was that they only played Brecht. It was very old-fashioned. During Brecht's own time only two or three of his own plays were staged here. There were German classics, young East German playwrights and so on.

RADOSAVLJEVIĆ: Presumably Brecht wanted to work with a permanent ensemble of artists for particular artistic reasons. How has that legacy lived on?

WÜNDRICH: It's not unusual what Brecht did – he did it the way other theatres do it. We work with an ensemble. The Deutsches Theater does the same, the Gorki Theater does the same, and so does every theatre in every city in Germany.

RADOSAVLJEVIĆ: Do you still have a permanent ensemble of actors?

WÜNDRICH: Yes.

RADOSAVLJEVIĆ: How many?

WÜNDRICH: About 60 people.

RADOSAVLJEVIĆ: Are they employed on permanent contracts?

WÜNDRICH: Yes, often.

RADOSAVLJEVIĆ: Who are the oldest members of the company and how long have they been in the company?

WÜNDRICH: There are only two or three who knew Bertolt Brecht. They are about 70–75 years old, but still acting. Most of them were engaged by Helene Weigel, as the managing director.

RADOSAVLJEVIĆ: How do you recruit actors now? Do they come to you from a particular school, or do you have auditions?

WÜNDRICH: We look around. If we are interested in someone we ask them, or they come to us.

RADOSAVLJEVIĆ: Do you have a formal audition process?

WÜNDRICH: Only for the young ones, people who come from the schools. The schools organise auditions and we attend them, and then we invite them for an audition here. But we only do that for the special acting schools.

RADOSAVLJEVIĆ: How long is the rehearsal period at the Berliner Ensemble?

WÜNDRICH: Between two and three months, it depends on the play.

RADOSAVLJEVIĆ: I presume it depends on the schedules of the actors as well?

WÜNDRICH: No, it depends on the play. If it's a big one, or a bit difficult, it needs a bit longer.

RADOSAVLJEVIĆ: How long do the actors rehearse each day?

WÜNDRICH: From 10:00 until 15:00, and in the evening they have performances, and if they don't then we start rehearsing again in the evening at 19:00 or 20:00 until 22:00 or 23:00.

RADOSAVLJEVIĆ: How do guest writers and directors work with the Ensemble?

WÜNDRICH: There are two directors with permanent contracts, the artistic director Claus Peymann and the other one is Manfred Karge. All the others are asked to come and make work.

RADOSAVLJEVIĆ: So do the directors choose the actors they want to work with?

WÜNDRICH: Yes, but we do not make a lot of new productions. Our productions often run for a lot of years, and we do not need so many new productions. We only make between six and nine productions a year – other theatres make about 15 or 20.

RADOSAVLJEVIĆ: Do you work with new writers?

WÜNDRICH: Yes, new writers, new plays. Botho Strauß, Peter Handke, Elfriede Jelinek.

RADOSAVLJEVIĆ: And do you develop new writers as well?

WÜNDRICH: No, we don't. They are already quite famous, and they give us their new plays.

RADOSAVLJEVIĆ: I noticed that you have the play *Freedom and Democracy* by Mark Ravenhill on here at the moment. How did that come about?

WÜNDRICH: Yes. It was the theme, the political point of view which interested us, therefore we did it.

RADOSAVLJEVIĆ: How would you define the artistic vision of the company at the moment, and Claus Peymann's artistic policy in particular?

WÜNDRICH: He is interested in Brecht, but in developing his theories further. We do not do Brecht the way Brecht did himself. We try to develop it, perhaps inspired by a playwright like Heiner Müller. We are interested in what we call 'Bürgerlicher Realismus', like Chekhov, Ibsen, Strindberg – plays from around the nineteenth century. We do Shakespeare too.

RADOSAVLJEVIĆ: So it's about upholding particular traditions?

WÜNDRICH: We are not very interested in experimenting, you could say.

RADOSAVLJEVIĆ: What would you say have been the most iconic and the most successful productions in this latest phase of the Berliner Ensemble under Claus Peymann?

WÜNDRICH: The most successful perhaps is *Arturo Ui* by Bertolt Brecht, which has been running for 10 years now. Also successful is another Brecht play which is relatively unknown, *Furcht und Elend im Dritten Reich*. And Shakespeare's *Richard II*.

RADOSAVLJEVIĆ: What makes these productions particularly successful?

WÜNDRICH: What the director did with the play.

RADOSAVLJEVIĆ: Are they mostly directed by Peymann or by other people?

WÜNDRICH: *Richard II* is by Peymann, *Arturo Ui* is by Heiner Müller and *Furcht und Elend* is by Manfred Karge.

RADOSAVLJEVIĆ: What was Müller's contribution to the company?

WÜNDRICH: He was the Intendant [artistic director] of the house until he died. He tried to develop the Berliner Ensemble, or to keep the Berliner Ensemble together during the very destructive years of change – the time of the fall of the Wall, which was very difficult for everybody. He also wanted to make Brecht new.

RADOSAVLJEVIĆ: Is his production of *Arturo Ui* representative of that vision?

WÜNDRICH: Yes.

RADOSAVLJEVIĆ: What was Claus Peymann's route to taking over the Berliner Ensemble?

WÜNDRICH: He was a very successful leader of theatres. He was in Bochum, in Stuttgart, at the Vienna Burgtheater, and then he came here. He got the invitation to bring the Berliner Ensemble back to its old glory. Peter Zadek, Peter Palitzsch, Heiner Müller, Fritz Marquardt and Matthias Langhoff were directors here after the fall of the Wall, and it didn't work. The city authorities then looked for someone who could make it work.

RADOSAVLJEVIĆ: Maybe we could talk about the dramaturgy department a bit more. I know it's a particularly German professional profile. There are currently four dramaturgs in the Berliner Ensemble and you all work on particular productions. Could you describe the process a little bit?

WÜNDRICH: Together with the director you come up with a 'Lesart' [a way of reading] for the play – a particular way of approaching a piece and what story you want to tell with it, especially when it comes to an older piece. Because we don't just want to tell the story, we want to tell the story for today: what is important about the play to us. On that level the dramaturg delivers some more or less scientific work at the beginning. As a group consisting of the director, scenographer and dramaturg, we develop what we call 'Lesart' – how we want to understand the play, and how we want to stage it. That happens before rehearsals. During rehearsals the dramaturg functions as the first critic. We are not there every day, maybe two or three times a week – we look at everything and think about whether it is developing the way it was imagined, or whether we even had wrong ideas and whether we should change something and discuss it further. That is the main job of the dramaturg. Otherwise the dramaturgy department is the strategising department. We choose which plays we would like to stage, and which directors we would like to invite.

RADOSAVLJEVIĆ: What was your favourite experience of working on a Berliner Ensemble production?

WÜNDRICH: Important for me was a German classic play by Friedrich Schiller, *Die Räuber*. Then there was the first staging of a play by Botho Strauß that was important for me. I also worked with a special director, Manfred Karge.

RADOSAVLJEVIĆ: What made those experiences special?

WÜNDRICH: We get along very well. He thinks a little bit differently, and therefore we can give one another inspiration.

RADOSAVLJEVIĆ: When you work with a guest director or a guest writer, do you feel like you need to represent the Berliner Ensemble?

WÜNDRICH: No, we just ask them to come here because we want them to!

RADOSAVLJEVIĆ: And in artistic terms?

WÜNDRICH: No, we know them very well. We have seen their work and talked to them, they know us very well. We want to make a good production – we have no ideology which has to be represented in every play or in every performance.

RADOSAVLJEVIĆ: Do you ever have to make any sort of intervention as a dramaturg?

WÜNDRICH: Of course – if something potentially destructive happens.

RADOSAVLJEVIĆ: For example?

WÜNDRICH: Well, a work of theatre is a work between many people in a group. Accidents can happen, quarrels. I've nothing against quarrels, quarrels can be very helpful, but I would try to resolve them.

RADOSAVLJEVIĆ: Quarrels between whom?

WÜNDRICH: Actors and directors, actors among actors, actors and dramaturgs as well sometimes.

RADOSAVLJEVIĆ: Have you been in a situation where you worked with a group of people who have only come together for that one particular production?

WÜNDRICH: Yes, when I was young.

RADOSAVLJEVIĆ: And how was that in comparison to working with the same group?

WÜNDRICH: I prefer to work with the same group of people, though not always for years and years. In every group there are changes, but I like working with people who have had experiences together; it doesn't necessarily make it easier, but the result can be better. People who don't know each other have to find each other first, and you may not get as far and achieve as much. You get farther with the people you know.

RADOSAVLJEVIĆ: How is working for the Berliner Ensemble different from working with other companies that you have worked with?

WÜNDRICH: Maybe we work under greater pressure here sometimes, because our expectations of ourselves are very high. That may not be the same in other theatres. But that may also have something to do with being in Berlin. We are competing with the other theatres in Berlin: with the Deutsche Theater, the Volksbühne, the Schaubühne. Unlike many theatres in Germany, we have no subscribers here, we live entirely on ticket sales. Each evening we have to make sure that we find enough audience. That creates competition. So we have to make an effort – just like the others, too.

RADOSAVLJEVIĆ: When the Berliner Ensemble came to England in 1956, it made a big impression. It is considered to have influenced a lot of people, like Peter Hall who then founded the Royal Shakespeare

Company as an ensemble. What do you think it was that created this impact?

WÜNDRICH: Everything Brechtian, Brecht's theatre theories. 'Verfremdung', 'Epic Theatre', and 'Sozialer Gestus' were new ideas, people did not know about them before. That resulted in a different way of staging theatre. That was new then, today it is old. The Brechtian theatre theories were shocking, he was all about breaking the illusion. But these Brechtian means are so common today that you cannot employ them in that way – because everyone is used to them. So we have to come up with other things today. Times have changed. The technical preconditions which we face today, our media and what we are used to being exposed to, have changed us in a way that the frame of reference that Brecht had is not appropriate anymore. Brecht was reacting to bourgeois illusionist theatre; he did not want to sympathise, or suffer with the characters, he wanted to break with that. But we have these breaks today naturally in our everyday lives, the technical conditions have progressed in a way that Brechtian ideas cannot counter anymore. Back then, in 1956 or in Paris in 1954 two years earlier, that was a new way of theatre-making. Brecht had had time to develop his theories during his time in exile in the USA, and he wanted to return to the German-speaking world to see whether they would work.

RADOSAVLJEVIĆ: When was the first time that you saw a Berliner Ensemble show?

WÜNDRICH: It was at the beginning of the 1960s.

RADOSAVLJEVIĆ: Which shows were these?

WÜNDRICH: *The Three Penny Opera*, *The Good Person of Szechwan*, and afterwards, when I was a student, I would come here to see performances.

RADOSAVLJEVIĆ: What do you remember about those first experiences at the Berliner Ensemble?

WÜNDRICH: For me they were old-fashioned. When I was a student, I saw *The Three Penny Opera* directed by Bertolt Brecht.

RADOSAVLJEVIĆ: How were they old-fashioned?

WÜNDRICH: The decor, the stage, the performances seemed as if they already had been played 500 times. But I came here because I wanted to understand Brechtian Theatre.

RADOSAVLJEVIĆ: How does the Berliner Ensemble negotiate between tradition and innovation? Do you encounter the problem of people attempting to honour a legacy?

WÜNDRICH: This problem does not exist to a huge extent anymore in this company. It does for some people, but traditional Brecht is only expected by people who have not been exposed to other theatre that much. Now that mainly applies to people from East Germany, and often there are sentimental reasons for this, remembering a state from 20 years ago. Most critics think that Brecht's theories are old-fashioned and are not relevant anymore. We are moving on, and the decisive first steps in that new direction were made by Heiner Müller, who has now been dead for ten years.

RADOSAVLJEVIĆ: Would you do things differently from the way they are done at the moment, would you run the theatre differently?

WÜNDRICH: I am doing it. I can bring things from my experience to the work. I can imagine that you can do things differently from the way that I do them, but I leave that up to the next generation. Most of us who are my age – we will do it for another three or four years, then we're finished.

RADOSAVLJEVIĆ: So what would you say to the next generation?

WÜNDRICH: I think that the means of Verfremdung – to use the old term – which was supposed to make it possible to regard a piece with the mind while experiencing it on a sensuous level, has not been found yet. One should try to find a way that allows for the use of both intellect and feeling, the use of the head and the heart at the same time, while watching a play. And I would say that one has to be careful that theatre does not slip and neglect the intellect. Theatre should not slip off in the direction of big effects designed to overwhelm the audience. Unfortunately that is a kind of theatre which I see more and more, and in which theatre increasingly becomes 'show'.

Bibliography

Bradley, Laura (2006) *Brecht and Political Theatre: The Mother on Stage*, Oxford: Oxford University Press.

Brecht, Bertolt (1964) *Brecht on Theatre: The Development of an Aesthetic*, ed. and trans. John Willett, New York: Hill & Wang; London: Methuen.

Thompson, Peter and Sacks, Glendyr (2006) *The Cambridge Companion to Brecht*, Cambridge: Cambridge University Press.

Berliner Ensemble
http://www.berliner-ensemble.de/

4 Directing as an art of composition

Yuri Butusov (guest director, Satirikon Theatre)

Yuri Butusov was born in 1961 in St Petersburg. He initially attended the Shipbuilding Institute in his city, and only graduated from the directing programme at the St Petersburg Academy of Theatrical Arts at the age of 35 in 1996. His graduation production of *Waiting of Godot* brought him instant fame and the Best Director Award at the St Petersburg Festival, as well as two of Moscow's prestigious Golden Mask Awards. This was followed by the Golden Mask award-winning production of *Woyzeck* in 1996, and a production of Pinter's *The Caretaker* in 1997, which won the Stanislavsky Award.

At the invitation of the famous Moscow actor, teacher and artistic director Konstantin Raikin, Butusov directed Ionesco's *Macbett* at the Satirikon Theatre in 2002. This created a bridge between his Theatre of the Absurd phase and an ensuing trail of Shakespeare productions: long-running *Richard III* at the Satirikon in 2004, controversial *Hamlet* at the Moscow Art Theatre in 2005, and highly acclaimed *King Lear* at the Satirikon in 2007.

The 2005 production of *Hamlet* featured a radical casting decision to have Hamlet, Claudius and Polonius played by three actors of the same age, his now famous colleagues from St Petersburg. In addition, Butusov also conducted major cuts to the play leading some critics to condemn the production as oversimplifying the play. Anna Shulgat reports that one critic branded this version 'Hamlet-shashlik', implying that the play was being served as a popular meal for the masses (Shulgat 2007: 43).

His *Richard III* however is seen as an undisputed success. The *Moscow Times* critic John Freedman has picked Butusov's 'tragi-farce' as one of the 15 most memorable productions of the last decade (Freedman 2011) and it is often a personal highlight of many international visitors to Moscow (see blogs: SBW 2010; Perkins n.d.). American freelance dramaturg Shari Parkins – who saw Butusov's version four times – singles this out as the 'best production' of the play she has ever seen. Most critics and commentators focus on the cartoonish black and white set, the highly poeticised representation of the numerous killings in the play, and the multiple casting of individual actors including Maxim Averin who also appears as the Duchess of York. 'But this is the Satirikon and, therefore, even the supporting roles are larger than life', concludes Freedman (2004).

Even though in the interview that follows, Butusov uses the analogy of composition to describe his directorial process, his notion of composition concerns the visual content of the stage. Norwegian dramaturg Njål Mjøs has aesthetically characterised Butusov's partnership with his designer since *Godot*, Aleksandr Shishkin, as a kind of 'theatrical neo-primitivism': 'without any post-modernist irony they play with the "primitive" conditions of the stage, the primal, ordinary elements of the theatre'. And echoing Freedman on the ensemble quality of the work, he too highlights its tendency to 'bring minor characters into the spotlight' (Mjøs 2007).

At the time of our meeting at the Moscow Art Theatre School in February 2010, Butusov was directing *Measure for Measure* at the Vakhtangov Theatre in Moscow. Simultaneous translation was provided by Anastasia Razumovskaya.

Interview

RADOSAVLJEVIĆ: How did *Richard III* at the Satirikon come about?

BUTUSOV: I found the actor who was able to do it. And I'd been dreaming my whole life about making a production of *Richard III*. When I started working at the Satirikon, it was a natural thing to do. I made some steps towards Shakespeare while I was still making absurdist theatre – I made Ionesco's *Macbett* first. So that was a pathway towards Shakespeare. I experience Shakespeare as very absurd, very paradoxical.

RADOSAVLJEVIĆ: And how did you go about creating the work? Was the text the starting point or was it something else in rehearsal?

BUTUSOV: My usual rehearsal process is that the text is the starting point, of course, but at the same time I create a series of etudes and improvisations. We approach a scene from a number of different perspectives. It's experimental work. And sometimes this leads to some paradoxical solutions which are contrary to the text. For me the text is not the law, which is something the critics chide me about sometimes. But that is a common issue in theatre – director versus the text.

RADOSAVLJEVIĆ: How does the directorial idea come about?

BUTUSOV: From the play itself, of course. But also from rehearsals – as we spend time talking about life and get to know each other – it is very important to me to be in agreement with the actors about our interpretation of the play. But above all, it comes from the artist inside of me.

It's probably very egotistical, but when I make a piece of theatre I am telling a story about the actor or about myself, not a story about the play. I get a lot of criticism for that. The show succeeds when my own desires and ideas and feelings coincide with those of the actors.

RADOSAVLJEVIĆ: When you say the first part of the process is talking to the actors about life, how long does that last? How long does the whole of the rehearsal process last?

BUTUSOV: It's always different. *Richard III* took four months in total. Sometimes it can take two months. We have a terrible time here in Russia because the repertory theatre system makes it impossible to plan anything, actors are multi-tasking and it's very hard to schedule anything, the process is really stretched – the actors could be shooting a movie and the rehearsals have to stop during that time – it's very bad. For example, when I made *Hamlet* here at the MHAT, the rehearsal process took nine months. As a result of this we lose the complicity – because they go away and come back different people, and I am different too, and I have already started thinking about something else – so it's very complicated. As for *Richard*, we had a completely different situation – four full months of rehearsals and we arrived at a more finished result than with *Hamlet*. The situation is different at the Satirikon, because it all depends on Raikin. And at that time, hardly anyone was filming anything. Here at the MHAT it's a real problem.

RADOSAVLJEVIĆ: Are they an ensemble company at the Satirikon?

BUTUSOV: Yes, it's a permanent ensemble. But they have a different organisational principle at the Satirikon – they have only one star. It's a group of people that really grew over time – I made three productions with them, and now they are really capable of some very big parts. But broadly speaking, it is a theatre of one star – that's neither good nor bad: it's just a fact.

As for the process of making *Richard*, I could say it was a success, because it started out with moments of confession. It was clear to me while preparing for this piece that childhood was going to be a very important theme – as it is in everyone's life anyway – but especially in the case of Raikin. As the son of a very famous actor[1] he had a childhood which was by all means extraordinary. And I knew that there would be a painful spot in there somewhere. Looking at the play itself, it could also be argued that the problem of Richard can be traced to his own childhood, to his illness and his personal view of himself within the world. And this became a kind of engine for the production.

So we talked about his childhood. Raikin has a unique nature. He never brings anything into rehearsals. You have to pull it out. If you open him up in rehearsal, he can create such emotions, and he can pursue your idea further than most other actors are capable of doing. But you have to find a way to provoke him and give him a very precise choice of words so that he can understand the character. And then something else starts to happen: he makes a transition from the head into the body – and this physical aspect is really important to me: when he becomes free, if he has a very precise understanding of what he is doing, he really starts to develop the character. I've been watching him over the last six years of playing the part, and he's been getting better and better. Not worse and worse, but better and better.

We had a specific circumstance in this composition because we were starting with a monologue from another play – one of the Henrys that precede *Richard III*. In the rehearsal of this monologue, it was just the two of us and a big carpet, and he was very excited, he took his shoes off and he was playing around on the carpet. You may have noticed that sometimes he is performing like a dog, or like a monkey, or like a bird, using his physicality. Those birds around the stage, and the whole space – it's all connected to the idea of a children's playroom. That's why the table is huge, and the bed is huge, but he is small. You could say that the main idea came from this notion of distorted proportions in the interaction between the soul and the outside world.

In the key scene when he is haunted by the ghosts of the people he killed – having the nightmare of the small man – he is standing on the oversize chair, very scared. And that's the point in which he grows up and releases all the pain. That's another reason I was criticised – because I was trying to justify the actions of Richard III, I was trying to find his pain. For me the historical aspect wasn't as interesting as the psychological aspect – the destiny of the human being.

RADOSAVLJEVIĆ: Is there any significance in choosing to make the whole piece in black and white?

BUTUSOV: I just like it quite modest. White is the colour of innocence. Of course, the colour scheme emerged from our feelings about the piece and from the conversations with the designer about the world of a children's playroom, the soft materials. That's why we have this carpet; and the birds are toys – it's his world. And this is connected to the fact that we found out that in the Tower there used to be a little zoo, and that the young princes used to play with animals.

RADOSAVLJEVIĆ: The princes are very prominent characters in this piece – they have the last word.

BUTUSOV: Yes, he dies because of this absolutely horrifying crime – that he killed the two princes. Because he killed the innocent children, in the end they kill him. Not literally, but in spiritual terms.

RADOSAVLJEVIĆ: So it becomes a revenge tragedy?

BUTUSOV: It's possible to say that. The tragedy of conscience, maybe.

RADOSAVLJEVIĆ: To me it looked a lot like German Expressionism.

BUTUSOV: I wouldn't argue with that. I do love German Expressionism and I do love German theatre. One of my first productions was *Woyzeck*, and it probably set off this Expressionist streak. I do use montage a lot. Even in *Measure for Measure* now, I like to start with breaking things down – like a kid's puzzle. I break the play down into scenes, mix them up, and then put them together into a new sequence, because I need this sense of Expressionism and the energy from the broken rhythm.

RADOSAVLJEVIĆ: So you are a Meyerholdian really?

BUTUSOV: Meyerhold was a genius, I am just a worker. But of course, I studied his work and he inspires me – the idea of the montage of attractions, and the idea of the show as a specific composition of attractions appeals to me. I do think that directing is actually the art of composition.

RADOSAVLJEVIĆ: There is a comic routine at the beginning of Act Two, when Richard is trying out the throne; was that rehearsed or did it emerge from just playing the character?

BUTUSOV: I proposed to him to make this Chaplinade – I proposed this interaction with the chair, because Richard is also an actor. And this acting trait is really strong in him and he gets a lot of pleasure from acting in front of people. When he woos Anne, for example, he inter-acts with her, and then he interacts with the audience, winking at us, really enjoying the process.

RADOSAVLJEVIĆ: How did you select the music for the piece?

BUTUSOV: It was absolutely a matter of intuition. At the time, I was very interested in this interaction with music, and very often the ideas for staging came from the music. I would include the music in the rehearsal process and then take it away. And using music is also very freeing for the actors.

RADOSAVLJEVIĆ: The music is a sort of impulse?

BUTUSOV: Yes, sometimes when I don't know what to do, I put the music on.

RADOSAVLJEVIĆ: And they do what?

BUTUSOV: I use it as an impulse for a scene. For example, it may lead to a clownade. Sometimes, I say 'Sing me this scene'. It's a kind of a train-ing workshop. But it's hard to say to the professionals 'OK, guys, we are now doing training'. Professional actors really don't like it. When you are working with students you can mix training and improvisation, but when they graduate, the training finishes. It's very hard. And that's how we get talking heads.

RADOSAVLJEVIĆ: In terms of the ensemble way of working, did the notion of the confession in rehearsal extend to the whole ensemble?

BUTUSOV: Yes, of course. But because this play has a clear centre it's more about the central character, the other characters are not as deep. We did try to flesh them out more, but anyway it's more linked to him.

RADOSAVLJEVIĆ: But you had worked with these people before?

BUTUSOV: Yes, it was absolutely the same team which I had worked with before, and some people were added. I do like to work with the same actors and develop them as actors. The same team is in *King Lear*. And when I make my next piece at the Satirikon, it will be them again.

RADOSAVLJEVIĆ: So you've made *Richard*, and *King Lear*, and now you are working on *Measure for Measure* –

BUTUSOV *(laughing)*: And am about to start *Othello* . . .

RADOSAVLJEVIĆ: So Shakespeare is a big part of your work?

BUTUSOV: I like Shakespeare. We say 'When you don't know what to do – do Shakespeare'.

RADOSAVLJEVIĆ: I am curious about what you said about the link between Shakespeare and the Theatre of the Absurd. Could you tell us a bit more about that?

BUTUSOV: Yes, of course. For example, the scene between Richard and Anne – I think it's impossible to find a more absurd and paradoxical scene than that one in the whole world. Of course, Shakespeare capitalised on these paradoxes of human psychology and I think that the Theatre of the Absurd is about the same thing. Then there is Shakespeare's inconsistent treatment of space and time. In my view, the space in the Theatre of the Absurd is the internal space of human psychology. My understanding of this notion began with my first production, *Waiting for Godot*. You completely lose a sense of reality and go inside. That's what helped me to create the space for *Richard III* looking so strange. It is linked to the play, but not literally. If I thought about this for a bit, I could probably think of other examples, but this focus on the paradoxes of human nature are the main and most important connection for me. This may be debatable, but in my view, Shakespeare's view of the world was very tragic, but this deep tragedy also makes it possible to discover the light. That is another connection between Shakespeare and the Theatre of the Absurd. It's hard to find something more desperate than *Waiting for Godot*. But in the end, if you stick with it, you will actually see the light. That's my feeling.

Note

1 Konstantin Raikin is the son of the Soviet star Arkady Raikin.

Bibliography

Butusov, Yuri, *Biography*, available online at http://persona.rin.ru/eng/view/f/0/ 35690/butusov-yuri (accessed 19 December 2012).

Farber, Vreneli (2001) '*Waiting for Godot* Review', *Theatre Journal*, 53(4): 653–5.

Freedman, John (2004) 'The Satirikon's Yury Butusov imagines "Richard III" as a cartoon fantasy, a tragifarce of blood and betrayal that would be laughable were it not so real', *The Moscow Times*, 5 March.

Freedman, John (2011) Fifteen Productions to Remember 2001–2010, *The Moscow Times Blog*, 16 January, http://www.themoscowtimes.com/blogs/432775/post/15-productions-to-remember-2001-2010/433227.html (accessed 19 December 2012).

Mjøs, Njål (2007) 'Director Yury Butusov's Shakespeare Frenzy', MHAT School website, http://mhatschool.theatre.ru/en/international/mosjournal2007/chapter2/ 1/ (accessed 19 December 2012).

Perkins, Shari (n.d.) 'Yuri Butusov's *Richard III* at the Satirikon', *Dramatic Impulse* (blog), http://dramaticimpulse.wordpress.com/2009/05/12/yuri-butusovs-richard-iii-at-the-satirikon/ (accessed 19 December 2012).

SBW (2010) 'Friday, March 12, 2010 *Richard III* at the Satiricon', *Dramatrekking* (blog), http://dramatrekking.blogspot.com/2010/03/richard-iii-at-satiricon.html (accessed 19 December 2012).

Shulgat, A. (2007) 'The new Russian Hamlet: without a hero', *Slavic and East European Performance*, 27(3): 38–46.

Teatr Satirikon
http://www.satirikon.ru/

5 A tried and tested ensemble methodology

Max Stafford-Clark (Out of Joint)

In a letter to *The Times*, dated 30 April 1968, Max Stafford-Clark, the then newly-appointed Artistic Director of the Traverse Theatre in Edinburgh, outlined his plans for a permanent ensemble of actors, observing that in 1968 'soccer teams and pop groups alone' expressed the spirit of the time (Stafford-Clark and Roberts 2007: 9). He had been profoundly influenced by seeing New York's La MaMa at the Edinburgh Fringe, and consequently admired the 'Arch Druid of this whole movement', Jerzy Grotowski, as the main influence on the American troupes (2007: 8). The Traverse company of actors would therefore be involved in continued training designed to 'increase spontaneity' and 'deformalise the relationship between actor and audience' (2007: 9). The plan was successful, but relatively short-lived as he eventually left the Traverse in 1972. Given these early ambitions, it is interesting that Stafford-Clark's most important contribution to the development of the ensemble way of working in Britain would be to build an ensemble around the figure of a playwright – a project he pursued with Joint Stock (1974–1979), Royal Court (1979–1993) and Out of Joint (1993 to present).

Joint Stock emerged within the climate of proliferating young companies in the 1970s and was founded by Stafford-Clark and Bill Gaskill with David Aukin. Its name was representative of the economic principles on which the company was based, i.e. that the members would own shares in the stock of the company. On the basis of this, and in terms of its own time, it is not surprising that Rob Ritchie (1987) and Simon Shepherd (2009: 73) have classified Joint Stock as a 'collective'. Its particularly renowned second production was David Hare's *Fanshen* (1975), about the Chinese communist revolution. Stafford-Clark agrees that *Fanshen* 'politicised' the company (Stafford-Clark and Roberts 2007: 96), but by Caryl Churchill's *Cloud Nine* (1978) they had abandoned Marx and made a 'passionate leap towards Freud' (2007: 68). More importantly, however, Joint Stock has yielded a 'Joint Stock method' of working, a longer rehearsal structure which provides a research period for the writer, and which has been adopted by other companies since.

It is insightful that Stafford-Clark progressed from a company named Joint Stock to one named Out of Joint – a play on words that suggests a certain continuity but also gestures clearly towards the poetic heritage of Shakespeare. Even though he continues to foreground the formative influence of the American avant-garde companies, Stafford-Clark's work can be seen as being chiefly dedicated to the development of plays. Consequently, he has discovered and developed playwrights with an exceptional understanding of the craft of playwriting who went on to become internationally renowned and hugely influential: David Hare, Caryl Churchill, Jim Cartwright, Mark Ravenhill, Robin Soans and many others.

This interview took place in the Out of Joint London office in April 2011.

Interview

RADOSAVLJEVIĆ: I have read the recent interview that you gave to Christopher Innes in the book of interviews on directors and directing. He covers some of the issues that I am interested in, but I would quite like to go into a bit more depth, especially in terms of describing Joint Stock as an ensemble, the way it came about, and how the methodology, that's now referred to as 'The Joint Stock Method', evolved.

STAFFORD-CLARK: It evolved really from the desire to have a greater time in rehearsal. We looked with envy at our brothers in Russia and Germany and Eastern European countries. I did a workshop in St Petersburg once with young directors, and it was pretty disastrous because none of my exercises or games had any relevance, and finally we ended up with a question and answer session. I was touring then with the play *Blue Heart* by Caryl Churchill, and they said 'How long do you rehearse a play normally?'. So I said 'Usually the conventional time is four weeks but this play, five weeks', and the translator looked a bit nonplussed and said 'Sorry, we did not understand your response – do you mean to say four months or four years?'. And that really strikes at the difference. So Joint Stock always undertook a period of research with the writer and with the actors in which the subject of the play was investigated.

RADOSAVLJEVIĆ: How long was the research period usually?

STAFFORD-CLARK: The research would be two or three weeks and then there would be a prolonged gap of eight or nine weeks during which the writer would write the first draft of the play, and then there would be five weeks of formal rehearsal.

RADOSAVLJEVIĆ: How did Joint Stock come about?

STAFFORD-CLARK: I had finished work at the Traverse Theatre in Edinburgh, Bill Gaskill had finished work as the artistic director at the Royal Court, so both of us were at a loose end. We were sitting in the sun one summer on the steps of the Royal Court, and we talked about doing some work together. We both came from very different methodologies. His big influence had been the Berliner Ensemble and Brecht, whereas my influence has really been the hippie American companies – the Open Theatre, the Living Theatre and the La MaMa. We both thought that a period of work would be mutually beneficial and we started work on a book called *The Speakers* by Heathcote Williams, which was about the eccentric personalities – one a Marxist speaker, but the rest really just eccentrics that spoke at Hyde Park Corner. With the actors we worked on this and the first thing they learned was to be speakers, so we could give an actor a subject like traffic wardens, or bumble bees, or fashion, and they would talk for five minutes, usually nonsense, on that particular subject. The play, when we eventually staged it, had multiple actions. The central configuration in the set was a tower that had lights, but it also had a tea bar so the audience could get cups of tea, they could wander round, they could listen to whichever speaker they wanted, and the speakers were in rivalry with each other. It was the first ever promenade production in this country.

RADOSAVLJEVIĆ: That was just a collaboration between Bill Gaskill and yourself before David Hare and David Aukin got involved?

STAFFORD-CLARK: David Aukin was involved as a manager right from the start. David Hare became involved in the second project which was *Fanshen*. But the company was really instigated and run by Bill Gaskill and me.

RADOSAVLJEVIĆ: How did the two of you as directors negotiate the division of labour?

STAFFORD-CLARK: Very easily, as it happened. We both admired each other. I'm 10–12 years younger than Bill so he was very much a senior partner. I would do a scene in the morning and then he would take over in the afternoon, or vice versa. For both of us it was very instructive to work with another director. Bill had a precision about his work and I had come from the wilder reaches of the fringe where overlapping and multiple staging could take place – I think we were mutually very fruitful.

RADOSAVLJEVIĆ: What training had Bill Gaskill had?

STAFFORD-CLARK: He was at Oxford University and he did productions there, but he went to the Royal Court as a very young man and worked under George Devine. His training was Royal Court through and through, and then he went to the National as an associate director under Laurence Olivier. But neither of us had formally studied theatre at university. He was at Oxford and read English and I was at Trinity College, Dublin, and read Irish History and English.

RADOSAVLJEVIĆ: What was the first play to which you applied the Joint Stock methodology?

STAFFORD-CLARK: I suppose *The Speakers* was the first one. We were never formally a collective and never politically that committed. But the second play we did, *Fanshen*, was set in China and based on William Hinton's monumental book about the coming of Communism to a particular village. The actors became politicised by the material, so decisions like how much should be spent on the set, how much should be spent on the actors' per diems when they were touring, were taken by the group. Although the group were dominated by Bill and by me because of our position as directors, it was certainly a more collectively organised group than most at that time.

RADOSAVLJEVIĆ: Would you have used another word to describe it at that time: would it have been a company or an ensemble or a group?

STAFFORD-CLARK: Certainly we had a permanent ensemble for a year, but since then I've become accustomed to, as it were, carrying a semi-permanent ensemble in my head. For example, a recent play I did, *Andersen's English* by Sebastian Barry, had a company of seven actors of whom four I had worked with before. You carry over actors from production to production – like Ian Redford who I've worked with half a dozen times in the last four or five years.

RADOSAVLJEVIĆ: When you put a group of actors together do you look for particular qualities that you think might work together well in an ensemble situation or is it purely on the grounds of casting by character?

STAFFORD-CLARK: I think that now Out of Joint's reputation and experience is such that people will only come forward to do the work if they think they're going to enjoy it. So an enthusiasm to do the work is crucial, but no, I think we look for character. Of course, if you have a permanent ensemble then you have to find plays that suit that company, whereas we commission plays and then cast according to the dictates of the play. There is a wider pool of some two dozen Out of Joint actors who I've worked with consistently over the years and I tend to draw from that. But that's always supplemented by another three or four actors that have not worked with the company before.

RADOSAVLJEVIĆ: How about other collaborators? Designers, composers?

STAFFORD-CLARK: I'm very conservative as far as designers are concerned, and once I find a designer I like working with, I tend to stick with that designer. I'm a serial monogamist! There's a designer called Julian McGowan that I've worked with for a long time who's now emigrated to South Africa, and there's Peter Hartwell who I've worked with for a long time. Tim Shortall who is designing *Top Girls* at Chichester, also designed *The Big Fellah*, so he's my designer of choice at the moment.

RADOSAVLJEVIĆ: Are there parallels in terms of how you work with Out of Joint and how you used to work with Joint Stock?

STAFFORD-CLARK: Yes, I think I took from Joint Stock some of the ways of working and applied them to a rather different company. Joint Stock, of course, had no particular commitment to touring and no affiliation to any London theatre. Out of Joint tends to co-produce with other theatres. *A Dish of Tea with Doctor Johnson* was an exception, but *Top Girls* was co-produced with Chichester, *Bang Bang Bang*, Stella Feehily's play, with the Bolton Octagon. So salary levels are always dictated in part by the theatre's policy. For example, at Chichester the actors would be on slightly different salary levels – the more senior ones will get paid more, whereas when they come on tour with us, at Joint there's a company wage that everybody will get.

RADOSAVLJEVIĆ: Is there any kind of training that you do as part of the rehearsal period for younger actors that are joining the company?

STAFFORD-CLARK: There are a number of status exercises and improvisations that I do that are always part of the rehearsals, and that's a way of bringing younger actors in. I tend to improvise things that don't happen in the play. For example, in *The Big Fellah* one of the actors is playing someone who is an enforcer or security guard within the Republican movement whose job is to winkle out informants. We had a rehearsal and I said to the actor who played the enforcer he had to come into a bar on a market day in this small town and shoot this man who was an off-duty RUC officer.

RADOSAVLJEVIĆ: This was in the research period?

STAFFORD-CLARK: No, that was actually in the formal rehearsal period. In the research period you're actually kicking the play itself about. Say *The Permanent Way* by David Hare – we met a number of people who were involved in the railways, particularly a policeman who investigated the crashes on behalf of the British Transport Police. And gradually through the workshop we found that there was a huge ongoing quarrel between the survivors and the bereaved, because the survivors wanted to forget the events as soon as possible, whereas the bereaved wanted to hold memorial services and wanted to commemorate the event. That was very interesting and totally unexpected.

RADOSAVLJEVIĆ: There is something else that is associated with your way of working and that is the notion of 'actioning'. Could you tell me a bit more about that?

STAFFORD-CLARK: Yes, behind you on that shelf there are a number of scripts, pull down any one with a little white label on.

That's *Top Girls*, that's the play I have yet to work on, rehearsal starts in May. Just open it, and you'll see that I have actioned an intention behind every change of thought.

RADOSAVLJEVIĆ: You've done this as preparation?

STAFFORD-CLARK: This is something that I've done by myself as you point out, but when I work with the actors I will go through it and will always be open to changing it – and say to them 'This is the action I have, what do you think?'. And some of them will be experienced in that way of working, some will be inexperienced.

RADOSAVLJEVIĆ: How did this evolve as a way of working?

STAFFORD-CLARK: I suppose it's straightforward Stanislavsky really. I worked that way when I worked with Bill at Joint Stock. But I think what's important is to be flexible about it. Certainly now, most actors that want to work with me know the way I work and are quite prepared to tolerate that. Within the *Top Girls* company there will be four out of the seven actors that I've worked with before who won't be surprised by this. But I always try and make sure actors know what I am going to do at the point where they take on the job.

RADOSAVLJEVIĆ: So that leads to a particular kind of clarity –

STAFFORD-CLARK: Yes, absolutely – hopefully. I think, when you are a young director you believe you have to win every argument and that losing an argument is somehow diminishing your own status. Whereas when you get to be an older director, and particularly when you get to be as old as I am, what's important is to lose arguments, and to really be flexible about the way that you are working.

RADOSAVLJEVIĆ: *Top Girls* is an interesting example of a play that you developed originally and are re-visiting again for a revival – how is it going to be different?

STAFFORD-CLARK: What is similar is that the play was written by Caryl after Mrs Thatcher won the election in 1979, so we were embarking on a Conservative era. The play deals with the glass ceiling that women encounter at work and that all of the women in the play have in one way or another given up babies. A lot of the dilemmas in the play, although the landscape has changed since 1982, are still very similar.

RADOSAVLJEVIĆ: Did working at the Royal Court change your approach to text and the rehearsal methodology that you developed for Joint Stock?

STAFFORD-CLARK: It didn't change its direction, but I think that it allowed me to develop it. And, of course, the Royal Court receives two and a half thousand scripts a year. So I had the finance to commission writers and to develop their work. At Out of Joint, we always make room for that. At the moment we're suffering under the threat of cuts from the Arts Council, but I'm determined that one thing we won't cut is standards – and that means rehearsal time and workshop time.

RADOSAVLJEVIĆ: If you think about Out of Joint in terms of its constellation, would you describe it as an ensemble or would you use a different definition for it?

STAFFORD-CLARK: I would call it an 'occasional ensemble'. When we played *Top Girls* in New York, interestingly I was asked the same question by Joe Papp, and I said 'Well, I wasn't against stars, and there would be no point in undertaking *King Lear* unless you knew very clearly who you wanted to play King Lear'. And he said 'Oh, ensemble stars', so I said 'Absolutely' – he used the term 'ensemble stars' after that, which is obviously a contradiction. I have worked with less real leading actors than most people, yet there are some actors like Donal McCann, who played the lead in *The Steward of Christendom* by Sebastian Barry, who is just an outstanding actor. Finbar Lynch, who is playing the Big Fellah is an enormously talented leading actor. As a director of any age you learn from working with actors like that – they're essential. I've nothing against stars.

RADOSAVLJEVIĆ: What's also interesting about your recent work is the way in which it slotted in with the trend of verbatim theatre when verbatim theatre became 'in' in the 2000s, but it's very clear from looking at your work that this owes a lot to the previous work that you had done.

STAFFORD-CLARK: That's right. You remember Madonna had a fashion of wearing underclothes outside her clothes? Verbatim is a bit like that – you're flashing your research. Usually with a play, you do your research and the writer writes the play. With this you do the research and the research is on the stage. There are plays like *Mixed Up North*, *The Permanent Way*, *A State Affair*, *Talking to Terrorists*, all of which were verbatim plays.

RADOSAVLJEVIĆ: Was the process exactly the same?

STAFFORD-CLARK: Similar, except that the first thing that the actors are looking for is the character that they are going to play. After about two weeks of doing the research one of them knows who they will be playing, but maybe two of them don't and they have yet to find that person.

RADOSAVLJEVIĆ: The actors go to interview their subjects in pairs?

STAFFORD-CLARK: That is correct. We don't take tape recorders, although there are people like Alecky Blythe who do that. The actors take notes so that the next day in rehearsal if you and Stella had interviewed somebody I would ask you both to improvise the conversation. You would brief us and say 'She sat down, she made us a cup of tea, she talked about her husband who had been killed in the Falklands, she started to cry a bit'. You would brief the other actress that was playing with you and then we would improvise it. But the two of you would play the woman who had been interviewed because then you would prompt each other. The energy is always sustained, nobody ever dries, and you always feel that the weight is shared by another person.

RADOSAVLJEVIĆ: How is it decided which actor takes on the character?

STAFFORD-CLARK: Oh, fairly pragmatic choices I think. The material is filtered through the actors' imagination before it reaches the writer. Then the writer would say 'Yes, this is what interests me a lot, I'm going to go and see her now', and then there would be a second interview which he or she conducted with the same person, and gradually the character would be built up that way. But it gives the actor a possession of the material, which is very important.

RADOSAVLJEVIĆ: Talking of possession of the material, what happens when a play is recast or revived later, how does a new actor who takes on the role that had been previously developed by some other actor, relate to that role?

STAFFORD-CLARK: I think you have to recount the experience you've been through and help them as much as possible, the same that you would do with any part. Obviously if it's based on a real life person then they too can meet the person. But that is also true with *A Dish of Tea with Doctor Johnson* where the actor who is playing Doctor Johnson has also adapted the play, so he feels a great possession of it in a way his personality has re-shaped the material, and it would be very difficult to recast it. *A Dish of Tea with Doctor Johnson* got very good notices, and possibly is going to transfer to the West End. Now, if a West End manager comes and says 'Yes, we would like to transfer it but Ian Redford is not a sufficient star, we want to get Ralph Fiennes to play Doctor Johnson' then I would say 'No'. I would say 'Fine, go ahead but you'll have to find another director', because I think you feel an obligation to the people who have helped you create it. Most people of course go to the theatre to see a particular actor, very rarely to see a particular writer's work, and certainly very, very rarely to see a director's work, almost never.

RADOSAVLJEVIĆ: The British attitude to theatre seems very much rooted in the idea of playwright's theatre. What's your view on that?

STAFFORD-CLARK: We find German and Russian theatre rather dictatorial, that the director dominates it. Caryl Churchill recounts going to Berlin for a production of her play, having lunch with a German dramaturg and a director and then trotting behind them to the rehearsal room, and the director saying 'No, no, you go that way' – she was excluded from rehearsal and put in the room with the dramaturg. Whereas those of us that were brought up particularly at the Royal Court are kind of well brought up directors who appreciate that the writer is really the senior collaborator. And when in question-and-answer sessions people ask 'Don't you argue with the writer?', the answer is 'Yes'. But argument is not a bad word – argument is a good word. All debate proceeds by argument and I think, as I say, that you have to be prepared to lose arguments as well as win them.

Bibliography

Ritchie, Rob (ed.) (1987) *The Joint Stock Book: Making of a Theatre Collective*, London: Methuen.

Shepherd, Simon (2009) *The Cambridge Introduction to Modern British Theatre*, Cambridge: Cambridge University Press.

Shevtsova, Maria and Innes, Christopher (eds) (2009) *Directors/Directing: Conversations on Theatre*, Cambridge: Cambridge University Press.

Stafford-Clark, Max and Roberts, Philip (2007) *Taking Stock: The Theatre of Max Stafford-Clark*, London: Nick Hern Books.

Out of Joint
http://www.outofjoint.co.uk/

6 'A group of people around a place'

Elizabeth LeCompte (The Wooster Group)

In 1968, a former metal stamping factory on lower Manhattan's Wooster Street was acquired by Richard Schechner and named The Performing Garage. It formed a base for his company, The Performance Group (1967–1980), and, as of 1980, for The Wooster Group.

The Wooster Group originated in the mid-1970s with works composed and directed by The Performance Group members Spalding Gray and Elizabeth LeCompte around Gray's autobiographical impulses. It was officially named The Wooster Group in 1980 with members including Gray, LeCompte, Jim Clayburgh, Willem Dafoe, Peyton Smith, Kate Valk and Ron Vawter. The works made since 1975 were retrospectively attributed to the company, which is still based in The Performing Garage.

In the late 2000s, Maria Shevtsova described the venue as follows:

> The Performing Garage offers an intimacy of space – without familiarity – in which spectators can see at close quarters the artifice of construction and not the verisimilitude of life.
>
> (Shevtsova and Innes 2009: 94)

Noting that LeCompte had long abandoned Schechner's 'environmental theater' approach to staging by reinstating the boundary between the performers and the audience, Shevtsova goes on to state that the act of witnessing this process of construction, therefore becomes 'the content of spectating' (ibid.). The Wooster Group's approach to the making and to presentation of their work is thus encapsulated as being inextricably linked with their own space, even though in recent years the company has performed in bigger spaces in New York such as St Ann's Warehouse and Public Theater. LeCompte confesses that they were also repeatedly advised over the years to change their base and system of production in pursuit of commercial success (Shevtsova and Innes 2009: 98). This has been advice that they have apparently ignored.

Instead, The Wooster Group frequently opened their space up to encourage the work of young and emerging artists. Alexis Soloski has noted that The Performing Garage has since 1978 systematically supported young talent, including the independent work of their own staff members, thus facilitating the emergence of John Collins' Elevator Repair Service, Jim Findlay's Collapsible Giraffe and Maryann Weems's Builders Association (Soloski 1999: 155).

John Collins, who has worked with The Wooster Group as a sound designer since 1993, notes that the company's collaborative structure 'exists somewhere in between egalitarianism and traditional theater hierarchy'. He has noted that LeCompte 'has explicitly resisted taking sole credit', preferring to be seen as a 'director in the group' rather than a 'director of the group' (in Britton, manuscript). The group is led by LeCompte and Valk together. In 2012, the company website listed 16 company members and 36 associates. The core longest-serving company members, apart from LeCompte and Valk, are Scott Shepherd and Ari Fliakos.

Renowned for its adventurous use of technology and bold revisioning of classics, The Wooster Group has become a highly influential company, not only for American performance and theatre-makers but also around the world. The Wooster Group's most memorable productions include *L.S.D* (. . . *Just the High Points* . . .) (1984) based on Arthur Miller's *The Crucible, Brace Up!* '*from Chekhov's Three Sisters*' (1991), Eugene O'Neill's *The Emperor Jones* (1993) and *The Hairy Ape* (1995), *To You, The Birdie! (Phèdre)* (2002) and *Hamlet* (2007). In 2012, The Wooster Group and the Royal Shakespeare Company collaborated on a production of *Troilus and Cressida* as part of the World Shakespeare Festival.

The conversation below took place in August 2010 following the opening of *Vieux Carré* by Tennessee Williams at the Edinburgh International Festival.

Interview

RADOSAVLJEVIĆ: How would you define The Wooster Group – would you call it an ensemble, a collective, a troupe, or a collection of individuals?

LECOMPTE: I've defined it in so many ways over the last 30 years and usually I try not to. I just say that we make work. Maybe I would define it as a group of people around a place because we own a theatre. Maybe it's people who congregate around a combination of that theatre space, the people who are working in our theatre now, and around a certain centre of people who have worked there for the last 35 years.

It's a place to come every day, and we all come every day and work on a project. So it's more like a regular traditional job. There're two or three projects going on at once in the space. There're people upstairs working on one project, people in the office working on another, and there're people downstairs in the theatre working on another.

I came to the space with The Performance Group in 1969, and in that company I was an assistant director. In the late 1970s, I already had a company set up, so there were two companies working out of that space, and when The Performance Group dissolved I inherited the space.

RADOSAVLJEVIĆ: How is The Wooster Group's way of working similar or different to The Performance Group's way of working?

LECOMPTE: With The Performance Group we did come every day but it was around a very strong director and someone much older than the rest of the company and a man, so it was a top-down hierarchy. And because the people that I was working with were all my own age and my own people to begin with, my own friends – it just had a different way about it. I think also The Performance Group was more academic because Richard Schechner was an academic, and so a lot of the things that he did related back to how he taught, so that gave it a different feeling.

RADOSAVLJEVIĆ: The work is characterised by the use of media, the use of sound, the use of imagery and so on; how does that emerge from the way that the company works?

LECOMPTE: It's very fluid and someone may join as a performer and find out that she likes video so she does video; someone who joins as a video person may perform as well; someone comes in as sound and they also do editing. So there's a lot of room for people to experiment with a lot of different things – like our lighting person came in as a technical person and became the lighting person; our video person came in as a costume intern and he went into video. There's a lot of fluidity.

RADOSAVLJEVIĆ: How many of the 16 company members listed on the website are performers?

LECOMPTE: It's approximately half and half. But then it shifts because some of the performers do technical and vice versa. I don't really make those distinctions when we work.

RADOSAVLJEVIĆ: Do people tend to stay on long-term contracts or do they go and come back?

LECOMPTE: We have no contracts. They just come and they stay as long as they want to stay, or as long as the project lasts, or sometimes they may only stay a few weeks. But I would say the average is probably around five to seven years, though we have people who have been with us for 20–30 years.

RADOSAVLJEVIĆ: Are there any training strategies for new people?

LECOMPTE: Just working. They train on the job because each project is different. I mean we have certain strategies that we use around performances, and for some people who have been around a long time, those strategies are really part of them now and they train the newer people. And then sometimes the newer people bring in new things that we don't know about so the new people train us; it goes back and forth.

RADOSAVLJEVIĆ: When you train the new people, is there a way in which you might be able to sum up the essential principles that they need to understand –

LECOMPTE: I think they just have to be interested in the whole process, and they have to be interested in the work itself. They have to want to be a part of that kind of work, that's all.

RADOSAVLJEVIĆ: When you say 'that kind of work' –

LECOMPTE: They have to have seen our kind of work and said 'I want to do that'. And again that's not everyone, because sometimes I will hire somebody that hasn't seen the work, and who just comes and says 'I've heard about you' and we do that, sometimes that works out very well, sometimes not so well, it depends. But the best thing is for you to come in as an intern and watch our rehearsals because when someone new comes in I always ask them to come and watch rehearsals for anywhere from a couple of days to a month or more.

RADOSAVLJEVIĆ: How long are the rehearsals normally?

LECOMPTE: It depends on the project, and because we work on so many projects at once we skip around. We'll work for four weeks on a project then put it away, go on tour with another piece and come back to the project. So it's hard to say. I continue to work like I'm working now, every day. That is why I have to go in half a hour – because we haven't performed *Vieux Carré* for eight months – we've been doing another repertory piece – we came back to this and I'm working on it now to complete it. I would say it takes me usually about a year, off and on, to complete a piece, and when I say 'complete' I'm always working on it, because there are new people that come into it, I have to change it to organise it around who they are and what their skills are.

RADOSAVLJEVIĆ: How much preparation do you do as a director before going into rehearsals?

LECOMPTE: I don't do any preparation without the company; everything we do is with the company. I try not to even think about the project before. Once we're working then I'm always thinking about it outside and preparing, but before we go in, I do nothing.

RADOSAVLJEVIĆ: Your work is also characterised by adaptations of classics and existing texts. I know that has not always been the feature of your work but can you explain why that happens?

LECOMPTE: No idea! I just like to direct, I like to make things happen on the stage. Somebody brings me something – I'll do it. I started working with Spalding Gray and because he'd been in theatre all his life, he was interested in some American texts, and I didn't know them because I didn't study theatre so I got involved in the American canon, and then people would say 'Oh, why not try this?'. I just go along basically. I go along until the moment when I have a take on it, and when I have a take on it – it's mine.

RADOSAVLJEVIĆ: What was your background before you came into theatre?

LECOMPTE: Painting and photography.

RADOSAVLJEVIĆ: How does that influence the way you work?

LECOMPTE: It's just the way I work. Visually orientated, and I have a feel for music, so I'm interested in those aspects of performance, but not from an intellectual perspective – it's just who I am. Like any director, I tend to put different tones next to each other, different rhythms, different colours, different personalities, conflicting and complimentary.

RADOSAVLJEVIĆ: If you think about the last 35 years of The Wooster Group, can you identify any important milestones in the company's development?

LECOMPTE: I guess the first big milestone was Spalding going off to do his monologues and the rest of the company continuing with Spalding coming in and out – that was a big milestone because other people stepped up to take his place. Another big milestone – it's hard though, everything is so fluid – might have been working on *Saint Anthony*, which was a very difficult text from Flaubert. Ron Vawter was sick and I had to face his imminent death during the making of *Saint Anthony* and figure a way of going on with the company. Ron suggested a play – Chekhov's *Three Sisters*. Even though I wove other elements into it, I really stuck to the play – some people might say 'Not quite', but I think I did. I found I kind of liked riding on somebody else's rhythm. I was free, because Chekhov's text was there as a structure, while before that I had to make the structure myself, which is much more difficult.

RADOSAVLJEVIĆ: Did that set the stage for working with more plays from then on?

LECOMPTE: I did another piece after *Three Sisters* – *Fish Story* – which I structured, but it had some Chekhov text in it. But yes, I think it did make it easier. I made a couple of pieces which I structured myself in between those, and they're really difficult, because in the old days when I was younger, I was structuring pieces around a narrative that I knew – which was Spalding's life. I knew him, I knew the narrative, and he did too. I never really did any structuring without a narrative of somebody else's life, with the exception of maybe *Route 1 & 9*. But by the time we did *Point Judith*, we had a writer come in and write sections of it.

RADOSAVLJEVIĆ: Did the writer have to understand the way in which you work?

LECOMPTE: No, because we knew him. He was a friend. And I liked his writing, and I told him 'Write whatever you want'. I tend to do that when I'm working with people. I don't tell them what to do – I just usually say 'Write whatever you want and we'll find out whatever it is'. Same thing with music – if I have a musician I tend to say 'Make some sound and we'll see how we use it'.

RADOSAVLJEVIĆ: And that presupposes that you will be free to use the text or the music in a way that suits the purposes of the piece?

LECOMPTE: Right. Or we don't get involved. Writers who don't know us wouldn't work that way. For instance with *Brace Up! – The Three Sisters*, we worked with an American translator, Paul Schmidt, and he played the part of the doctor so he was on stage re-writing as we worked. So he wrote his part. He had made a rough translation, and then as we rehearsed he listened to everyone speaking. He re-wrote sections of it and it was published from our production.

RADOSAVLJEVIĆ: Was he previously an actor as well?

LECOMPTE: Yes, he had been an actor, but he was also a translator and a poet from the beginning.

RADOSAVLJEVIĆ: Are there any particular stages of the creative process that you might be able to identify as being particularly characteristic of the way that The Wooster Group works?

LECOMPTE: I don't really know because I've never really worked with any other ensemble. I wish I had the time and a grant that I could go around and find out. I assume we work pretty much the same as everybody else, it's just – I'm directing instead of another person, and I assume that that's it. We get in a room, we're all together and we start immediately putting the play up, listening to it moving around. Only we have the lighting people, the video people, the sound people there with us, fooling around also. That doesn't happen as a separate process, it all happens together. We come up with ideas, and some ideas might seem to have nothing to do with the play. We allow the ideas to work towards the play – so it's kind of a joining, overlapping and stitching that goes on between the technical and the performers, me, and the play.

RADOSAVLJEVIĆ: That doesn't necessarily mean that you would start working on a particular play from the beginning from the first scene?

LECOMPTE: Right, we often go right in to the middle and then move out or start at the end perhaps. I actually don't work that sequentially, now that I think of it, except for something like O'Neill – O'Neill's plays I have worked from scene one to the end. I don't know why.

RADOSAVLJEVIĆ: How did the video become such an important part of the pieces that you make?

LECOMPTE: I was a photographer and a visual artist, and I always liked television. TV and I grew up together, and I'm still influenced by it. We had our first grant in 1978 and I just bought four televisions, put them on stage in *Route 1 & 9* – and that was it. I didn't think much about it because in the 1970s a lot of artists were working with video. I was just in the stream although I didn't go to see theatre and I had no idea what people were doing in the theatre. The only time I remember TVs onstage being seen as something odd was when we toured to Europe. In Europe sometimes we would come up against – and still do come up against – these people who are resistant to technology, thinking about it as some kind of alien thing. And maybe it is, I don't know. It doesn't feel that way to me. In Amsterdam people were more accepting of us although there was a little trouble with The Wooster Group when it was too personal – Spalding's autobiographical monologues in *Rumstick Road*, for example. They didn't mind the televisions so much, until we got to Switzerland in 1983 and people came with tomatoes and eggs and threw them at the televisions. It was surreal, I was so surprised, and they were yelling 'Go back to Disneyland!'. That was the first time we had travelled out of Amsterdam and Brussels. The Mickery in Amsterdam and Kaaitheater in Brussels were eager to see new forms – they seemed excited about the televisions.

RADOSAVLJEVIĆ: Does the use of the moving image on the stage have a particular dramaturgical purpose?

LECOMPTE: For me it's all visual sound and story. I use it like somebody else might use another actor. It's another device on the stage for me to tell the story. I get bored sometimes because if I've used it to put in a character that I don't have an actor for, then I don't like to do that again, so it takes a while for me to figure out what its uses are in each production. For something like *Vieux Carré* I didn't figure out what it's useful for until months into the process. The video people were there and they were doing what they were doing and nothing hit until I got some 'heat' on it.

RADOSAVLJEVIĆ: And with *Hamlet*, for example, did the idea to use that particular footage come very early in the process?

LECOMPTE: No, I only wanted to do that piece because of Scott. He wanted to perform. He was obsessed with the play. He did a small workshop and I thought it was terrible, but his performance in the middle of it was interesting. Because he had such a bead on the language, but it didn't have a style or a take. So we started going way, way back listening to the early audio-tapes for style, how to do the iambic, how we would both be interested in the iambic. And in watching all these things I discovered the Burton film,[1] and remembered that I had gone to see it when I was a child or pretty young, and it was a stage version on film. There's quite a few *Hamlet* films, but they're usually redone for the camera. This *Hamlet* was the actual stage version. So, then I tried to combine what Scott was interested in with what I was interested in, which was: what was Gielgud doing and what were they doing with these multiple camera angles? And I was curious to try and bring it back, bring back what I remembered from the performance, to see if I could recreate it.

RADOSAVLJEVIĆ: So it was an archaeological exercise.

What would you say has been the main thing that has contributed to the longevity of The Wooster Group – you have mentioned the space . . .

LECOMPTE: That's big. I guess there are other places that have spaces but they're usually not ensembles. I would like to believe that it's me, and I think I do have something to do with it because I still want to make pieces. But I also think that the space gives people more sense of a place and a sense of ritual that's not around one person. I do direct all these pieces and it's a very powerful position. So the space allows people to think that they're coming to the space, they're not coming to me, and I am functioning in the space as they are, and that's my job. I think that helps to keep people healthy, to keep a sense of themselves clearer and allows them to stay longer.

RADOSAVLJEVIĆ: Are you able to survive without subsidy?

LECOMPTE: We're subsidised in the sense that we get money from some foundations, and about two per cent from the federal government, so it's very small. Individual contributions are also pretty small. I think somewhere around 60 per cent of our income is from box office and touring, and the rest is a big mish-mash of individual grants and teaching and some foundations. No corporations – they won't touch us! Even in the UK there's a lot more funding from the government. We own our own theatre which makes a difference. I think that the young people that I'm watching, that are coming up and trying to maintain companies, they have to be a lot more responsive to what the audience and critics want than we've ever had to be.

RADOSAVLJEVIĆ: When you say you do teaching – is it just you or other members of the company as well?

LECOMPTE: It's very rare because we don't have much time, but some members occasionally teach.

RADOSAVLJEVIĆ: Would that be teaching based on how the company works?

LECOMPTE: That's what we've been doing. We've developed this technique with in-ear audio feeds and visual stimuli for the performance. It's
controversial – when they see the pieces, audiences don't know that
we're working with so much technology because it's often hidden.

RADOSAVLJEVIĆ: Does that mean that all members of the company are
able to teach a similar kind of class?

LECOMPTE: No, the only people that teach performance are the more
experienced members, people like Kate and Scott and Ari. Sometimes
the technical artists teach.

RADOSAVLJEVIĆ: You also use your theatre for receiving other people's
work?

LECOMPTE: Yes, when we can, we never rent it but we invite people in
and we subsidise them by giving them the space very cheaply, so
cheaply that we lose money on it. But it's part of the community, it's
part of how we can support people like Richard Maxwell and a number of other companies that come in, and that makes me very happy;
I like to do that.

Note

1 This was the 1964 production of *Hamlet* directed by Gielgud with Richard
Burton in the lead.

Bibliography

Collins, John (forthcoming) 'Elevator Repair Service and The Wooster Group:
Ensembles Surviving Themselves', in John Britton (ed.) *Encountering Ensemble*,
London: Methuen.

Mitter, Shomit and Shevtsova, Maria (eds) (2005) *Fifty Key Theatre Directors*,
London: Routledge.

Quick, Andrew (2007) *The Wooster Group Work Book*, London: Routledge.

Savran, David (1986) *The Wooster Group, 1975–1985: Breaking the Rules*, Ann
Arbor, MI: UMI Research Press.

Shevtsova, Maria and Innes, Christopher (eds) (2009) *Directors/Directing:
Conversations on Theatre*, Cambridge: Cambridge University Press.

Soloski Alexis (1999) 'Garage Music: The Wooster Group's Emerging Artist
Series', *The Village Voice*, 44(28): 155.

The Wooster Group
http://thewoostergroup.org/blog/

7 On regional theatre-making

Lyn Gardner (The Guardian)

Throughout the 1990s and 2000s, Lyn Gardner's work as a theatre critic for *The Guardian* newspaper has been characterised by a continued focus on young and experimental companies, the Edinburgh Fringe and, significantly, on regional theatre.

The interview below took place in the context of a specific research project concerning the Northern Stage Ensemble (1998–2005) in Newcastle-upon-Tyne, which Gardner frequently covered despite its considerable distance from London. One of the key moments for regional theatre in the UK at the time, according to Gardner, was the Arts Council-commissioned Boyden Report in 2000. Prior to the Labour Party victory in 1997, the Conservative government had made minimal investment in the arts, and most arts funding was administered centrally from London. The Boyden Report revealed that only 14 per cent of the overall theatre repertoire comprised new work, and that regional British theatre suffered major deficits (British Theatre Guide 2000). This eventually led to a Theatre Review in 2001, increased support for 'new writing' in the UK, and a £25 million funding boost for the regional sector in 2003. In this context, Alan Lyddiard's ensemble project at the Newcastle Playhouse was highly unusual in two ways: rather than looking to London, it took inspiration from the internationally renowned artists Lev Dodin, Peter Brook, Alain Platel, Robert Lepage and Pina Bausch, and more importantly, it was already thriving in 2000. Having received two years of funding through the Arts Council Arts for Everyone scheme, the Northern Stage Ensemble achieved enough financial success to be able to continue. Similar projects were subsequently piloted in the Dundee Rep, Clwyd Theatr Cymru and Mercury Colchester.

The interview with Lyn Gardner, which took place in May 2010 in Wimbledon, yielded valuable insights into the broader topic of ensemble theatre in the UK. It also introduced a useful distinction between the terms 'actor' and 'theatre-maker', forming part of this book's key terminology.

Interview

RADOSAVLJEVIĆ: You have had a very broad understanding of the British theatre scene for quite a long time. What was your perception of the Northern Stage Ensemble (1998–2005) and the way it sat within a broader context at the time?

GARDNER: What was unusual was indeed the European influence, which was apparent in the setting up of the ensemble itself and in the work that went on the stage. Alan Lyddiard had a very particular vision about a way of working, obviously inspired by Lev Dodin, but he also found his way of doing it. The way that he found, if I recall correctly, was that he looked at the way that Northern Stage was structured, which like most rep companies, was artistically a triangle the wrong way round (very top heavy with administrative staff), and when it came down to how much of the subsidy actually went into art itself and into the creative people, that amount was very small. He did something that, funnily enough, in the coming few years when we end up in a very difficult financial climate – may yet be seen as having been absolutely visionary and actually very radical, which was to turn around and say 'Let's cut our administrative costs to the bone and instead put those into what goes on stage'. What was remarkable, both there and I think in Dundee as well, was how much immediately it raised the game. And I'm not saying that every piece of work that I saw at Northern Stage I loved and liked, but there was always something very distinctive and very interesting about it, in a way that was not necessarily true of all British theatre at the time.

The other thing that was interesting about it was the point when he did it, which was 1998. It is very important to remember that that was before the Boyden Report and before the injection of £25 million into British theatre, which absolutely changed British regional theatre. British regional theatre at that time, in 1998, was really in the doldrums. I suppose from my point of view as a critic – I did leave London and I left London quite a lot – but it often felt that what was going on in the regions was in no way competing with what went on in London. That wasn't true at Northern Stage – Alan Lyddiard was a very good reason to leave London.

RADOSAVLJEVIĆ: When I first arrived in Newcastle from Leeds in 2002, there were artists of various kinds living in the city. It seemed very much that this was a place which had a very strong sense of local culture. Might it have been this very particular context that gave birth to this way of working? In your review of *The Ballroom of Romance*, for example, you said that with Lyddiard's work 'the important things are

on the periphery' and that it 'takes the lives of ordinary people surviving on the margins and makes them seem special' (Gardner 2000).
GARDNER: That was very true. One of the things that was so apparent in the work was that it had so many influences – and again it was work that generally at the time was perhaps not seen very much in the regions. So for example, *The Ballroom of Romance* very distinctly had that sense of things fraying around the edges. I also remember there was an extraordinary *Romeo and Juliet*, which again had that similar sense that everything that took place took place on the edges. What was really clear about that *Romeo and Juliet* was that its influences were Alain Platel and Fellini – so the cultural references that were in a sense a rather magpie borrowing from European work – rather than being very distinctly British. What Alan's productions never did in the nature of the things that he chose to stage was that idea – that so much British theatre is really about – of actors sitting there or standing somewhere and hurling situational chat at each other. None of the work was like that. The work owed as much to movies, to dance – it bled, it always bled.

The other thing that was fantastic, that was interesting and that I always remember about *Romeo and Juliet* was that it was subversive in terms of piercing the idea of romantic love. Because actually Romeo and Juliet were quite plump if I remember. But that was fantastically interesting because it immediately pricked the way that you think of Romeo and Juliet.

The point that you're making about the strength of locale in Newcastle – I think that's always been true in Newcastle. If you think about something like Live Theatre and the kind of work that it is doing – it is very much new writing but grounded in the local community. I think that that's unusual. And it is one of the things that I would use in terms of measuring health of a city – which is one of the reasons therefore why I've written a lot about regional theatre buildings. Not only did Alan just create an ensemble, one of the things that he did was that you knew that you would see a lot of local actors, whereas I can think of plenty of other regional theatres where they cast in London. One of the responsibilities of any regional building – and it seems to me that most of them are funded as national resources and also as local resources – is to get that balance right and that means also encouraging local actors, local writers; basically allowing local artists access to the citadel. And too often what happens is that the citadel pulls up its drawbridge and doesn't allow that to happen.

There's been a legacy with what Alan did at Northern Stage – which is the introduction of that international element combined with the local theatre – a kind of legacy which you don't really see in other cities in regional theatres. One of the things that led to, for example, is that Newcastle audiences are very open to seeing a very wide range of work. Even now at Northern Stage, you can see the programming where you can have Robert Lepage in there, and it isn't just lots of people trotting up from London to go and see it. Local people will go and see a work in progress for Robert Lepage, and I think that's very much due to what happened with Northern Stage and the ensemble. It was as though it introduced people to something different from what was British theatre at the time, and let them have a head start. It's like that Jean Miro quote – 'To be truly universal, you also have to be local'. Like *The Ballroom of Romance*, which was not of course set in Newcastle, it was a rural piece – and how many plays can you think about which are about rural themes? They do not exist, on the whole, on metropolitan stages.

It seemed to me one of the things that always went on was that the work was brave. It was brave and it was distinctive and that certainly wasn't true of British theatre at the time.

RADOSAVLJEVIĆ: When you say that you think that theatre might move in the direction of cutting out the administrative element and enhancing the artistic element – do you think that there might be more space for the ensemble way of working?

GARDNER: That's very problematic because the truth is of course that ensembles are expensive to run. There have been other examples of ensembles. The Mercury in Colchester is such an interesting example of a regional theatre that was absolutely on its last legs and Dee Evans came in and took it over. The theatre was about to be shut and she just said 'I am going to try and make a go of this'. It's a small theatre in a small town. I don't think they do now run as an ensemble though they do use a lot of the same actors – but for a short period of time, certainly for several years, it did run as an ensemble. One of the things that was very interesting there was that the same actors that would appear on stage would also be the same actors that would go and do the education work in schools during the day – so it really was a genuine ensemble. Mostly the education departments are entirely separate from the creative departments.

The other thing that she's done was to be completely brave about programming. It's quite interesting that you can take an audience with you. I think that it is to do with conditions in a particular city. We often forget that theatre does not sit outside of everything else that's going on economically. Theatre during the late 1990s and early 2000s was enormously successful. In part it benefited from the fact that we had a boom-time at the time generally. A good example that you may recognise if you lived in Leeds would be Jude Kelly and the West Yorkshire Playhouse.[1] That theatre opened just at the time when Leeds became a boom town and started changing from flat caps and whippets to Harvey Nichs and so on. Jude Kelly did something fantastically clever with that building on the Quarry Hill which is in the wrong place and should never have been a success – she recognised what she needed to do was to get local people in. You walked into that building and at 10 o'clock in the morning it would be full of old age pensioners and mothers and babies, and it became a community. She understood that very well and latched onto the coat tails of regeneration within Leeds. To a certain extent, that was less true of what was happening in Newcastle at the time, which in some ways makes the achievement only the greater really.

I think ensembles take time to grow and to mature. An ensemble is, in fact, people working together over a relatively long period of time. And that's why it's very hard to do it in a building context. It's much easier to do by people like Complicite because one of the things that they can do is have people come and dip in and dip out and go on and do other projects. But I've always thought that theatre benefits enormously from people playing together, sleeping together, living together and really being bound up.

RADOSAVLJEVIĆ: There is something about that way of working emerging naturally from how people train, and it doesn't seem to be the way that necessarily survives. When we think of Complicite or DV8 now, we tend to think of one person who represents it.

GARDNER: It's true. The company that's quite interesting in that way would be Forced Entertainment. Although, of course, people tend to think of Tim Etchells and quite clearly it seems to me that the work of Forced Entertainment has very distinctively Tim's voice in it, but if you think of people like Cathy and Terry, it has been pretty well the same kind of personnel the whole way through. When Forced Entertainment is represented it isn't necessarily represented by Tim, it is as likely that it might be somebody else. And I think that that comes from being in Sheffield and from people – particularly in the early days – living together as well.

The problem is that it all comes down to economics. It is enormously difficult to sustain these things over a period of time and to have a loose enough arrangement that allows people to dip in and dip out – and go and do other work. Particularly when you are older. It's easy when you leave college and say 'We get on incredibly well and we are always going to work together'. But actually, by the time you hit 30, and maybe you've got a relationship and a child – these things are very hard to do. And other things have changed. It's difficult to get the actors to commit to a longer period of time because, of course, if they've got agents, effectively they are expected to do commercials and to get that TV part. The idea of being in an ensemble if you are a young actor, for example, is less appealing to your agent.

The area where we are seeing it more is perhaps the devised work and the work of what I would call the theatre-makers rather than actors. Because, actually, if you're an actor, why would you want to go off to Newcastle or Dundee for the next three years now? I think on the whole, your agent will turn around and say – 'Don't do it!' because no casting director that casts for TV or films is going to go to Newcastle to see you. I certainly know people who run touring companies who say it's harder and harder. The agents would prefer you to be doing a little unpaid fringe production somewhere with a good reputation like Theatre 503 or the Arcola where a casting director may go, than tour out of town even though that may be paid.

RADOSAVLJEVIĆ: So it remains a London-centric theatre scene.

GARDNER: Oh, yes, it does.

Note

1 Jude Kelly was the Artistic Director of the West Yorkshire Playhouse in Leeds between 1990 and 2002, during which time the theatre became a major regional centre.

Bibliography

British Theatre Guide (2000) 'Is Regional Theatre Dying?', 20 February, available online at http://www.britishtheatreguide.info/articles/200200a.htm (accessed 19 December 2012).

Gardner, Lyn (2000) 'Distilled Emotions', *The Guardian*, 23 September, available online at http://www.guardian.co.uk/culture/2000/sep/23/artsfeatures1 (accessed 19 December 2012).

Radosavljević, Duška (2012) 'Shared Utopias? Alan Lyddiard, Lev Dodin and the Northern Stage Ensemble', in Jonathan Pitches (ed.) *Russians in Britain: British Theatre and the Russian Tradition of Actor Training*, London: Routledge.

Lyn Gardner
http://www.guardian.co.uk/profile/lyngardner

Part II

Working processes

8   Beyond words

Anton Adassinsky and Elena Yarovaya (Derevo)

Since their first appearance at the Edinburgh Fringe with *Red Zone* in 1997, members of the Russian troupe Derevo have evoked a mixture of fascination, curiosity and – with *Islands in the Stream* (2003) and *Ketzal* (2006) at St Stephen's church – even cult-like worship. Their distinct physicality and almost uniform outward appearance characterised by lithe, slender bodies, shaven heads and bony faces, even gave rise to a certain mythology concerning the company's dedication to their work. The group's leader, Anton Adassinsky has over the years veered from being very evasive about the company members' personal lives, to providing the kind of detail about their unorthodox working ways that would fuel even more intrigue: according to Rimmer (2003), Derevo's rehearsal strategies involve metronomes, endurance tests and dark imaginings. Nevertheless, a number of articles in the British press over the years (all archived on the company website) concur about several key facts: Adassinsky was born in Siberia in 1959, he trained with Slava Polunin and his St Petersburg-based Licedei Company from 1982 to 1986, and then left in order to develop his own work. He was briefly the frontman of the rock band Avia. An oft-quoted story goes that in 1988, having run a year-long, arduous training session for 50 volunteers/students, he ended up with four successful 'graduates', who went on to become Derevo.

As the Soviet Union began to open up during the Perestroika years, Derevo acquired international exposure. The Butoh master Kazuo Ohno took them under his wing at one point, and so did Flavio Fo, the producer brother of Dario Fo. In the run up to their first LIFT appearance in London in 1989, the company were described as the 'Beckett zombies' and 'anti-clowns' (Connor 1989), and later as 'violent-souled jesters' (Hutera 1998). Derevo's 'circus of despair' (Bishop 2002) eventually led *The Scotsman* to proclaim it 'one of the most exciting theatre companies working in the world today' (Rimmer 2003).

Derevo changed bases several times in the early 1990s – Prague, Florence, Amsterdam – and in 1995 they settled in Dresden, where they were given a disused ammunitions factory to turn into a rehearsal space. They remain active and continue to bring their theatre work to Edinburgh at regular intervals, though their style and subject matter keeps evolving, and their interest is also captivated by music and film-making. Anton Adassinsky has played Mephistopheles in Alexander Sokurov's *Faust*, which went on to win the Golden Lion in Venice in 2011, and in 2012 Derevo presented their new show, *Mephisto Waltz*, at the Edinburgh Fringe.

The interview below took place during the run of *Harlekin* at the Edinburgh Fringe in August 2010.

Interview

RADOSAVLJEVIĆ: I'd like to start with the beginnings of Derevo. I understand you worked with Slava Polunin, which may have been one influence on your work, but also you come from a rock music background.

ADASSINSKY: I worked with many people, not just Slava. He is a good friend of mine. We are still working together on some projects. As for rock'n'roll – I graduated as a classical guitarist, but I worked as a photographer, and a movie director, many different things. I took workshops in different kinds of dance: ballet, flamenco, tango – all the things connected to the body. I even went to Japan and worked with Japanese dancers – I worked with Butoh quite a lot.

Derevo just emerged. Nothing like putting a list together through casting – people just came together one day, like a real rock'n'roll band. It was five or six or seven people at the beginning; we started speaking about the arts, what we liked to do, what we didn't like to do, we spoke about dance and movement and step by step we started to train together. We started to make 'actions' outdoors – not physical actions, but mostly explosion-actions just to shock people on the streets, in winter or in summer. Then we found pleasure in working with the body more and more, without speaking. We started training, and the training was developed by ourselves. At that time in Russia there was no information about the kind of work we were doing – there were no video recordings available.

RADOSAVLJEVIĆ: Which period was this?

ADASSINSKY: 1985–86. It was a complicated situation. We knew nothing about contemporary trends in art, we just did what we liked to do. We went to perform in Prague for the first time, and the big master of Butoh, Kazuo Ohno, saw our performance and he said 'Wow, it's Russian Butoh!', and we said 'What's Butoh?'.

We didn't know anything about it, we were just using our bodies. That's how the company started and, from that time till now, all five members including me have stayed together, because I couldn't find better masters, better quality people than Elena Yarovaya, Tanya Khabarova, Dimitry Tyulpanov and Alexey Merkushev – they are the best.

I have my school in England, I have my school in Italy, a school in Poland – my students are living and working there and if they want to see me they come to Dresden or if I have time to do a workshop I go to them. I give them some exercises for the next two or three months, and they follow their own way, but they regard Derevo as the beginning of everything. I don't need them to follow the Derevo style, it's too hard, they need to find their own way. Because in theatre you must have your own way. Derevo is Derevo, and they have to be something different, because they are the future.

RADOSAVLJEVIĆ: Do the five company members always work on all of the shows together?

ADASSINSKY: *Once* was five members, *Red Zone* five, *Islands* five, *La Divina* four, now *Harlekin* three, *Gospel of Anton* is my solo – so we are flexible. Because we are not living together, Tanya is living in Italy, Dima in Israel, Alexey in Berlin, we are living in Dresden, so ... We don't need to see each other every day – not any more.

RADOSAVLJEVIĆ: Was there a time when you were all spending a lot more time living together?

ADASSINSKY: Yes.

RADOSAVLJEVIĆ: I remember reading that there was an aspect to your work that was about training being incorporated into the lifestyle and the lifestyle becoming part of the training.

ADASSINSKY: If you are living for the theatre, if you're living for the performance every day, it automatically includes your lifestyle. You wake up on the morning of the performance, you do your training, you go to the dressing room, you change your costumes – you spend the whole day just living for the performance, no time for anything else. You go to sleep and you start again in the morning. Then you just speak about the performance, no time to see anything else, to read anything new.

RADOSAVLJEVIĆ: You moved to Dresden in 1995. How did that change your way of working?

ADASSINSKY: Not really. Before that we lived in Florence for two years, before that we were living in Amsterdam and before that in Prague. It didn't change our way of working but it changed our social status. We have a beautiful space, we have a theatre, we have subsidy, the town helps us with money – it's amazing. Before that it was a struggle, fighting for every square metre, spending a lot of time organising our life.

RADOSAVLJEVIĆ: What prompted you to move to Dresden?

ADASSINSKY: First of all the town liked a lot what we were doing. There was some connection between Dresden and St Petersburg. We played a few of our performances in Dresden so the town saw us and said 'Yes, Derevo is a good company, so we can give them a space'. I was almost afraid to take something from someone because they could ask for something in return. So I said 'What do we have to do for that?', and they said 'Nothing, just play 15 shows a year'. I said, 'OK, with pleasure'. Now we have our castle, we can close the door to be alone, to concentrate on our performances and our ideas; it's a useful place to be.

(*YAROVAYA arrives*)

RADOSAVLJEVIĆ: Do you live in the same place where you work?

ADASSINSKY: No, no, we live in a different part of town. Sometimes we sleep in the studio, when we've had a nice long rehearsal.

RADOSAVLJEVIĆ: How would you define Derevo as an ensemble by comparison to how other people work?

ADASSINSKY: In Derevo as a company, everybody is of the same high quality, which is very difficult to handle. Because when you are working with young people, you are always talking to them from the top. When you are working with stars – and everybody is a star in our company – you have to be very strong. I still have to close my mouth and show things on stage when I'm working with these people. Words don't work with our company. When I want to comment on what Elena is doing and what Anna[1] is doing, they can ask me 'OK, just show me how you see it', and I have to show it. And I have to show it better than Elena, who can do it better than me, and there's always competition – and a very fast growth. It's again like a rock'n'roll band, everybody is equal, I play the drums, he plays bass-guitar, somebody plays something else, but everybody can bring a song to the table and everybody will play the song of this band. There's no real boss. If you imagine a rock'n'roll band, there is no-one to regulate how you play music, everybody is the same. It means we are always working with our own material, we never play a piece written by someone else. Once we tried to work with a director, but it didn't work.

RADOSAVLJEVIĆ: How do you start developing a piece of theatre?

ADASSINSKY: Nobody can remember a moment when the show starts. Even now, if we say, 'Let's try and remember the day when we started talking about *Harlekin*' – no idea. I can't remember how it started. Really I can't. Maybe it was some improvisation, or just speaking about commedia dell' arte – we are always missing the starting point. But then, suddenly everybody's moving in the same direction. It's like we have some kind of a common brain in the company. In this common brain some ideas come up and they have a certain power, and everybody immediately agrees to do this. This was the case with all our shows.

The funny thing is, when I compare, for example, *La Divina Commedia*, *Islands* and *Harlekin*, they are totally different things, totally different styles of work, styles of mentality, styles of movement. It looks like it's a different company playing. It's so easy to think that the style of, for example, *Islands* is the style of Derevo – it would be so easy to do that. But it's hard to keep changing things radically: you have to invent new training strategies, you have to make new creative exercises, a new way of living, a new way of preparing yourself for the show. Everything from the beginning. Which is refreshing.

RADOSAVLJEVIĆ: Does that mean that your training continues all the time and ideas for new shows emerge from your training routine?

ADASSINSKY: We have improvisation evenings for friends – sometimes once a week, sometimes twice a month – you can just go on stage and improvise something. And for these evenings we have no rules. You can sing a song, you can do a dance, you can do drama, speak, read poetry – it doesn't matter. And then you might notice: 'There's something about commedia dell' arte in there' . . .

RADOSAVLJEVIĆ: How long does it take to develop a show?

ADASSINSKY: One year, one and a half. And Edinburgh always brings a lot of energy, a lot of opportunities to clean up the show. Every day the show is developing. It's incredible.

RADOSAVLJEVIĆ: Can we ask Elena some questions?

ADASSINSKY (*jokingly*): She doesn't like to speak about any of this. She just likes to speak about dreams.

RADOSAVLJEVIĆ: OK, we can speak about dreams.

(*ADASSINSKY goes for a cigarette*)

RADOSAVLJEVIĆ: How did you become involved with Derevo?

YAROVAYA: I saw Anton on stage and I joined the company the next day.

RADOSAVLJEVIĆ: And were you an actor before, or a dancer?

YAROVAYA: I was studying Technology. And theatre was my hobby.

RADOSAVLJEVIĆ: What kind of theatre?

YAROVAYA: Mime, dance, ballet. But I was studying to be an engineer, and I had to choose between Derevo and my diploma. And I chose Derevo.

RADOSAVLJEVIĆ: How long ago was this?

YAROVAYA: It was 21 years ago. Nobody lives so long. Normally people have already stopped making theatre after 20 years.

RADOSAVLJEVIĆ: How would you describe the Derevo way of working by comparison to other ensembles?

YAROVAYA: I think the other ensembles consist of a few members all of whom are thinking about the future. They think: what we have now is temporary and in future we will become a better ensemble, I will make better work. With Derevo it's 'here and now' – I am in the best ensemble, I am in the best play, I do not look around for something better. I do my thing.

RADOSAVLJEVIĆ: What does a typical Derevo week look like?

YAROVAYA: There is no typical week. We might have a run, like here in Edinburgh. It's very special. Then we will have a month to relax, to slow down and to collect new ideas. Look back on what we have done this month and look forward to what we will do half a year or one year later.

(*ADASSINSKY returns*)

RADOSAVLJEVIĆ: Shall we talk about music? Music is quite a strong feature of both your backgrounds as you've described them and of the shows themselves.

ADASSINSKY: All of us are musically educated. Elena is a very good Russian singer – she has had special training. Tanya plays the piano. I play the guitar, all sorts of guitars. We all play the drums – to quite a high level I would say, because our teacher of drumming was the best drummer in St Petersburg – Roman Dubinnikov, a fantastic drummer. So the musicians and composers who come to work with Derevo really like to work with us because we understand music. We can consider detail and nuance and it makes them really happy when we understand what they are doing. Daniel Williams is a highly educated piano player and teacher of electronic music and we have a very good working relationship. We also use our own music. In *Harlekin* there are three pieces by me on the guitar.

It's a big thing for me, because some people can see something on the stage and some people can hear something. It's 50:50. The same channels are open on both levels, so if you make a mistake on one level, you can compensate. We've worked with five different composers in our time. I've worked with Daniel for five years I think and I am very happy about it. We don't speak much. I don't know much about his life, we are just working together. We have drinks together maybe once a week – but that's enough. He is a very shy person, very closed, but what he does for the show is amazing. There are maybe 20 or more layers to the music, and it means every day it is different, because he plays live. He plays everything live with his fingers and every day is different, and that's what I need. I never ask people to record the music and fix it. I know it's hard work not to fix the music, but I always say 'Play it live, make it better, make it different' – otherwise it's just dead. All our composers always work live with us. They might use computers, huge drum sets or instruments – but it must be live. Nothing recorded.

I see theatre-making as poetry. Because poetry has rhythm. And we all see the work first of all rhythmically. Not melodically but rhythmically. That is important. The brief of the piece is the energy – and peaks and beats – and then on top you put some notes, you put some melody, but they just make life better. Normally, we can rehearse the piece and we can play all of *Harlekin* with just a metronome. We can do this. And you can sometimes feel the same energy even stronger because we are building music by ourselves through movement. That's what we call dance. You don't need to jump like a ballet dancer, you don't need to make stupid strange movements which people call dance, but if you just make clear movement, or clear energy, a clear image – that is dance for me.

RADOSAVLJEVIĆ: As a director and a performer, how do you negotiate being inside the piece and being able to see it from the outside?

ADASSINSKY: I really don't direct the shows any more. I don't like it. I like to be on the stage. I know it's very difficult for the others because they need an outside eye, they need advice – I need advice too because I can't see myself – but I prefer to keep going, rely on our feelings, keep playing together and day by day we can make our show. Sitting outside makes for faster work of course, you get results more easily, but I lose myself. If I open my mouth to explain to people what's good and what's bad, I stop being an artist.

YAROVAYA: The position of a director is a kind of sacrifice of the artist – to be off the stage and to look. Two months before the performance of *Once* which came to Edinburgh in 1998, Anton had an accident and injured his leg, and he had a replacement for his part. He saw the performance for the first time from the outside. And this was the moment he made such perfect corrections that it came to Edinburgh absolutely ready. Often we use video nowadays.

ADASSINSKY: We put cameras around the rehearsal room, and then you can see yourself what it looks like. This is how the video can help the artist.

RADOSAVLJEVIĆ: Elena was saying earlier how the way in which Derevo is different from other companies is because there is a sense of being present in the moment, rather than looking to the future. I was also wondering: are you aware of the way in which your way of working might be changing over time?

ADASSINSKY: Each piece itself dictates what we have to do. First you build the show, or just build the shadows of the show. And the show tells you which way you have to go. It's a strange moment. And from that moment on you are not free any more. Because you can't just put anything in *Harlekin*. Not because you can't make it fantastic – yes, you can make it fantastic – but *Harlekin* asks 'Please don't do it'. You have to be very flexible, very free; and don't have any pretensions such as 'I would like to make sure I put my number in' – no, think about the whole piece. In the beginning I played with Elena, just the two of us, we made a show in two parts of two and a half hours – with an intermission in the middle. This was one year ago. Now, it's one hour and twenty minutes – so many things were thrown away, many good things!

As for other companies, I don't know what other people are doing now, but I think people are just expecting results. We don't expect results, we enjoy the show. We need to be here and now, not tomorrow, not yesterday – today. People think too much. Many things we see on the stage are about the mind. Mind games, not from the heart.

RADOSAVLJEVIĆ: It's true.

ADASSINSKY: We isolate ourselves. We haven't watched TV for twenty years. We don't listen to the radio. We don't even listen to the music, it's very rare. I stop myself from collecting information about the world. Because not all of the things that are happening around me are good for the show. We like to sit alone with a glass of red wine, or to play music – to play music is the best thing you can do because it's so healthy. Music is always good. Even if you can't play a melody, but even if you just make some small noise, it's already good because it brings good vibration. All music is good, you can't play a bad sound. But when you open your mouth and start to sing you can make a mess. Because of the words.

YAROVAYA: You can get an impression that we want to isolate ourselves, but working on a show we ideally want to work with the collective subconscious of all the people around – what people are dreaming about, what they feel like they want to be.

RADOSAVLJEVIĆ: Do you still think of yourselves as a Russian troupe?

ADASSINSKY: None of us are really Russian. Elena is from the far North of Russia – Chukotka, Kamchatka. I am half Jewish, a bit Polish, and a bit Scottish. The name of my family was Gordon. A huge cocktail.

YAROVAYA: What is common to us is not Russian blood, but Russian language. It's interesting because it collects maybe 12 languages. For one object we have many different names, and when you say something it can have many meanings. So that's why during the show you can see that sometimes we turn it upside down. It's because of the absurdism in the language.

ADASSINSKY: Russian is really good for putting things upside down. We have such long sentences, such a lot of things inside them. It's rich. When we work in the company we don't speak much, and when we start speaking we just speak bullshit like five or six main words. Something in between the lines.

Note

1 Anna Budanova, playing in *Harlekin* with Adassinski and Yarovaya at the time of the interview.

Bibliography

Anonymous (1997) 'Derevo', *The List*, 22–28 August.
Bishop, Clifford (2002) 'If it's hurting it must be working', *The Sunday Times*, 4 August.
Brown, Ismene (2001) 'Absolute clowns', *The Daily Telegraph*, 16 January.
Connor, John (1989) 'Dawn of the anti-clown', *The Guardian*, 14 July.
Hutera, Donald (1998) 'From zero to fever pitch', *The Times*, 6 January.
Slater, Emi (1998) 'Seeing red', *Total Theatre*, 10(1), Spring.
Rimmer, Louise (2003) 'Russian Unorthodox', *The Scotsman*, 2 August.

Derevo
http://www.derevo.org/

9 From a community to the West End

Emma Rice (Kneehigh Theatre)

Cornwall-based Kneehigh Theatre was founded in 1980 by the former teacher and actor Mike Shepherd. Originally conceived as a theatre-in-education company, it grew and performed in village halls and site-specific places (quarries, beaches, fields, etc.). Kneehigh often worked with a core group of collaborators and had a strong connection with the Cornish community.

Emma Rice originally joined Kneehigh Theatre as an actor. In 2001 she directed her first piece for the company – *The Red Shoes* – which became a significant success and won the Best Director Award and Barclays TMA Award for Best Touring Production in 2002. This led to Rice taking over as the Artistic Director of Kneehigh Theatre and producing a string of box office hits – including *Pandora's Box* (2002), *The Bacchae* (2004), *The Wooden Frock* (2004) – as well as an increased audience following both nationally and internationally. Over the years Kneehigh forged successful creative relationships with various regional theatres as well as the National Theatre with *Tristan and Yseult* in 2005 and *A Matter of Life and Death* in 2007, and the RSC with *Cymbeline* in 2006 and *Don John* in 2008. In her review of *Cymbeline*, the Arden3 editor, Valery Wayne proclaimed that she was 'impressed by how fully Kneehigh conveyed not the letter of the text, but its spirit' (Wayne 2007: 231), even though there were only 200 lines from the original text in Kneehigh's version. The company's work is mostly characterised by adaptations – particularly screen to stage adaptations, which offer what Hesse (2009) has defined as 'surplus value' for the viewer. In the case of Kneehigh, this 'surplus value' is often contained in being able to feel part of a community. The adaptation work culminated with the West End debut of *Brief Encounter* at the Haymarket Cinema in February 2008, which went on to tour the US.

The interview below took place on 9 April 2009 at the Battersea Arts Centre, London, days before the opening of the London run of *Don John* at the same venue.

An earlier version of this interview appeared as an article 'Emma Rice in Interview with Duška Radosavljević' in the *Journal of Adaptation in Film and Performance* (3(1): 89–98), and is reprinted by kind permission of the editors.

Interview

RADOSAVLJEVIĆ: How would you define Kneehigh as an ensemble company?

RICE: I don't know whether it's possible to define an ensemble. There are lots of answers to it because it's very changeable. The very nature of an ensemble is that you are trying to stay together as a group, and the very nature of life is that the only thing that's definite is change. So the only way that you can keep an ensemble together is with quite fluid thinking. And you don't get it right all the time either. There is a British phrase 'familiarity breeds contempt' – but familiarity also breeds a shared language, a shared understanding and a shorthand, and a bravery, a fearlessness that, if you balance [it], the dividends can be so extraordinarily high. So I am really passionate about it and certainly, as I get older, I am very, very passionate about people coming back as well.

As a younger director it was all 'Are you going to stay?' and 'Are you committed?'; and actually I am much more thinking – 'Go away and come back, go away' – and actually it's a lifetime relationship. More and more as an employer I also think – understanding that actors are human beings with very rich lives is one of the keys in keeping an ensemble together. And it's one of my criticisms of what I would call a 'bought ensemble' in that you just pay them, you contract them, but you also burn them out. At the end of two years of rehearsing-performing-rehearsing, you just want to get away, you never want to do it again. We work very, very hard at making sure that people do get time off and good hours, and it's not a very good business model – it's an art model. But we work very hard financially and administratively and creatively to say 'Yeah we're going to work really long hours, we're going to sing and work late into the night, but you will go home and you will see your family and you can come back fresh'.

I think Boal talked about the five main attributes of being a human being and I am very keen on accepting that as a director as well: they are human beings and they do need company, they do have sex, they do move – real basics. I think that the work is what is at the heart of it – the people have to want to come back, and I think we all believe in the work and I think we are very lucky. It was once said of Kneehigh that we're not only part of our community but a community in ourselves – and that's when an ensemble takes on a life of its own. Because if Kneehigh finished tomorrow we would still all meet up and we would still go to the christenings of each other's children and the funerals of each other's parents. Now, how we manage it and how we nurture it is another matter, but it's a real thing and – I almost want to cry saying it – that's the most precious thing.

RADOSAVLJEVIĆ: Obviously Kneehigh has grown over the years. Would you say that there was a group of core members as well as associate members of the company?

RICE: Yes, absolutely. Again, we've talked about labelling it in the past and it doesn't go anywhere because your core members might suddenly say – 'That's it, never going to see you again', while of course, most people do come back. And associate members: somebody might come and it might be their first job, but they just get it and they are the beating heart of the company for however long it lasts. So absolutely there are core members and there are people that I would always try and cast, and it's not just casting, there's people that I think about on a strategic level – I think I must keep those people involved and part of the company. So yes, there are core members, but I am also very careful of labels.

We've never had a contracted ensemble, and never will. I can't bear the institutionalised poverty of artists and I feel very strongly that they should be paid very well, but if I've managed to get somebody sign up to say that they're going to work for me for a year, the element of choice is gone. And we still have that moment – it's like relationships, it's like sex, it's the moment when you go – 'Do you want to do this?', and they say 'Yeah, I do'. And actually I think that's priceless; what I couldn't bear is 'You're going to do this because I paid you'.

RADOSAVLJEVIĆ: How long are they contracted for usually?

RICE: It varies entirely. This *Don John* contract will eventually have run from the beginning of November till middle of June.

RADOSAVLJEVIĆ: So when you bring new members of the company into the process, do you have any particular training that they have to do?

RICE: No, although we do talk about it. The process itself is our training, but I do think we should have more. We work in our barns and there isn't anywhere else to eat and there isn't any mobile signal. So we really do end up spending a lot of time together because there is nothing else to do, and we eat together because there is nowhere else to eat, and the only warmth is a fire and it does work an immediate magic. That sort of immediate fear 'Will I be accepted and am I any good?' – there is no room for it, it just vanishes very quickly. Everybody is accepted. One of my principles as a director is that I run a room that's free of fear, so I take the responsibility for 'fearfulness' very quickly.

RADOSAVLJEVIĆ: How do you achieve the 'no fear' philosophy in the rehearsal room?

RICE: I can't guarantee that I achieve it totally. My background is in acting so I feel I understand actors. I take responsibility. I tell them what to do a lot; we don't sit around. I run the first bit of the process quite tightly. There's no notion of anything being wrong. Sometimes people say to me 'Why are you letting that happen? It's rubbish'. And I think, well, because it's all right, when there's something good it'll drop away, but there's no point in judging too soon, so there's no judgment at the beginning of rehearsals. Also it's good discipline for me because that's when strange ideas happen, so it's quite good to keep very open. And then as we devise, I lead people quite carefully through the process. We wear costumes and we put lights on and I help people so it's not them saying 'I have to be brilliant'. I've worked out quite a careful process. Which I know, if I was an actor, I'd go 'OK, I'm not in control of what happens, somebody else is in control', and then they have a space to be free.

RADOSAVLJEVIĆ: Is it possible to summarise the process?

RICE: We always run first thing in the morning. We always sing. And the music is a great leveller because everybody likes to sing and everybody is the same. Every day we do physical work, we touch each other, we sweat a lot, we pick each other up. We always play games, which is a skill that we lose very quickly. So we spend a lot of time playing games: Keepy Uppy we play for hours – keeping up balls and trying to get them into the bin. Volleyball we can play for hours. Blind Man's Bluff, Grandmother's Footsteps, whatever – it's just keeping those mechanisms quite free.

The next thing that I would always do is start building the foundations of 'why'. Now I've made an awful lot of decisions, and I know the world, and I know why I'm doing it, but what I do next is try and get the ensemble to key into why they might do it and to begin to fill in the blanks. So on huge sheets of paper we do quite a lot of 'What's your first instinct about the story?' – I'm not working with the script at all, so it would be a story. We'll write down the themes. I'll often say 'What do you not like about it?', and we write down the problems – very quickly, no censorship at all. And I'll say 'What's the colour?', 'What's the season?', 'What are the key moments?', and we are filling the room up with instinctive feelings about the story. That really forms the agenda. I leave that up in the rehearsal room for the whole process, because five weeks in when you are thinking 'God, I can't make that moment work', you might look at the wall and go 'Oh God, the moment before that was the moment everybody loves!', and it might give you a key as to how to adapt. The other thing I always get people to do is to draw pictures of the story to use different parts of their brain.

In terms of removing fearfulness, most actors – not necessarily my lot – but most actors would come to a rehearsal room thinking 'What's my part?', 'How many lines have I got?', 'Have I learnt them?', 'Am I going to be brilliant?'. Those are the questions that an actor can't help but think. In this process, nobody has read a script and all I'm saying is 'What's it about?', 'Why are you doing it', 'Why would *you* tell the story?'. And the answer might be as simple as 'Because I had my heart broken once' or 'Because I am afraid of the dark', or it might be 'Because the world has to know that care is the only way through it'. It might be an epic reason, it might be tiny. It doesn't matter. But it means that everybody in the room has a connection to the story.

The next level is characters. We all work on every character. We brainstorm what words might describe this character. From that I would choose a core set of words that I feel balance each other, and are playable and fun. Then I'd lead the company in an improvisation for each character, and I'd get them to move and talk and work on some of this key set of words that we've chosen and find some surprising things. And then eventually, at the very end, we leave that person to carry that and be that character . . .

RADOSAVLJEVIĆ: Do members of the company know which characters they would play?

RICE: Yes, they would know, but that first bit of groundwork is everybody, so you could look around and see what other people are doing. At the very end we take out that person who will play that character, the rest of the company goes and watches, we dress up, we put some costume on this person and I basically talk to them, and we find out about this character: 'Do they dance?' or 'Do they sing?' or 'How do they feel?', and it's as much physical as it is words. And without fail, with my genius-people, they will create wonders in that moment and it's a very magic moment of alchemy. I am absolutely part of that, I'm not watching them, I'm with them, I'm in the space finding out who they are. For me as a director and an adapter, that's my agenda. What happens in that moment of chemistry is that I know the heart of the person playing that character, and that will guide then how that character sits within the structure of that work.

So now I've got the themes and I've built all the characters up – that's when I start putting situations in and that's when the characters can start meeting. But if I've started that process well, things happen very quickly and very instinctively. So once you've done that, there's the point when you say 'What happens when Iachimo comes and meets Imogen?'. And you say 'You've got a bed and you've got five minutes and I'm going to put some music on' – pshhh (*mimes chemical explosion*)!

I'm not saying everything does, but more stuff works than doesn't work. You end up with a huge palette from which to start creating – again, if I've done my job well, people's ideas will tend to be good ideas, and they will be within the world of the show and within the world of what we want to do.

RADOSAVLJEVIĆ: How long is the rehearsal process on average?

RICE: I'd say five weeks.

RADOSAVLJEVIĆ: And this final process of putting scenes together, how long does that usually take?

RICE: I would start putting scenes together in week two. I would do a week of preparation, which in five weeks is a bit airy. But in that time we would have learnt a lot of music so that by the time you start putting scenes together it's amazing how quickly a sort of a world emerges.

What I just described is the process – I work on the iceberg and the words are the sprinkle on top of the point. And I think that most theatre works the other way round – you work on the words and then you keep finding meaning.

RADOSAVLJEVIĆ: With adapting films, do you watch the film as a company?

RICE: When I decide to do a story, I don't tend to go and read or watch it, I tend to work on what my cultural memory of it is, because that's my truth. So rather than going 'Hey what is it, I'm going to pull it apart!', I say 'What do I remember about that film, what did it make me feel, what are my favourite bits?'. I do a lot of work from my memory and my emotional recall. Then I will of course watch and read it later, but in any case, my foundation will be my memory. And I'm sure that's one of the reasons why I want to do adaptations – I want to work with that emotional memory. I want to retell the stories, whether it's *Brief Encounter* that I saw when I was ill off school aged 12, or whether it's *The Red Shoes* which I must have been told as a child.

RADOSAVLJEVIĆ: With *Brief Encounter* there was the film and then there was the original play *Still Life* that played a part in this adaptation, but also the songs.

RICE: *Still Life*'s brilliant because it doesn't move location – it's all set in the station. And it's five short scenes of the couple meeting up at different points of their affair. Most of it is in the film, but other characters are painted more vividly. It really gives you the groundwork for a chamber piece, which is great for an ensemble director. The film has been much more guided towards the two stars and the other people just support them. I didn't have two stars to cast and I didn't want to cast two stars. That's where *Still Life* worked, this was about six people. Two of them happened to be middle class people – but actually it was about six people. I did the first rough adaptation very quickly, literally sticking bits of paper and looking at a different structure going through.

RADOSAVLJEVIĆ: At one point you had three shows on the road and that must have affected the way you think about the company and the ensemble work itself – what kinds of challenges does that have for you?

RICE: We're just beginning to realise that, for all sorts of reasons, we are having to do it more commercially. And I don't have an instinctive problem with that – I wish to create income and I wish to be popular – I am not elitist in any form. The more money that passes through the company the more opportunities there are, so I don't have a problem with the basic mechanics of business. But if you are led commercially it can destroy work and sometimes destroy people in the process. At the time when there were three shows on the road – we'd already committed to *Rapunzel* being in New York, *Brief Encounter* was being run by a separate team in London which was fine, and then we got invited to Brazil and Columbia with *Cymbeline*. We're just not going to say no. And that's because when we tour abroad, they are the best moments of our life. And again an ensemble – not just a group of individuals – but a community, lands in another community and tells stories, and parties, and all of our lives are better for it.

But I do worry. Sometimes recasting works really well. But it always rips your heart out. What's hard is when you are sort of grafting new people – so you've got one person who doesn't know what they are doing and everybody else who knows it backwards, and it's quite a mismatch. To go back to describing how we build the work – these aren't just characters on a page that anybody could pick up, they are characters that have come from somebody's very being and because we are multi-disciplined – I've got a Polish cleaner in *Don John* who is also a virtuoso violin player – that's tough to recast! You can't just, like in the West End, get an assistant director to teach that role, you have to find somebody else – who will definitely not have the same skills – and you have to find a way of getting a new set of skills and a new person in.

RADOSAVLJEVIĆ: So is the process of recasting as long as the process of creating the work? How does the handover of characters happen?

RICE: No, we haven't done it that often. *Don John* we knew that there were going to be some character changes, and what we did was we got the people that were going to come into the show into some of the rehearsals, so they knew the company. They were in and out and then we did a week's re-rehearsal and quite a hard, tough, getting them into the tech. But we spread it throughout the process so that they didn't feel they were just coming with their suitcases.

RADOSAVLJEVIĆ: You say you trained as an actor, but you also trained in Poland. Did that experience inform your way of working in some way?

RICE: Yes, blissfully – I do feel that it's taken years but I do feel that I am me now. I no longer feel that I am trying to assimilate other brilliant people. I am sort of in my own skin as an artist now. Poland was simply the most influential thing that happened to me. It was really tough, really difficult. I am over it now but I have had lots of issues about it as well. I do think it was punishing, I think it was controlling, I think it was authoritarian, I think it was full of fear – and all of that gets results. They did lots of things, but the single thing they did to a British actress is to go 'This fucking matters! We will hide in the forest from the military to do this, we will stay up all night to do this, we will not piss about'. I mean just the level of sacrifice that they make to make work, the level of seriousness, and then the wonders that that creates. You can't go back, once you've seen that. I've never really freelanced since, because I think once you have worked in the way that's completely dedicated, it's very hard to sit in a green room and read a paper, and say there is no work about – you can no longer be that person.

Kneehigh is a million miles from Poland, but the similarities are there – it's rural, it's isolated, it's completely dedicated, but I would say, I've developed and we've developed a way of working that's based on joy, not on pain. And ultimately I don't feel guilty or judgmental about that. So actually it's also to do with me saying I'm British, it's not very exotic, I come from Nottingham, but it is who I am. I think I spent a lot of my twenties just wishing I was Eastern European, so I could be exotic. So there is also a level of saying 'This is what I am, this is the culture I am in, but I am as passionate and we do care as much'.

RADOSAVLJEVIĆ: Did the music element of your creative process emerge from that experience perhaps?

RICE: Yes, is the short answer to that. But I also played music a lot as a child. I played the French horn to Grade 8 and played in orchestras. My dad was a jazz musician. And Gardzienice obviously – they taught me how to sing in a different way, taught me how to own music in a way that I never had with a classical training. So as a performer I felt cracked open by Gardzienice in a way that three years at Drama School hadn't touched me! And then you go out there and you feel like you've had your rib-cage ripped apart and you sound different and you look different. I started sweating in Poland and have never stopped, literally – things change. And I love that. I feel that I was sort of born out there in many ways. In the 1990s all of us got very obsessed with the Balkan singing. There wasn't a show in England that didn't have the Bulgarian voices. But that has evolved. We now have our own band of musicians. My very close relationship is with Stu Barker. I think I have my own process of the way that music works. And I think it's much more informed by pop culture. Gardzienice is very much folk culture, which I'm still very much interested in, but I am more interested in what the British folk culture is. Now, we didn't sit around fires and sing songs – we listened to Bay City Rollers, but that's still folk culture. That's really where *Don John* is my letter of love to my childhood. It sounds like punk, it is punk, but it's still my folk culture, it's what I listened to with my mates in my bedroom. So I've moved away from an 'exotic' folk culture, which isn't my own.

RADOSAVLJEVIĆ: What is Stu Barker's background musically? Would you say that he belongs to a particular genre?

RICE: You'd have to ask Stu that. When I first worked with Stu, he had dreadlocks and a dog on a piece of string. He is into the folk tradition, so he plays the Uilleann pipes and the hurdy-gurdy, but he has also done a lot of punk and was an anarchist in his youth. He's not a classically trained musician which most of my musicians aren't. The way that we score our work is the same way that we devise our work, which is that it happens through improvisation. So the way that a band would work.

RADOSAVLJEVIĆ: They are part of the rehearsals as well?

RICE: From day one. They work alongside.

RADOSAVLJEVIĆ: Do the words come first or the music?

RICE: Words, probably. Stu likes to write tunes to words. But we also work on themes early on. Long before rehearsals I'll say 'I want the theme of hell', 'I want the theme of desire', 'I want the theme of frustration'. So we'd start putting things together. And then of course in rehearsals, what is interesting is that maybe the theme that we wrote for hell becomes the theme for frustration. They might not sit where you think they were going to sit.

RADOSAVLJEVIĆ: They are very well integrated into shows. Sometimes some of the singing – I am thinking primarily of the young singer in *Cymbeline* was in fact coming across as filling in a dramaturgical function of the storytelling. Is that simply because they are part of the rehearsals? How does it work?

RICE: Dom [Lawton], who is in *Don John* as well, is an exceptional talent. He isn't an actor – he'd be the first person to say that, but he is an artist and he is a storyteller, he is an amazing musician. That's interesting for me – how do I use a talent like that? In *Cymbeline* he became the lost son. And that becomes very interesting because then there is this young man who is angry, who is calling from somewhere different – and meaning comes out of that. Having Dom singing out the action, but from the outside, had dramaturgical weight. He is the child that got taken away from the family when he was two and he is on the outside. In *Cymbeline* I love that little car which signifies children trying to find their way back. In many ways that's what *Cymbeline* was for me – a family finding itself, not in a sentimental way, but just saying 'who am I?' – and eventually finding your way back.

I've got Dom doing a similar job within *Don John*. He's narrating more, but I've got him as a paper boy, and I really wanted somebody quite innocent looking in from the outskirts. In Britain there was a famous murder trial, for a paper boy who got murdered in 1978 – Carl Bridgewater. For me he is like the ghost of human horrors – to remember what human beings are capable of. Nobody ever needs to know that – but we do. When we look at Dom, we think he stands for every child or every person who's needlessly tortured in that way.

RADOSAVLJEVIĆ: Do the musicians get involved in the character formation?

RICE: They come and go. I don't make anybody do what they don't want to do. I don't make musicians act if that's not what they want to do. But they'll often watch and I'll often get them to improvise.

RADOSAVLJEVIĆ: Does Stu work with other people as well?

RICE: He does. He tells me he prefers working with Kneehigh. I'm sure he does as I use music very strongly, as to my knowledge there aren't that many theatre practices that have so much music. As a composer you tend to do scene changes which is more frustrating than what he is doing here which is creating whole scores, which is fantastic.

RADOSAVLJEVIĆ: How do you deal with the notion of being faithful to the original?

RICE: It comes back to the way that I answered before, which is that I work a lot with my emotional recall. I've never done a single piece of work that I don't care passionately for. There's never any pastiche in my work, even if people sometimes say there is. And there's never any cynicism. Therefore the absolute heart of everything I do is being honoured. I only do A *Matter of Life and Death* because I think it's the most beautiful film of all time. I only do *Brief Encounter* because I think it charts that elemental human condition of 'falling in love when I can't do' so beautifully. I don't think about it, because to not honour it isn't part of the equation. And I'd argue really, really strongly about that. What I always say is that you can watch *Brief Encounter* the movie an hour and a half before you come and see the play, you can see the play, and then you can go and watch the film again and – nobody's touched it, nothing's altered, I haven't touched anybody's work. All I've done as a storyteller – which Shakespeare did, Brecht did, I'm so not alone in that – is taken an existing story and done what we've all done throughout the entire history: told stories.

Bibliography

Costa, Maddy (2008) 'Troupe Therapy', *The Guardian*, 1 December, available online at http://www.guardian.co.uk/stage/2008/dec/01/kneehigh-theatre-cornwall-maddy-costa (accessed 19 December 2012).

Hesse, Beatrix (2009) 'From Screen to Stage: The Case of *The 39 Steps*', in Monika Pietrzak-Franger and Eckart Voigts-Virchow (eds) *Adaptations: Performing Across Media and Genres*, Trier: Verlage, pp. 143–58.

Wayne, Valerie (2007) 'Kneehigh's dream of *Cymbeline*', *Shakespeare Quarterly*, 58(2): 228–37.

Kneehigh Theatre
http://www.kneehigh.co.uk/

10 On being an ensemble actor in the UK

Joanna Holden (freelance actor, Northern Stage, Kneehigh, Cirque du Soleil)

There is a nuance to be observed regarding the perceived distinction in the British theatre context between drama school-trained freelance actors and alternatively trained ensemble theatre-makers. As already noted, longevity is a challenge for many ensembles which may over time become associated with the individual figure of a director (Complicite's Simon McBurney or DV8's Lloyd Newson). This has, however, led to an emergence of what might be called a 'freelance ensemble actor' – a type of actor who is accustomed to collaborative ways of working which may include devising and physical theatre as well as text-based mainstream work. Actors such as Paul Hunter and Hayley Carmichael, the founders of Told By an Idiot, have both worked extensively with other ensembles, such as Kneehigh, David Glass Ensemble, Complicite, Northern Stage and Shared Experience, but also at the National Theatre (Carmichael) and at the Shakespeare's Globe (Hunter). Hunter and Carmichael had trained at Middlesex University with John Wright. Another actress of this kind is Bretton Hall graduate Amanda Lawrence, who worked extensively with Fecund Theatre, Compass Theatre, Northern Stage and Kneehigh before pursuing an increasingly successful screen career.

Similarly, Joanna Holden, the founder member of the Northern Stage Ensemble, has since 1992 performed professionally in productions at the Royal Court, the Bush Theatre, Soho Theatre and the Royal National Theatre as well as working with John Wright, Told by An Idiot, VTOL, Ridiculusmus and Cartoon de Salvo. Holden has a drama degree from Royal Holloway, University of London, and she has studied Clown at École Philippe Gaulier. As a clown she has also worked with Cirque du Soleil on *Varekai* (2004–2008). In 2004, she appeared in the Northern Stage production of Ionesco's *The New Tenant* directed by Gabor Tompa.

The interview took place in May 2010 in London shortly after her tour of *Hansel and Gretel* with Kneehigh Theatre.

Interview

HOLDEN: I guess, for Kneehigh, working in an ensemble way means that they create a process that's all-enveloping. It's not about going along as a jobbing actor and being in a room and having a director, and there being some kind of a gap between you, and one of you tells the other what to do. With Kneehigh you join the rehearsal process – for the first two weeks you are at the barns, where their headquarters are, so you eat together, you sleep together (well, not completely sleep together), in the morning you get up, you go running on the cliff tops. And because of where it's based – out in the countryside, with the crashing sea against the cliffs – that is an inspiring experience that can be taken into the rehearsal room. You get a lot of work done because the work never stops – by the time you've finished rehearsals, you are having dinner together, and I find, ideas come to people sometimes, not when they are under pressure in the rehearsal room, but quite often it's in the break that you go – 'Well, I could try this', and 'What about this!?'.

They do a great thing where you dress each other up in costume – nothing is tied down, they don't go 'This is what I think Gretel should look like' – they put any costume on you and you play in that costume. Of course the big emphasis is on play and on working together: finding the structure, finding the characters, finding ways you want to tell the story – whether it's through puppetry, whether it's through music, whether it's through movement, whether it's through you as a performer. It was a company of four actors, two musicians and an acting stage manager, plus lighting and sound, plus Mike Shepherd the director. The three actors that I was working with have worked together on and off for 15 years! They absolutely know the vocabulary of Kneehigh, they know the vocabulary of each other, which I think is great about the ensemble work.

The idea of ensemble can mean many different things. Within a week you can begin to create and start moving together as an ensemble. You can almost interpret each other's ideas before the person has even thought of it. And that is a beautiful environment to be in. Very creative, very free because of the trust that has developed between you. The other idea of ensemble is a group of people that go together on a long journey of discovery, and that can't be done within a week. This is what Kneehigh has with its core group, of which I was only on the periphery. I only worked with them for six months, and it was my first contact with them. They used a lot of tools that I'm very familiar with in devising and the technique was

really 'rough theatre'. Broad brushstrokes, an outline, and then carefully filling in the details. Just before we opened we didn't even know
the running order really, but we played together so much that we felt
absolutely comfortable with each other.

RADOSAVLJEVIĆ: Was there a text or did you devise it from scratch?

HOLDEN: Prior to the rehearsal we were sent a rough idea of an outline of
various scenes of *Hansel and Gretel* by Carl Grose. He is not a founder
member because they are 30 years old, but he's been there for a very,
very long time; he started as an apprentice. The core members often
only work for Kneehigh – they are not into the commercial thing of
having an agent, looking for other work; their work is Kneehigh.

Carl Grose was the writer on the project. He would come in with a
structure, with certain more poetic bits of the text – the Witch, for
example, spoke in rhyming couplets. So that wasn't improvised, that
did come already written. What we did was flesh it out. They had
done an R&D beforehand and they decided that the rabbits – we had
white puppet rabbits that are constantly being killed by traps – would
act as a chorus for the story. We had two chickens and the two chickens act as a chorus too. They were plump chickens in the beginning
and by the second scene they were already skinny chickens, and
through the chickens you can see the hard times that the family have
fallen on. So there were those really interesting ways of telling the
story – not just through the main characters which were the Mother,
the Father, the Father doubling as the Witch, and Hansel and Gretel.

And so then you're improvising, and sometimes you came on and
you ramble on, and sometimes you come up with fantastic lines and
ideas. And Carl would go home every night, and he would write up
some of the stuff that we'd improvised. There was probably a new
script every day – a new script that was constantly evolving throughout the rehearsal process, along with the structure as well. They had a
big blackboard, and you would move scenes around. The day would
be split so we would be looking at structure, character scenes, choreography, music sessions. They had two great composer-musicians that
went away with some of the lyrics that Carl had already written, and
put music to them. And then you had to learn an instrument. And I
took my trumpet thinking that in four weeks I would learn it enough
to be able to play, and I ended up playing the washboard . . .

It's all about adapting!

What I do love about that kind of theatre is that there isn't a star
system – the only thing that has status and priority is the work. And
what I find beautiful about theatre, and certainly the theatre that I am
interested in, is using what you have in front of you: using the beauty

of those people, whether they might have a club foot or be a terrible singer, or have a beautiful voice. It's taking all the ingredients and making a big birthday cake, to be served up on the opening night.

RADOSAVLJEVIĆ: How was that different from working at Northern Stage?

HOLDEN: Even though Kneehigh do work as an ensemble and the process is that everyone is equal in the rehearsal room – I was there for such a short time. Whereas at Northern Stage, I was part of the ensemble for a longer time. That familiarity leads to an absolute sense of freedom and an opportunity to work and develop with the same people every day for two years.

RADOSAVLJEVIĆ: Had you worked with Northern Stage before you joined the ensemble in 1998?

HOLDEN: I had done *Animal Farm* with Northern Stage in 1997 and the ensemble was set up in 1998. Alan Lyddiard had met me when I was doing a show at the Gate Theatre, *Ubu Roi*, and he auditioned me for *Animal Farm* – a show which in no way I could do now, it was so physical!

RADOSAVLJEVIĆ: You were with the Northern Stage Ensemble for the first year and in the second year you went away?

HOLDEN: In the second year I went to work with VTOL dance company. Why did I do that? I think I was young – I was offered something, and I wanted to try something new. At that time we had done two shows, *Romeo and Juliet* and *A Clockwork Orange*. I think my appreciation of what Alan was trying to do grew retrospectively. Ensemble is about the company and its vision. What did I really love and what did I find most difficult? I guess what I really loved was moving towards that feeling that the whole is greater than its many parts, that complete comfortableness, that learning process and that journey that you went on together. And the fact that we were constantly being trained – which was great! Normally when you do a show, you go there as a trained actor and you do what you do. Whereas at Northern Stage, Paul Hunter came and did some stuff with us, we had the Linklater voice training workshops, there was some space for personal projects. I remember doing a workshop on the *House of Spirits*, and I guess if I pursued it, there could have been a possibility to put on a small production at the Gulbenkian. You were rehearsing, performing and training all the time.

One thing that I did really enjoy was the fact that we would all have meetings, we would all discuss a way of working even if that way of working came from Alan. I don't know if it was easy for Alan to impose that on a young, quite wayward company that we were when we first started, and not all of us were as disciplined as the others. How did I contribute? I certainly felt a great freedom. And I certainly felt able to voice my opinions. I seem to remember that if there was something we specifically needed in terms of training, we could make a request for that.

What I really now understand and love as part of the training we had was structure and repetition. I think of the 'Slow Walking Exercise' which was an absolute signature exercise that Alan did. We did it every day. And I remember when I first did it, I loved it. And then I went through a phase of naively thinking 'What is this, why am I doing this every day?'. And now when I think of the ensemble, that is one of the exercises I think of and admire the most – to be able to just stand there. Reminds me a bit of the neutral mask exercise. And also a meditation exercise. To just stand there and be naked, as it were, and be you and understand the beauty in human beings in yourself, and theatre of course is about humanity and being human. Another thing I love about those exercises is they teach you discipline. Of course your mind wanders and you are constantly holding it back, and it's a good thing to check in with yourself, with what's going on through your mind that day, how you feel before you go into this room. It brought you into the space where you were ready to play. And we also used to do a movement piece every morning as a warm up.

RADOSAVLJEVIĆ: The 'Frank piece'?

HOLDEN: Yes! By Frank McConnell. I didn't find it easy, because I am not the most physical person in the world. But what I loved about this was – and I found this when I was working in circus repeating the same routine every day – that you find delight in the structure! Because in that structure you find moments of playfulness and moments of reflection, in the tiniest of moments. And the more you have to work within that structure, the more the slight differences seem immense.

RADOSAVLJEVIĆ: I remember you saying that when you did *Romeo and Juliet* at Northern Stage it was the first time you ever played Juliet and it was an opportunity made by the fact that this was an ensemble company.

HOLDEN: Yes, I always remember the moment: we were all sat around some big boardroom table, and Alan was announcing what the next production would be and the casting of the next production. And I was just doodling with my pencil, and he said 'We are doing *Romeo and Juliet*', and I kind of looked up and then I was doodling a bit more, and he said 'And I'd like Joey to be Juliet', and I literally lent on my pencil and the lead broke. I don't know how old I was then, 32? I thought 'That's amazing, I'm a little bit plump, I'm 32 – a really unlikely casting for Juliet!'. Even from the age of 12, I was nurse material as opposed to Juliet . . .

So that was a fantastic opportunity. And I loved that production. I know it wasn't without its problems, but then again creating is a bit like giving birth. You are never working in a paradise, you are working with different people's passions and different people's ways of working. And it was one of those productions that absolutely split the audience down the middle. People either loved it or they absolutely hated it. But because the casting had to come from the ensemble, it allowed for more adventurous casting.

RADOSAVLJEVIĆ: What do you remember about that process? Did you have a work in progress and was there a text?

HOLDEN: In the same way as with Kneehigh, the text was constantly evolving throughout the process. Alan and the writer Kitty Fitzgerald were going away and writing bits. It was 'A Factory Romeo and Juliet', so there was a factory framework which was developed through improvisations and was shaped by Kitty. Alan worked out how the original Shakespeare would interweave with the modern.

RADOSAVLJEVIĆ: Did you have any say in that as actors?

HOLDEN: I think we had more of a say in terms of the framing device of the show, in terms of developing the characters and where they fitted into the factory world. And when we went into Shakespeare's world and language, it seemed more intimate. The contrast between the two styles brought out different elements.

RADOSAVLJEVIĆ: So the frame was that these people work in a factory and then they put on the play?

HOLDEN: On 14 February every year, they would put on a production of *Romeo and Juliet*. I was playing somebody with special needs, and so was Mark Calvert, as factory workers – hence the idea of forbidden love. And then we were given these parts as Romeo and Juliet, and of course we fell in love in the 'real world' and in the 'world of the play'. The way I understood it was that when they could speak Shakespeare – they became more articulate. It was almost as if through that language they became their other self.

RADOSAVLJEVIĆ: It's really interesting to consider that experience by comparison to circus – which is obviously very different and yet a very intense way of being together.

HOLDEN: Yes, it is, a kind of ensemble in a different way. It's ensemble in that you live, eat and travel together and they become absolutely your family. Circus by its nature is the idea of travelling and family.

Because Cirque du Soleil is a commercial circus, the acts are so defined, each act exists on its own, although they are put together as a show. In terms of an ensemble feeling when you are performing, within those acts there is a great sense of working together, but in the show as a whole, there are some people that have been there for eight years and there are some people that have just come in and taken over from somebody.

RADOSAVLJEVIĆ: It's not an organic process?

HOLDEN: No. And there is not much movement or change. You don't go through a process together, but because of the domestic and other sides of things, you do have that family feeling. But if you are going to do that 'eat, sleep, live, breathe the work' together – it's a sacrifice of other aspects of your life. And that's always difficult, because there are other aspects of your life that feed into your creativity.

Bibliography

Best, Jason (2010) 'Hansel and Gretel', *The Stage*, 20 December, available online at http://www.thestage.co.uk/reviews/review.php/30792/hansel-and-gretel (accessed 19 December 2012).

Joanna Holden
http://www.castingcallpro.com/uk/view.php?uid = 144558 (accessed 19 December 2012)

11 An actor's journey between Wales and Wroclaw

Ian Morgan (Song of the Goat)

Founded by Grzegorz Bral and Anna Zubrzycki in 1996, Song of the Goat (Teatr Pieśń Kozła) spent four years as a company in residence at the Jerzy Grotowski Centre for Theatre and Culture Research in Wroclaw, and then moved to premises of their own in the same city. They consider themselves an 'international ensemble company with members from the UK, Finland, France, Norway, Sweden and Poland' (Song of the Goat website). Over the years they have developed a singular aesthetic and training methodology which combines movement, text, song and voice through the so-called 'co-ordination technique' rooted in Bral and Zubrzycki's personal practice of Buddhism:

> an approach that seeks to create a profound sense of harmony within and between each actor and every element of his or her work through training, improvising, and research on diverse songs, dances, myths, and rituals.
>
> (Porubcansky 2010: 261)

The company's Edinburgh Festival Fringe debut in 2004 with the multi-award winning *Chronicles: a lamentation* was an instant success and led to a series of further engagements in the UK and internationally. In 2004 Song of the Goat teamed up with Manchester Metropolitan University to deliver an MA in Acting, run on a bi-annual basis. In 2006 they were invited by the Royal Shakespeare Company to participate in the year-long Complete Works Festival with a work-in-progress of their version of *Macbeth*, featuring Siberian and Corsican polyphonic singing. In his review of the work-in-progress, Paul Allain singled out an instance in which the singing is deployed dramaturgically, for example in Ian Morgan's 'touching sung duet that became the motor for Macduff's resolve' (Allain 2007: 256).

Over its first 15 years, the company created only three full productions. Anna Porubcansky noted in her article:

These three productions represent the body of Song of the Goat's artistic work and demonstrate the group's strong commitment to the creation of a holistic exploration of their varied source material.

(Porubcansky 2010: 268)

Then in 2012, they presented another Shakespeare-inspired work-in-progress *Songs of Lear* at the Edinburgh Fringe. Despite the fact that this was only a recital, discursively framed by Bral, it has received five star reviews and the Fringe First award. *The List*'s Matt Trueman declared it 'a full-body detox; catharsis pure and simple and transcendent' (Trueman 2012).

Originally from Wales, Ian Morgan is an actor and teacher who has developed an impressive international portfolio of work and training practices. Having graduated from the University of Hull Drama Department in 1990, Morgan went on to train with Monika Pagneux in Paris in 1991, and then with Jerzy Grotowski and Thomas Richards at the Workcenter in Pontadera 1992–1995. As of 2004, Morgan has been a performer with the Polish company Song of the Goat (Teatr Pieśń Kozła). An experienced teacher in his own right, as a member of Song of the Goat, Morgan also teaches on their MA in Acting. In the interview that follows, which took part in writing in the course of 2011, he contextualises his work with the company through some of his earlier experiences. This is accompanied by a short statement from Song of the Goat co-founder Anna Zubrzycki.

Interview

RADOSAVLJEVIĆ: Could you describe your background as an actor, your training and your work with any other ensembles prior to Song of the Goat?

MORGAN: As a teenager I experienced making theatre at the National Youth Theatres of both Wales and the UK. From there I went to study Drama at the University of Hull, where, in the late 1980s, there were no performing skills classes on the curriculum. It was essentially an academic course, studying theatre history and dramatic literature. However, there was a module in directing (which I did) and there were plenty of opportunities to appear in Departmental productions and smaller projects. The presumption was that if you wanted to perform, in all probability, you would go on to complete a Postgraduate Diploma in Acting at one of the recognised drama schools. At the time, I had no awareness of actor training practises, theatre laboratories, ensembles, performance, live art, etc. Instead of going to Drama School I joined my graduate colleagues in a student company, Z Theatre, and went to Edinburgh (in my second year) and then to France (after graduation) to a festival called Harlequinart, in Metz. There I met Annabel Arden (ex-Theatre de Complicite) and Monika Pagneux.

As a result of that festival, I enrolled in Monika's studio (which she held with Phillipe Gaulier) in Paris in 1991, and ended up in a small company associated to the Theatre du Soleil. I experienced *Les Atrides* in the early part of that year. The beauty of the spectacle, its immersive nine hour journey, the quality of the physical work on the stage and the musicality of the whole experience was life defining. I also sensed that these people lived for this work. Many of the actors had worked in the Soleil for a long time, and they seemed to treat the theatre as an extension of their idea of home and community. It seemed to me a precious and intensely personal part of their life, where they spent most of their time and where they seemed to devote a lot of their energy. The company seemed to have excessively long working hours, which were amorphous, to the extent that the borders between work and going home were blurred. And the passion for the work was distinct. Everyone had something at stake. More than being anxious about their own personal performances, the actors seemed to have an ownership over their roles and the identity of the whole work. It didn't seem something they walked away from with ease. I think I was meeting the first actor-artists I'd ever encountered – people for whom theatre was central to their way of encountering and communicating with the world.

I instinctively followed the Soleil's work during that period and managed to get an audition for a project to be directed by one of the company's performers – the Mexican actress and director Esther Andre Gonzalez. The company – Teatro Pirequa – was formed to go to Mexico and create a piece about the rise and fall of the Aztec empire and their relationship with their gods. This experience gave me a taste of many aspects of being in a particular type of ensemble, as I now know it. I was introduced to many of the characteristics we recognise and sometimes romanticise as European laboratory/ ensemble theatre groups. It was my first experience of a certain way of making theatre in an ensemble of artists whose work dominated a large part of their life. It seemed a way of life and a choice made of how to experience human encounter and existence.

Rehearsals took place in the evening (to allow people to work to gain money) and on weekends. This was the case at the Soleil and in

various informal workshop spaces around the twentieth arrondisse-
ment in Paris. The sense of meeting and group forming through exercise, physical improvisation and song was a profound experience for
me. Slowly there developed a codified energetic way of meeting and
experiencing each other that I hadn't encountered in the conventional
theatre work I'd had already. I was experiencing the creation of a group
that was sensitive, responsive and supportive to all its members, and
that had something seductive and compelling. There was an energy of
'gang', we hung out after rehearsal and relationships formed.

We also worked with local cultural groups in Mexico, who taught
us songs and dances from pre-Columbian sources, which we studied
and adapted into the structure. The experiencing of this culture was
the vehicle by which we created our culture – the culture of the group.
I wouldn't use the word family in this case, or in fact any of the ensembles I've worked with.

A group's culture can be made up of many diverse relationships that
continue both inside and outside the working environment. The
dynamic of hierarchy is also important. Each group – like each family –
has its own social structure; with age, experience, shared histories and
acquired roles – imposed and/or evolved – all being clear factors in
this. A group ensemble can feel like a tribe or gang and I've heard
some use the term 'conscious community'.

On returning from Mexico, the Pirequa ensemble slowly disintegrated and I ended up in another type of ensemble theatre practice,
with Grotowski and Thomas Richards at their Workcenter in Italy. I
stayed there from 1992 to 1995. It was obviously very different, as the
group was not explicitly making performance. It was the period in
which Grotowski was handing over his leading of the work slowly to
Richards, but was still very much involved in the space. This work
involved aspects of so-called training and the making of 'performance' structures and went on for 11 months a year, six days a week
and on average eight hours a day.

In this case, for financial reasons, initially, the majority of the
group were communally housed in accommodation found by the host
theatre. My first year was spent in an unheated, unkempt countryside
villa, with cracked everything. But we all pulled together and made it
sustainable. At first – in 1992 – new members of the two work groups
that existed at that time, lived together, relied on each other to get
by and shared time outside the work – an enforced community that
slowly became a real one. Maybe that is the pattern with a certain
type of working group that retires away from the metropolitan areas
to gain some quiet and concentration to work?

The Workcenter groups, in my experience, were co-dependent communities brought together by the work. There is a bond between those who spent time there together and even between those who spent time there in differing periods.

Later we split into smaller living groups and found better shared accommodation, and later still I lived alone in a flat in Pontedera and even had a part-time job, but the work was always the dominating factor, governing all aspects of my life for three years. It was simply a vocation that one lived and breathed – taking responsibility for various aspects of the Workcenter's running.

After those two experiences abroad I returned home to Wales to work in and around the Centre for Performance Research at the University of Wales, Aberystwyth, and devise work with Welsh companies such as ManAct, Equilibre and U-Man Zoo. These companies devised work and had a sense of communal identity but didn't exist as permanent ensembles. One could say there existed communities of artists around these companies, that returned once or twice a year to collaborate with the lead artists who organised the company's ongoing processes. This period lasted about four years, during which I developed a teaching/facilitating practice.

Then I was invited by Peader Kirk, a theatre artist from London, to be a part of a new performance collective called Mkultra. The work with Mkultra didn't have a training practice, but did have a rigorous and established way of making work, involving performer-led propositions, often made from personal material. I was involved actively in the collective as a central practitioner until I left to join Song of the Goat in 2004, although I remain a member of this collective to this day. Because Mkultra is a collective, the responsibility to being ever present doesn't exist. Each work has a shuffled list of participants made up of those who are available at the time of making.

RADOSAVLJEVIĆ: How and when did your association with Song of the Goat come about?

MORGAN: In 2002 I did a workshop led by Song of the Goat performers Christopher Siversten and Maria Sendow in Wales, and they recommended my partner, Zoe Crowder, and myself to the company for a one-month making/training exploration. The work in Poland, with exercises that stimulated highly physical, immersive flows of action, was something we both found attractive. My partner ended up studying on the first MA in Acting cohort run by the company in Wroclaw and I was invited to join the company in the last stage of creating [their second piece] *Lacrimosa*. At first, this was a short-term involvement, then I was invited to take over a role in *Chronicles*, and then decided to join the *Macbeth* process when it started in 2006.

RADOSAVLJEVIĆ: How does working with Song of the Goat compare to working with any other ensembles you have worked with?

MORGAN: Each ensemble I've been involved with has been distinct in terms of their working processes and organisational structures.

Each has its own interests and its own approach to creativity and the performer has different roles in each case, within the creative process. Maybe that is what they have in common, their uniqueness.

Many of the creative teams I've worked with have engendered enormous loyalty from their members. There is a sense of belonging that exists in a type of work that is unique; an ownership and identification of one's personal creative identity with that of the company that has much to do with the fact that work is made through a collaborative practice – it could only exist in the way it does because of the people involved. Also just by the fact that one spends a long time in such companies and in the presence of colleagues, they do lead to incredibly powerful relationships, that often are very difficult to move on from. This is very different from the situation of the conventional independent actor.

RADOSAVLJEVIĆ: How would you define your personal involvement with Song of the Goat?

MORGAN: I am committed to the company, and I think of the people in the company as my respected colleagues, above all things. We are drawn together and stay together through a commitment to making a work that takes time to emerge. It is a group. But we often jokingly refer to ourselves as 'The Goats' – the way that a band might name themselves, and hence declare themselves a part of something cohesive. Having time is one of the most crucial aspects attracting me to this way of making work. The work is never finished – in the way that some performances are 'done when they're done' – the work is always in process and can be because we continue to commit to that level of engagement. The performances have been and continue to be 'places of meeting', creative activities that we simply continue to do together, because we find value in them, both personally and professionally. There is an unspoken, continual commitment, through the performance structures, to explore our capacity for feeling, exploring, sensing. Entering on a journey together into a known yet always surprising territory of experience and togetherness, without pretension, in front of others.

RADOSAVLJEVIĆ: How much time do you spend together as an ensemble and how do you manage your life between the UK and Poland?

MORGAN: When we are preparing a new piece we will rehearse every weekday six to eight hours, including preparation of songs as well as the work in the space. Otherwise we are free to spend our time as we wish and work in other contexts. During performance weeks we will meet up to three to four days prior to the performance for rehearsal, to tune to the performance.

As an international group, some of us are where we are for the work. Wroclaw is a wonderfully vibrant and culturally diverse university town, with lots happening. So, it entertains and enriches our lives outside the company's working hours. Simply by the fact that we are in this place for the work and that our primary contact with the community is, at first, through work, then inevitably some of us have lived together. It has been convenient. But over time people have found their own places and/or split into smaller friendship groups. With the city being served by an international airport and two flights or more to the UK each day, it is easy and relatively cheap to spend time working and living in both the UK and Poland. After seven years the displacement effect is small and the commute relatively short.

RADOSAVLJEVIĆ: To what extent is Song of the Goat similar, and to what extent is it different from any Grotowskian heritage?

MORGAN: Song of the Goat's founders worked with Gardzienice, formed by Wlodek Staniewski who worked with Grotowski in his 'parathea-tre' phase, so there is obviously a relationship. But, personally, I don't believe in any conscious Grotowskian lineage or heritage. In my experience, most people who worked with Grotowski directly went on to be inspired to create their own distinct way of making work. Grotowski never seemed to hunt disciples, he encouraged excellent rebellion. Those who worked with him hardly ever cite him as being an aesthetic influence on the work. Influential on the quality of their process and even themselves as people, yes, but in a way that has been liberating and empowering as opposed to limiting.

The influences are personal, varied and idiosyncratic, fluid and not useful to fabricate.

RADOSAVLJEVIĆ: How does the company divide and combine its pedagogical and creative work – when do you teach, when do you create? And what are the interrelations between the two?

MORGAN: Song of the Goat runs workshops throughout the year, but a workshop season has emerged over the years, during the months of June, July and August. Then every two years we run a Postgraduate Diploma in Acting, followed by supervising some of those students through an independent study MA lasting one year after that. The taught part of the PG Diploma lasts approximately 24 weeks and includes two terms, one taught by members of the company, then an expedition followed by a performance-making process, culminating in a sharing of work.

Rehearsals are organised into six-week to two-month blocks, depending on the company's work agenda and some visiting artists' availability.

There is a flow between the pedagogical work and the creative work, they influence each other subtly in ways that cannot be fixed. The way of making work is a living process, and our way of training is similar in that it contains a fluid set of exercises based around principles and sensations as well as technique. So the teaching practice of different members reflects that. Of course principles do exist, but their formulation/expression changes as the creative process of devising performances changes. The deeper we go into our creative processes through our body and voice, the greater our understanding of them is and that is reflected in how we pass on knowledge. Also, the process of teaching is a living process for us; it automatically deepens our awareness of 'creative material', inspiring and challenging us to go further.

RADOSAVLJEVIĆ: Is there a way of summing up – in terms of any principles or in terms of constituent stages – Song of the Goat's rehearsal process?

MORGAN: It would be dangerous to present the existence of a formula – but one could say there is an initial stage of gathering inspirations around the territory, narrative, theme, texture, etc. Then we might explore these elements – often starting by learning and tasting music and song in the space, then possibly combined with elements of text. And at some point, we might start exploring what we might call the physical vocabulary of the piece, the physical texture. In a long process of maturation, all these elements will become the ground for our own creative reactions. Often long improvisations ensue – out of which elements of action, text and music will start to change themselves and emerge organically. Eventually Grzegorz will make an initial montage, not based on narrative logic but on energy and musicality. This montage will only be a first draft of many, as the unique journey the company intuits appears from the clay. These are some steps we may take. But each process is different.

RADOSAVLJEVIĆ: To what extent is ongoing training of the ensemble members part of the rehearsal process itself, and is this the performers' responsibility or is it facilitated by the director?

MORGAN: A consistent but fluid body of exercises over the years has emerged and are the basis for teaching on the MA and workshops. A binding principle exists – 'co-ordination'. Exercises come and go depending on the company's process, but 'co-ordination' is always present. It, in itself, has basic aspects that we always have present at the heart of the physical work.

In rehearsal, we may start from something that resembles exercise, in that work may revolve around some clear, simple principles of physicality or music – it's not focused on expressing something creative. This sometimes leads to the beginning of an exploration of material for the performance. A piece of action or vocal material may break through the exploration work and start to represent something specific from the material we're working on.

In fact, we might say we don't do training in rehearsal – in the sense of training in preparation for a moment of creativity – instead we're always exploring a creative engagement in whatever we're doing. This is led and stimulated by both actors and director. However, the director will inevitably work from the outside to navigate the way forward.

RADOSAVLJEVIĆ: What discernable directions can you see for the company or for yourself as a performer?

MORGAN: Personally speaking, I can sense the company entering into an expansive stage, which may involve many different types of smaller projects emerging alongside the central process that acts as a focus point for the company. That will be *King Lear* over the next few years.

ANNA ZUBRZYCKI: The company began as a group of unpaid performers interested in creating theatre with Anna Zubrzycki and Grzegorz Bral, and after *Chronicles* won prizes at the Edinburgh festival, it entered a more stable phase of creativity where its actors could rehearse full time, and be paid a very modest fee. As the company members get older they have other responsibilities, which take them outside of Wroclaw so the pedagogical work has become more prominent, with the MA Acting taking a large percentage of the core company members' time. New members are being added now and rehearsal periods are shorter and more intense. The company is still committed to and investing in keeping its core members in each new project, and adds two or three new members per performance. Which ensures both the continuity of the Song of the Goat approach through common training, as well as fresh new energy and commitment on the part of younger colleagues.

The phases of the creation of each performance seem to be: a two-year gestation period, then about three to four years of performing it, after that the performance enters the final stage of its growth. The performances are never 'finished' products in the sense that each time we perform it is different. They are always analysed and re-rehearsed.

The company is an NGO and is funded on the basis of annual funding applications, which support its projects. This funding has been in place since 2005, and has grown from a modest one-off grant to support the development of a performance, to a three-year grant from the city of Wroclaw which allows the company to be paid retainers and to keep two administrators. It also receives small grants from the National Ministry of Culture and partnership grants investing in projects (for example, the RSC supported the initial creation work on *Macbeth*, and that first stage was shown during their Complete Works Festival). The company also has given birth to projects such as the Brave Festival, which now receives a separate grant and new educational projects, which are not yet funded. The company has applied and is waiting for permanent funding from the City Council of Wroclaw.

Bibliography

Allain, Paul (2007) 'Goat Theatre *Macbeth*', *Contemporary Theatre Review*, 17(2): 255–8.

Porubcansky, Anna (2010) 'Song of the Goat Theatre: Artistic Practice as Life Practice', *New Theatre Quarterly*, 26(3): 261–72.

Trueman, Matt (2012) 'Songs of Lear', *The List*, 17 August, available online at http://edinburghfestival.list.co.uk/article/44625-songs-of-lear/ (accessed 19 December 2012).

Zubrzycki, Anna and Bral, Grzegorz in conversation with Maria Shevtsova (2010) 'Song of the Goat Theatre: Finding Flow and Connection', *New Theatre Quarterly*, 26(3): 248–60.

Song of the Goat
http://www.piesnkozla.pl/about_the_theatre,en.html

12 'Comic figures repurposed'

Dan Rothenberg (Pig Iron)

Co-Artistic Directors of Philadelphia-based Pig Iron Theatre Company, Gabriel Quinn Bauriedel, Dito van Reigersberg and Dan Rothenberg, met as students at Swarthmore College in the early 1990s. They formed the company in 1995, following which Bauriedel and Rothenberg took some time out to train with Jacques Lecoq in Paris. The company's artistic affiliations have repeatedly changed over the years – they call themselves a 'dance-clown-theatre ensemble':

> Individual pieces have been called 'soundscape and spectacle', 'cabaret-ballet', and 'avant-garde shadow puppet dessert-theatre'. We have a hard time sitting still.
>
> ('About' page, Pig Iron Theatre website)

Pig Iron has performed at the Edinburgh Fringe Festival six times and they have also toured to numerous other European countries. In 2005 they won an OBIE award for *Hell Meets Henry Halfway* on which they collaborated with Adriano Shaplin, and this was followed by another OBIE for James Sugg's performance in *Chekhov Lizardbrain* – a production which was one of the Top Ten picks for 2008 in *The New York Times*.

In a *TDR* article, Nick Salvato characterised the company's work as being defined by 'cultivations of movement and adaptation' and by presentation of 'aberrant and marginal subjectivities' (Salvato 2010: 210), though his conclusion ultimately underlines Pig Iron's creative and pedagogical interest in collaboration.

The interview below took place at the company's base in Philadelphia in October 2011, some weeks after the premiere of *Twelfth Night*, the company's first Shakespeare production.

Interview

ROTHENBERG: I had contact with some clown theatre folks at high school in New York and Connecticut. And also my high school drama teacher had worked with Joe Chaikin and Andre Gregory, back in the 1960s. Bill Irwin was a big hero of mine in the era of New Vaudeville, but I knew Chaikin and Gregory from books, I'd never really seen any videos. Then at Swarthmore College, there was a new scholar at the theatre department named Allen Kuharski. His area of expertise was Polish theatre, specifically of the 1980s, and he knew Joe Chaikin after his stroke. He knew a lot about ensemble theatre, and he was also very interested in Theatre du Soleil. There was certainly a focus on reinterpretations of the Greeks and of Shakespeare by Ariane Mnouchkine. Allen Kuharski had no direct contact with Lecoq, but knowing that Mnouchkine had studied with Lecoq, he became interested.

We were theatre majors. Theatre at Swarthmore was very academic. Right when we arrived Swarthmore had started to make peace with the idea of the arts as a serious discipline. All the arts were really bending over backwards to prove their scholarliness so we did a lot of reading. But Allen Kuharski did make sure that we were put in touch with various theatres so that in the summers when we weren't at college, we were able to get internships, sometimes apprenticeships. I worked with the San Francisco Mime Troupe which is an ensemble and a collective, with a couple of other Swarthmore people including Jeff Sugg who designed a lot of our early stuff, and is now a pretty accomplished projection and lighting designer in New York. I worked at American Repertory Theatre. People did different things that exposed them to how things worked in the real world. At Swarthmore, we had a really good, almost graduate level training in theatre history – especially this kind of theatre history which is so spottily documented – Ariane Mnouchkine, Joe Chaikin, Jerzy Grotowski, the world of ensembles.

Pig Iron was founded by a group of undergraduate liberal arts students at Swarthmore College. Quinn [Bauriedel], Dito [van Reigersberg] and I have been there since the beginning, and now we are the Co-Artistic Directors of the company. About half of the people left, and half the company stayed together in the first couple of years.

RADOSAVLJEVIĆ: Did all three of you direct or were any of you involved as performers?

ROTHENBERG: When we started the company in 1995, I was the director of the project. I think in those first couple of years there was some thought that I would write. We tried that in 1998 and I thought I was much better editing other people's work and collaborating with

writers than I was actually writing. When we started the company we
were interested in studying and making work that was dance, clown
and theatre. Some folks had trained in dance – both the Martha
Graham technique and the release technique of the day – some of us
were trained in clown. The early work that we did was very much col-
lage: a section that had a dance value, a section that had a theatre
value, and then a section that had a clown value – they were stories
that moved in between these different modes of expression. After
starting the company Quinn and I went to Paris and studied with
Lecoq who was still alive. A couple of years after starting the company, as the Swarthmore people left, we brought back to America
three people we had met at Lecoq to work with us.

Answering your question: I've directed almost all of the work. I've
co-directed twice. Quinn has directed twice by himself. Quinn does
direct sometimes, does design sometimes and now that he is the head
of our new school he is absenting himself from creating new work for
several years. Dito is always a performer, and he does co-write some
of the work.

RADOSAVLJEVIĆ: How is it having three artistic directors?

ROTHENBERG: It's personal. It really works for us. There are some things
that are frustrating. As we grew beyond just us working as self-taught
administrators – and now we have staff – it's been hard for us to
evolve our decision-making process in a way that can communicate
efficiently with those guys. But it works so far – I don't know why it
works. It's totally chemistry. And I think we've evolved pretty clear
communication and pretty good delegation as well.

RADOSAVLJEVIĆ: The website says that there are about six artists that are
associated with the company – are those artists present on a daily
basis as well?

ROTHENBERG: We've never had artists on a year-round contract, for a
couple of reasons: we didn't think we could afford it, and we also
thought we would drive each other crazy. A lot of us have worked
with other ensembles, and seen other models of ensembles and we
felt that the ensembles that worked only with each other year after
year for 10 or 12 months out of the year generated a kind of family
dynamic that seemed really toxic. We make a lot of different kinds of
work, we are really curious, everybody who works with us is pretty
curious, and the whole endeavour has been a balancing act between
maintaining contact with one another so that we can keep working
and building our vocabulary together, and giving everybody space to
do things which not everybody was interested in. I think there was a
fear – a good fear – that we would end up with the lowest common

denominator instead of highest common denominator: 'Well, this is the thing that nobody objects to, and therefore this is the thing that nobody really cares about'.

We've always believed that there has to be strong leadership and passion and provocation in the process. As Pig Iron became more successful, we the artistic directors said to the company members 'Do you think you would want to be on a year-round contract?', and everybody said 'No'. So we haven't worked towards that. It makes scheduling a real nightmare. And actually the methodology and the agreement between the artists and the artistic directors and the company is not clear right now. I think it's in flux and we are struggling to find a rubric and a contract really that everybody can work with. But it keeps changing. People's personal situations keep changing, so I don't think I can fully articulate it right now.

RADOSAVLJEVIĆ: How did your experience of going to Lecoq change the way in which the company worked?

ROTHENBERG: I think about four of the plays right after we went to Lecoq were heavily influenced by his vocabulary – very much his work on clown, chorus and melodrama. One of our early big successes was almost cookie-cutter Lecoq vocabulary made into a full-length piece. I do think that as we started to move away, sometimes, we became diametrically opposed to what Lecoq was interested in.

There is another way of looking at Lecoq's language. I started talking about the spirit of enquiry at Lecoq and about impossible questions as being something that an ensemble was really uniquely suited to addressing. Some of Lecoq's questions were: 'How do you make the audience cry?', 'How do you make the audience laugh?' – this almost Socratic research and development method, which really was over by the time we were there in the 1990s. We sensed an endless resentment from Lecoq at how little we knew – I mean he still had a passion but he didn't really have much patience... He would talk about things that had emerged from the school 20 or 30 years ago. You didn't get a sense that he believed that anything could emerge from the school now. But these questions were fascinating, and to go back to them and wonder if Lecoq got his answer right, or if they were a product of his time ... We made projects, and we still do make projects based on 'How do we want to represent violence on stage?', for example. Violence is either lurid and it's sexy or it's fake and it's embarrassing – so it's a formal problem and a moral problem. That led to an installation with a lot of puppetry called *Anodyne*.

There is a kind of demystification that's important to me and I share at least in part with the rest of the people in Pig Iron, although some of them have more of a necessary dreaminess that's a good counterpoint to my practicality. But one of my things is: all training is made up, we humans like to worship a mask, we like to worship an idol, but there's really nothing to stop us from developing our own training every step of the way. And really every project developed its own training and developed its own ensemble. There are some things that we do every time, and there are some things that we do only because it seems appropriate to that project. We've always been interested in a kind of a middle way where it's not necessary to reject rebelliously but it's important not to follow slavishly.

RADOSAVLJEVIĆ: What was it like to work with Joe Chaikin on *Shut Eye?*

ROTHENBERG: Remarkable. A real change. I feel like it operated in three really different ways. There is the fact of working with this hero of ours – and the particular space that put us in. There were some sympathies between him and me in terms of things we cared about. He once said 'I prefer yearning', and I was like 'Oh, yeah, I prefer yearning too' – it was just very succinct and clear. And then there was the particular paradox of working with somebody who has aphasia.

After about a couple of years I realised how much I'd learnt from that particular experience. Being in a theatre company with someone who cares about rhythm and breath, and working with somebody who had damaged the part of his brain that allowed him to put syntax together – that was its own part of this encounter. That was really important to me. I'd been a long-time reader of Oliver Sacks and his neurological tales. And I see his project as 'Well, let's look at these deficits and these moments of damage and they can reveal to us things that seem invisible to us about how we perceive the world and understand ourselves'. Working with Joe had that impact of reading Oliver Sacks.

In a way, all of us, when we work with somebody we play a kind of a character. We figure out a rhythm in any field. But sitting next to Joe and co-directing with him, I would put myself into a mental state, in order to communicate with him. I would watch people talk to Joe, and sometimes people didn't know – because you wouldn't be like 'This is Joe Chaikin, he's had a stroke and he has aphasia'. It would be 'This is Joe Chaikin, he is co-directing the piece with us'. They'd say 'Hello', and they'd start to understand from his speech that something was wrong. And then they would start to talk loud, and they would start to over-articulate their words. And I would watch Joe struggle more to understand them. They sensed that he was having trouble understanding, and they made exactly the wrong decision – they took out all the music from their voice and they tried to be really clear with their syntax, which was exactly the part that he couldn't get. I found out through working with him over the summer that the more I relax, the more I assume that he is fine and understands everything – the more he gets. Because I allow myself all the dynamics.

The anecdote I like to tell about that is that an actor was upset about something and giving me some attitude, and she walked away and under my voice I went 'Thank you very much', with light sarcasm. Joe was sitting next to me and he started laughing really hard – he understood all of the energy and music that was going on in my most unconscious moment. Through that process I allowed myself to be more and more unconscious – and that interaction became a really important parallel for me in the production of sound on stage – something I worked with as recently as the last Shakespeare project I did, where I just said 'So much of theatre in America is just shouting and indicating' – and there's so many other rhythms that remain unexploited. All the things which I allowed myself in my conversation with Joe became important things to allow on the stage.

RADOSAVLJEVIĆ: How long was that process?

ROTHENBERG: It was 13 months although the period of contact was probably more like seven weeks – in total.

RADOSAVLJEVIĆ: How would you say the piece emerged from that collaboration in terms of the various kinds of input that came from you or from Joe or from the ensemble members?

ROTHENBERG: Joe couldn't tell us what we were going to do – so that by default made us more open; and – we'll never know if it was by coincidence or it was by design – it made it more personal.

Another thing that we had taken from Lecoq that was important in those first five years was playing characters that were different from ourselves. Plays that were about transformation, and plays that demonstrated the actors' ability to transform. A play we made and revisited several times was called *Cafeteria* in which three people in their twenties play junior high school students, and then they play 35-year-old business people, and then they play 75-year-old retirees and then a bunch of insects – the same three people play all these different things. I think of that approach to character as almost drawing a silhouette with a big indelible marker around the character – which I think of as coming from Lecoq and from his mask work.

The work after Joe was formally different – we allowed ourselves to play characters closer to ourselves and trusted that there were other kinds of transformations, and other kinds of playfulness that could be found even if the description of this character would be not unlike what I am in real world. And this new vocabulary emerged which was called 'ordinary' – this idea came from a very short set of instructions he gave very early on. That word 'ordinary' became our way to apply the language of mask training to the style of hyper-realism. In simple terms, it meant that things that Lecoq claimed to hate, we found a way to love – which had to do with very regular, mundane, pedestrian activity. Things which Lecoq spent a couple of years really beating out of people as being untheatrical – we then found very theatrical.

We realised that many of us had a real interest in the margins, diametrically opposed to something that Lecoq said 'That character's marginal – we don't do that in the theatre'. We found that many of us had our own excitement about characters on the margins, marginal movement – I started to call it 'the dramaturgy of nothing happens'. But I phrase it as a provocation: 'How can nothing happen on stage but we still feel fascinated?' – which to me is a version of 'How do we make the audience cry?', it's another iteration of that kind of a question. So many plays would answer that question in different ways with different constellations of collaborators.

Another chapter in this 'journey of ordinary' was *Love Unpunished*, a collaboration with the choreographer David Brick. I felt David's impact on the ensemble was similar to Joe Chaikin's impact: I saw these people I'd been working with for ten years doing things that I didn't know that they could do, I didn't know that they cared about. David was fascinated with the ordinary. And I was fascinated with his work, his performance values – again it was the opposite of Lecoq, it was the opposite of having a level of tension in breath, in the body, and playing at the level of a mask; it was all about the kind of movement and interaction which happens from a place of tactile awareness. He comes from a deaf family and he says that he's moved to this tactile world because his parents are deaf and he's got a hearing impairment, so in a way there is an Oliver Sacks connection as well. David and I took his sensory vocabulary and we married that to this ordinary world and made it even more ordinary. It was the most ordinary. So we had just people walking downstairs for eight minutes. Very, very much 'nothing happens'.

RADOSAVLJEVIĆ: So there seems to be a pattern of constantly reinventing your aesthetics?

ROTHENBERG: Yes. But I don't advise other people to do that any more. I do look to painters too, people like Picasso and Gerhard Richter who went through very different stages of expression and style – but theatre people don't do that very much. It's just really hard to reach an audience if you insist on changing it up. I feel like we've invited a very curious and somewhat intellectual audience because we are always trying to surprise ourselves and them. There are other examples like Rude Mechs and also Elevator Repair Service who are like that. But I think of ensembles like Richard Maxwell's New York City Players or The Wooster Group, certainly Theatre du Soleil – they do different things from time to time actually, but the band of stylistic enquiry is narrower.

Our belief, my belief was: if we're an experimental theatre company, we can't do the same experiment again and again. But I think there is a paradox hidden in there. I think even if you try to not do the same experiment again and again, there's something you're always doing – you have values, you have a bedrock fascination. And even if you do do the same experiment again and again, like Richard Foreman – things change. So I've tried to become less prescriptive, as I've done this for 15 years now.

RADOSAVLJEVIĆ: How do you perceive your work in relation to the heritage that you've received from the other American companies?

ROTHENBERG: I feel most closely associated with Chaikin, from even before I knew him. The book *Presence of the Actor* was my bible and our playbook in a way. He also began with questions – 'What is original sin?', for example. And in particular there is one line in *Presence of the Actor* where he says 'The study of acting, like any study where one aims to go to the root, requires a new discipline'. And that's a sort of impossible question – a study that requires a new discipline. That one sentence became the launching pad for the company.

I knew that I was more interested in design than Joe ever was. I was interested in design the way that Mnouchkine was interested in design. And we tried to make our company include designers in a real tug of war so that they can actually communicate with each other – which I think is one of the unique things about our methodology.

Also Joe said 'No methodology' – and that's us too. Our attitude is: 'Methodologies are going to be useful for a certain amount of time, and then they are not going to be useful any more, for me or for anyone'. Even with the school that we've set up now which is going to use a fair amount of Lecoq vocabulary as well as our vocabulary, our guiding principle is: fundamentally, it's us interacting with these students and then them interacting with each other. That's the basis of ensemble theatre, and that's the lesson we can teach, too.

RADOSAVLJEVIĆ: What level are they at?

ROTHENBERG: They are postgrad. The median age is 27. That was really important to me. We've taught professional workshops between three days and three weeks-long since the 1990s – since we were too young to do so, I suppose.

RADOSAVLJEVIĆ: Is it a daily training programme?

ROTHENBERG: It's about five or six hours a day, five days a week, 30 weeks a year. They are on a two-year programme.

RADOSAVLJEVIĆ: Presumably all the company members are involved in the pedagogical work?

ROTHENBERG: About five or six of us are. And we have Jean-Rene Toussaint teaching voice – he has his own pedagogy that's similar to Roy Hart's vocal work, but different. For ourselves, even before the school, we've had a practice of bringing esteemed teachers to Pig Iron to train us. Partially that came from folks like Joe Chaikin coming in, but also when we collaborated with writers like Adriano Shaplin, who had a very different vocabulary, part of our work was: 'Well, train us to do your writing'. Part of it was, when we worked with live music: 'Let's all sing together'. We brought the Swedish group Theatre Slava and workshopped with them. We've had Giovanni Fusetti come and work with us for a couple of weeks. So we developed a model where we bring in a master teacher, he or she works with Pig Iron for a while and with Philadelphia community – and over time relationships can happen.

RADOSAVLJEVIĆ: How long is the Pig Iron rehearsal period?

ROTHENBERG: The model that we've evolved – involving a mixture of funding and people's schedules – is that every year we do two weeks that we call 'the island' which is an open 'play and invent' time. The idea is it's as though we go off on an island with nothing. In those two weeks we have no production pressure, we just have each other and we mess around with some provocations, some open time. Sometimes it's been a place where we bring an outside provocateur, a clown master like Giovanni Fusetti, or musicians to work with us specifically on music and singing – there's been different things that have happened in that island period. So two weeks are 'the island'. Two weeks are initial workshop of the piece – that's us plus some collaborators and we know 'something'.

RADOSAVLJEVIĆ: How far apart are they?

ROTHENBERG: Nowadays, it's at least six months. Sometimes a whole year. And then another six months or a year after that we'll do a development and creation process which is between five and eight weeks. That five to eight weeks leads up to performances. Then usually what happens is the piece, if it's good enough, stays in the repertory and there's probably another two-week workshop to continue to refine the work. That's less formal but we tend to feel that we need that. We learn all this new information once we start the performances: these things we care about turned out not to be important, these things that we didn't spend any time on are in fact the backbone of the piece – and we need to revisit it after that first encounter with the audience. Sometimes a piece will go for three years and we'll go back to it. The piece that was a big hit, *Gentlemen Volunteers*, back in 1998 – in 2003 we rewrote the central ten minutes and reorganised it after having performed it for five years. I guess an important aspect of this is that I attend almost all the performances. And there are notes and discussion and sometimes some rehearsal.

RADOSAVLJEVIĆ: What brought Shakespeare into Pig Iron?

ROTHENBERG: I've cared about Shakespeare for a long time. The dramaturgical project of Shakespeare, at least my reading of it, which comes from some theorists who look at genre, ended up being a set of guidelines for me as I was making original plays. It had to do with – in very simple terms – imagination and death, so that in the early comedy you see death is actually mocked – there are these fake deaths and badly performed deaths, and then in the later tragedies you have these comic figures repurposed. 'Comic figures repurposed' – that ended up being very important to me. I said that it's a different experiment every time, but I'm starting to see that there are some things that I care about that are in every project: this playful energy released and then shown to be powerless – that is my project. And when I've tried to do something else – it hasn't always worked.

So I knew Shakespeare. Really hated most of the Shakespeare that I saw – very declamatory acting and very little complicity between actors. Then a couple of years ago I said 'I keep asking you guys to do less and less but you're very inventive performers and creators, what if we did *A Midsummer Night's Dream*? What if we took the lid off and let it be super-inventive and playful?'. But for whatever reason *A Midsummer Night's Dream* didn't click, it's as though we were too old for it all of a sudden. And that yearning quality found its way into *Twelfth Night*, and all that music research, and all that work that we did with Joe on the music of communication – found its way into *Twelfth Night*.

I think I was interested in the question of audience. I was 21 when I started the company and all of us said 'We're going to change the face of American theatre'. And the deal is: even if you made the best play in the world, it's only a play and there's only a certain number of people who are gonna go and see it. There's only a certain number of people who wake up in the morning and think 'I'd like to see something in the arts'. We have no outside marketing, we're the marketers, we work closely in-house, and we dream and we scheme and we try to trick people into coming. And our favourite thing to hear is

'You know I really don't like theatre but I like what you do'. We heard that, we even heard it in different countries – and in terms of someone who wants to change the face of theatre, that means you're succeeding. But the fact of the matter is: we live in America and people choose their arts and entertainment the way that they choose their jeans. They say 'I'm the kind of guy who likes movies with Kristen Wiig', 'I'm the kind of guy who likes action movies' or 'sweet love songs' or 'live music'. There are certain curious people, too. But presenting Shakespeare was very much about 'Let's see what other audience we can reach' – and if we can still do the things that we care about, if we can still make a physical world, if we can still infuse the piece with the playfulness and the acting qualities that are important – and I think we got 70 per cent there. It was a big success. A lot of people said 'I've never understood Shakespeare so well' – and I specifically didn't work on the talking, I worked on everything else, the stuff that we would normally work on –

RADOSAVLJEVIĆ: Did you have any verse specialist come into your rehearsals?

ROTHENBERG: No, several of us had done that, including me, and I don't believe in that. I think that's a bad idea. I had thought about it, and I'd done some of it, and – I just trust the intuition of the performers and my ear to make more of it. I felt vindicated by many people who said 'I'd never understood the language so well'. And it actually goes back to the Joe Chaikin experience – of what he understood.

I think when people work with these verse specialists they build arias and they build a little wall around themselves. So, this person who's in the scene with me and who I'm communicating with stops interacting with me, stops listening because he or she is letting me do my aria and my verse work – but that's not the basic building block of theatre.

RADOSAVLJEVIĆ: You mentioned that when you worked with Adriano Shaplin you had to bring in a different methodology into the rehearsal room. What is it like, working with writers?

ROTHENBERG: The Pig Iron writers are Deborah Stein and Robert Quillen Camp. They come in and go, 'OK, I'm shaping the improvisations, I'm taking the characters, inventing characters'. Quill did a remarkable thing when we did *Chekhov Lizardbrain* – he worked with existing characters and ideas, but he really made some very different writing proposals for us. Adriano very much had a different voice, his own voice.

It's many things, it's a tug of war. I don't think the playwriting system is set up to deal with theatre very well. I think that it's actually a weird, very American, property-based problem, that's sort of unique to the past couple of centuries. Theatre have always been groups of people doing stuff so there's always been a push and pull. I'm thinking of these dramatists like Chekhov and Shakespeare – they were working fast and they were working for an ensemble of actors that they knew. The notion that they came up with all their ideas because God spoke to them – 'I'm now delivering a perfect play' – is opposed to the way that we work which is 'I like that funny thing that you do in the bar, and I'm gonna bring it into the play because I know how funny you are when you do it'. I just see that all over Shakespeare's work.

I tell playwrights 'You need to think about this as writing for television – you are generating material, the characters and the actors are a big part of it and they have input too – what they can make work is part of it; you are not crafting a perfect work'. I just find a lot of plays overwritten.

Our model looks a lot different from the regional theatre model. I think it's a real shame that these scripts emerge and people feel like 'I must protect them from any changes'. That's just not how it works in film and television. Everybody knows that script is a platform on which you launch this other thing which is a visual artform. And I feel theatre is also mostly visual, although also musical artform. And for it to become literary is like 'I don't really want to read the book so I'll go see some dressed up literature at Lincoln Center or something'.

Bibliography

Apple, Krista (2010) 'A Wild, Wild West of Their Own: Pig Iron Theatre Company Heads Wherever Its Rowdy Collective Spirit Leads', *American Theatre*, 10 February, available online at http://www.tcg.org/publications/at/feb10/pigiron.cfm (accessed 19 December 2012).

Babb, Roger (2005) 'Hell Meets Henry Halfway', *Theatre Journal*, 57(2): 284–6.

Cook, Amy (2003) 'Who's Dreaming Whom?: The Dissolving Boundary Between Wake and Sleep Reality and Dream Me and You in Pig Iron's "Shut Eye"', *Theatre Forum – International Theatre Journal*, Summer–Fall: 58–61.

Salvato, Nick (2010) '"Ta daaaa": Presenting Pig Iron Theatre Company', *TDR: The Drama Review*, 54(4) (T208), Winter: 206–23.

Pig Iron Theatre
http://www.pigiron.org

13 Ensemble as a musical 'intersubjective unit'

Adriano Shaplin (The Riot Group)

Adriano Shaplin is a New Jersey-based playwright, actor and artistic director of the Riot Group theatre company. Since its inception in 1997, the company consisting of Shaplin, Stephanie Viola, Drew Friedman, Paul Schnabel and Maria Shaplin has won the prestigious Fringe First award four times at the Edinburgh Festival. Well before Shaplin's 25th birthday, they achieved even greater international acclaim with a tour of their 2004 piece about the Iraq War – *Pugilist Specialist*, which alongside some of the other Riot Group plays, has also been translated and performed in several European countries.

Characterised by minimalist and highly presentational staging, the Riot Group works are often noted for their strong ensemble spirit and 'baroque language' (Kuharski 2005; Soloski 2008), which combines 'Elizabethan syntax with vernacular profanity' (Soloski 2011). In terms of its theatrical exploration of politics, Kuharski places the work within a Brechtian tradition, although textually he finds resonances with Mamet, Albee and Oscar Wilde too. Ultimately, however:

> In this embrace of the actor-playwright, the Riot Group in its downtown fashion revives and honours the actual practice of the Greeks, Shakespeare, and Molière more than any classical repertory company.
>
> (Kuharski 2005: 525)

Shaplin's apparent refusal to artistically specialise or compartmentalise his professional profile is seen by Kuharski as a potential challenge to the American theatre system, both in terms of the mainstream expectation that a playwright is a free agent and the nonprofit sector's emphasis on process rather than content.

Shaplin maintains a dialectical interest in methodological experimentation and artistic reinvention on the one hand, coupled with a preservation of his company's core values on the other. In 2004, he collaborated with the Pig Iron theatre company on an adaptation of Witold Gombrowitz's novel *The Possessed* under the title of *Hell Meets Henry Halfway*, which received an OBIE award. From 2006 to 2008 Shaplin was the International Playwright in Residence at the Royal Shakespeare Company, which culminated with a production of his play *The Tragedy of Thomas Hobbes*. More recently, Shaplin and the Riot Group have began a collaboration with another Philadelphia-based company, New Paradise Laboratories, and its artistic director Whit MacLaughlin. MacLaughlin has directed a revival of Shaplin's play *Victory at the Dirt Palace* (2008), as well as *Hearts of Man* (2009) and a premiere of a co-production between the two companies, the double bill *Freedom Club*, shown as part of the Philadelphia Live Arts Festival in September 2010. In 2012, Shaplin and the Riot Group collaborated with McLaughlin on *The Poet Laureate of Capitalism*, and with director Rebecca Wright of Applied Mechanics on *Sophie Gets the Horns*.

This interview took place in November 2009 in New Jersey.

Interview

SHAPLIN: The beginning. I arrived at Sarah Lawrence College in 1996, and was enrolled in Theatre Studies. Stephanie Viola was also in the first year and we were in a class together. In my first semester I submitted to a student-run space a play called *Settle* – written to be spoken from music stands. I staged the first movement in my first semester with some friends, with some music that I had put together. Then I wrote three more movements. Later I produced a play on campus called *Infanticide*, and I had eight people that were my friends that I asked to be in it. Two of them were Stephanie Viola and Drew Friedman. Drew had never acted before. He was studying poetry and he was really good at reading his poems so I cast him in the show. And I had a particular interest in Stephanie and Drew after that.

In 1998, we did *Why I Want to Shoot Ronald Reagan*, and that was the first show we brought into Edinburgh. We took our reviews from the Sarah Lawrence Newspaper and attributed them to *The Village Voice* when we sent out our Press Packets. The next piece we made at Sarah Lawrence was *Wreck the Airline Barrier*, we brought it to Edinburgh and that was the first show that won a Fringe First.

The first time that I worked with Paul Schnabel was when I was 16 in my home town in Burlington, Vermont. He was an actor, and we were both cast in a show. What we made when Paul came in, and when we restarted the company after graduating from Sarah

Lawrence, was *Victory at the Dirt Palace*. We brought that to Edinburgh and that won another Fringe First. That was the first show of ours that transferred from Edinburgh to London, to Riverside Studios. Right when we got back from that, I started writing *Pugilist Specialist* in March 2003, and we debuted it in Edinburgh in August 2003. By that point we had moved to California: me, Drew and Stephanie lived in one two-bedroom apartment, I lived in the living room. And we rehearsed all of *Pugilist* there, in Stephanie's bedroom, which was the biggest room. We managed to throw together one pre-performance in a borrowed space before Edinburgh. And then that show won a Fringe First and moved on to London, and we toured the whole year of 2004. Then 2005 – *Switch Triptych*; 2007 – *Hearts of Man*.

Since *Pugilist Specialist*, all of our rehearsal periods have been paid rehearsal periods. We went from paying nothing to paying Equity minimums to all the actors whenever we rehearse, and for all performances. We've become a not-for-profit organisation. That's curtailed our activity to a certain extent, because it's become much more difficult and a somewhat grown up operation. Since *Pugilist Specialist* we've been inviting new actors – so we've worked with Sarah Sanford, Cassie Friend from Pig Iron theatre company, Kristen Sieh from the TEAM, Tara Perry from Neo-Futurists New York. We worked with Dennis McSorley who is a Burlington actor. Now we are working with New Paradise Laboratories. In addition to paying ourselves and everybody we work with now, and hiring designers instead of just doing it ourselves, we are trying to bring in and experiment with new actors, to change the dynamic and the chemistry of the ensemble.

RADOSAVLJEVIĆ: You had a very specific way of working when it was just the three or four of you. Could you tell me how that process would unfold, and how the script was developed through that particular way of working? Maybe it would be useful to explain how you write parts for particular actors, rather than characters?

SHAPLIN: That certainly can be traced to the fact that my earliest dramatic texts have very little space – they are just voices on stages. They were very much conceived for the impoverished non-theatrical stagings that they were going to be given. All the plays were written with the knowledge that they were going to be performed with clip-lamps and folding chairs somewhere. In other words, there was something about my entrance into theatre that was very, very far from narrative or character. I do think of my way into theatre as being like a kind of a frustrated musical impulse that's combined with acting. My way into theatre is as an actor. Within the medium I'm really a singer and a performer – not a literal singer, but I use my voice.

Once the relationship between me and Drew and Stephanie as performers became established and we found a way of working together musically and in our aesthetic, it seemed natural that what I would write would be just entirely written for them. The actors – myself as an actor and them as actors – are the inspiration for the plays. From *Wreck the Airline Barrier* on, all these plays are written with these particular actors in mind.

I don't think about creating a character so that the actor has to transform themselves to embody it. I think of the role much more like a tailor – I'm building a suit for the actor that has to fit them right, I'm building a part for their voice, for the sound of their voice and their morphology. The script is also like a set of accomplishments for the actor that it's going to be pleasurable to watch them struggle through. I don't know if that means that I set up the play in such a way as to present a series of obstacles to the actor, but I also feel that I'm greasing the wheels for them so that they can do what they do best. That's the way I write. And that's the way I want to have it when I've written outside of the Riot Group, for Pig Iron and for the Royal Shakespeare Company.

I never have finished the script before rehearsals. I always start with some kind of proposal for the first bit of the play. The first bit, where I find the play, I hear that aloud usually. The closest formula is that if I'm working on page six it means that I have heard the pages one through five aloud already, because now I have the idea about the next place to go. I'm constantly adjusting the script based on how it sounds and how it feels to try and do it with my actors.

RADOSAVLJEVIĆ: Do the other ensemble members contribute to the script in any way?

SHAPLIN: No. In Riot Group, no one has suggested a line within the context of a rehearsal. I'll maybe take phrases that we've said. I might take slang that comes up from our relationship or some catchphrases we use, and quote things – all the Riot Group texts have lots of quotations, both secret and apparent. We're quoting things that we've said to each other, but we've never improvised anything. I'm improvising the text at night and during the day, and then we come together in rehearsal and then we build it bit by bit. I do think of writing as improvising, yes, as an actor. So I don't know if it's really true that there are playwrights or writers that wake up and sit at a desk and work for eight hours. I guess, maybe people that write prose can work that way. I can't imagine that playwrights work that way.

Certainly for me writing is like an acting exercise. I prepare myself to feel some things and say them in my head and say them on the page. And I'm imagining, I'm acting my way through, I'm carrying with me a model for Stephanie's voice and Drew's voice and Paul's voice, and if I'm working with an actor for the first time I've usually seen them before. I'm thinking about what they've played before, and I'm thinking about what interests me, I'm following my pleasure definitely, I'm saying: what do I want to see this body and this face do, what's most interesting?

RADOSAVLJEVIĆ: Can we revisit the story of how *Victory at the Dirt Palace* came about?

SHAPLIN: *Victory at the Dirt Palace* is a confluence of a bunch of different things. Every play certainly seems to have some seed in a previous work. I recall *Victory at the Dirt Palace* being an idea about a relationship between a father and a daughter, because it was rarely done. And because I've always liked to think about my plays as foregrounding gender, whether they are presented that way or not. I thought: a relationship between a father and a daughter, not only is it unknown and unnatural to me, I'm neither a father nor a daughter! I need a lot of imagination to get within that relationship, and that presents a challenge. And then, I'm thinking: newscasters – that seems to work, we did it in *Why I Want to Shoot Ronald Reagan* and it was really funny, it allows for a way of naturalistically justifying the facing forward [which is a characteristic of the Riot Group's work].

So I write these first 20 minutes which is about father and daughter, they are both newscasters, they are in a competitive relationship. And I remember thinking: I know that at Edinburgh whenever people adapt Shakespeare everyone pays attention. So I went to Drew and I said 'Drew, are there any Shakespeare plays that are about fathers and daughters'. And he said '*King Lear* is'. And then I decided that *Victory at the Dirt Palace* is an adaptation of *King Lear*. I didn't go back and rewrite the 20 minutes, I just assumed that it already was an adaptation of *King Lear*. I read the Cliffs Notes and I read the first scene, and that's why the few quotations are either from the first scene, or some of the most famous lines from the play.

It's a totally hip hop approach to sampling. I'm not trying to sample the most obscure parts of *King Lear*, I'm trying to sample the most obvious parts, that everyone might know. And then I've very recently started to think about and realised that every work of art is a series of repetitions – certainly I'm repeating the same cast over and over – and then once I create the first part of the play that works, in some ways, the rest of the process is just finding ways to repeat that same first few moments in different ways so it doesn't look like a repetition, but it is also registering on a subconscious level as a repetition:

to the extent that every artwork has to repeat itself in order to have coherence as a work of art.

I am usually using an intertext. That's a principle of ensemble creation without it being a devising process. There are companies and principles of ensemble devising out there that are sometimes based on the idea of creative democracy, but as most would admit, there are democratic parts of the process but then there's also an electoral college and someone who signs it at the end. And I am maybe old enough to say now that I think it is true that a work of art on some level needs to be filtered through a single consciousness in order to present itself as properly singular to the singularity in the audience.

An audience can be brought to function as a collective, but at best it's momentary, it's also illusory. Sometimes you'll harness it, and you can get the audience to perform as a collective, but it's wrong probably to think of them as really thinking like a collective. And ultimately you are communicating to a group of individual subjectivities, despite their proximity and the lubrication of alcohol – they are still each an individual subject, and it seems that, in my experience, it's more pleasing to each individual subject to apprehend a work of art that has been created, and has been dominated somehow by another individual subjectivity.

And just to finish: now we have lots of long extended conversations and everybody gives their feedback, but it's not like we have some sort of democratic discussion about the play. They are not giving feedback, they are not writing lines, we are not improvising, and we are not devising, but to me that doesn't mean that I am inherently more in control or that it's less collaborative. Because I'm collaborating with who they are. And it might just be my personal idiosyncratic and inaccurate interpretation of what they are and certainly I don't actually have access to their inside, but I can play with their subjectivity as they present it and the confluence of their subjectivity and their morphology and the voice that exists in between them. I'm stealing their soul.

RADOSAVLJEVIĆ: You have previously referred to a notion of your collaborators as instrumentalists.

SHAPLIN: I do think of actors as instruments. Like a cello, or a bass guitar. I think that I have their lung capacities inscribed in my wrist. When I'm writing, I now know how big Stephanie's lungs are. In my muscle memory, I know where Stephanie is gonna take a breath versus where Drew is gonna take a breath. And I've often wondered: why after working with eight random actors did I choose Stephanie and Drew for the very next project and continue on with them for the next

12 years? And somehow, it might be literally because of their lungs and their voices. I know for a fact that neither of them has ever lost their voice in 12 years of doing shows that involve a lot of screaming. And we worked with a lot of other actors who definitely do lose their voices. I wasn't thinking about it at the time, but it seems it was an unconscious decision.

RADOSAVLJEVIĆ: Would it be friendship then that's primarily kept the company together? Or is it some sort of a creative chemistry?

SHAPLIN: If we break up in a month, what kept us together – I don't know; if we are together for another 10 years, what kept us together – I don't know. But I do think that intimacy is what makes the work the way it is. And that intimacy is part of the process. I don't know how other people work, but I desire to get intimate with the cast and let the piece be intimate for each of us.

I know that when I am performing and acting as an actor I can connect personally to the things that I've written because they personally come from me. But I also want the other actors to feel that way. So the play contains riffs on their own personal mythology too. And certainly the plays also contain stories about the Riot Group, embedded within them, that we experience as stories about us. It's not just a job. I don't like the division of labour model of theatre that separates everybody up into specific artisans with specific skills, I don't respond well to professionalisations of theatre. I fully admit, I don't like professional rehearsal rooms. I don't like union rehearsal rooms. I don't like institutional theatre. I would always rather see a piece of theatre in a room that is unlicensed, or purpose-built or stolen or borrowed, than I would want to see theatre in an institution.

RADOSAVLJEVIĆ: So how did working at the RSC challenge you as a playwright?

SHAPLIN: I gave in as a collaborator very much to a process. I didn't try and fight it. I went to work with Pig Iron in 2004 and I felt like I was totally myself and I had intimacy with all of the actors and connections with all of them and I was deeply embedded in the process and the work was really great, but several of the relationships were destroyed afterward by the process. There's no other way to put it.

In a lot of ways I tried something different at the RSC and I was completely outnumbered in every way. The only American, living in a foreign country, working for an institutional theatre with tons of rules and regulations. I didn't try and fight it. I just went with the flow. I worked the way that I work, and there was a lot of room made for the way that I work, but the way that I work is more than just writing the script during rehearsal. It's also about whether or not I can connect with the performers and whether or not I can personally connect to the story that I am trying to tell. There is a lot of people involved, a director that I am working with for the first time, 15 actors that I am working with for the first time – and for most of them, the last time – as part of a contract. For a lot of those actors it's just six months in their life. And my experience with the Riot Group is that it's a bunch of people that are in a gang, in a family, and committed and everybody just has the right attitude; it's much more cult-like. The bonds are familial. They are like a surrogate family. I did my best to function with the bunch of people. Some of them are great actors that I really hope to work with again. Some couldn't give a shit about the project really and were just waiting for their contract to be up.

RADOSAVLJEVIĆ: You have said that when you teach playwriting you start with getting students to pose an unanswerable question.

SHAPLIN: Yes. I'm now trying to find a deeper way of stimulating a paradox in them. 'Unanswerable question' is a bit of a crude way of doing that. What I essentially try and do is get them to write outside of what they know. To present an obstacle. Somehow a play has to be an obstacle or a problem. I think of it as: it needs to be a short-circuit in ideology and in fantasy.

I find almost always when I'm teaching playwriting, I'm teaching it at a university to students who are taking academic classes when they are not taking playwriting. And to function in those institutions, what you're writing is mock empirical research papers. Your point in almost all other classes if you are taking the humanities – even more so if you are taking science – is to present yourself and your ideas as legible coherent thesis-based reckoning with source materials, plus an original idea. And I think plays are not supposed to have theses. I think they're supposed to have questions.

So on some level you have to choose a question that is not possible to answer. That's the only thing that's going to keep the play going in my view. Otherwise you are just stalling for time until you tell the audience what you think. What I think is not for the audience really. What I think is maybe for my friends. What 'turns me on' is a secret that I need to conceal from the audience. And in part, I try and cultivate a not knowing of what I think. I've been writing plays now for so long that it's pretty habitual to think dialectically, and when I encounter an idea, or an image, or an ideology, or an emotion, I immediately try and identify the unresolvable paradox, in order to think about how I'd write about it. How I'd translate it into a dialogue.

As we discussed before, it needs to be filtered through a single consciousness, but one of the whole tricks of theatre is to make it appear as if there are multiple coherent subjectivities on stage. So you are masquerading as a multiple, whilst also communicating that you are singular through the coherence of the art. And in the linear world of writing papers, in order to communicate a thesis and demonstrate yourself as a legible, intelligent, responsible person, it's almost like making a play is all the opposite of that. You have to make yourself illegible, you have to not know what you are writing, you have to keep secrets, rather than reveal everything.

And I do think of playwriting as writing music for instruments. The title of my playwriting class now is 'This Playwriting Class is a Music Class'.

RADOSAVLJEVIĆ: What are the principles?

SHAPLIN: That the text is not a work of art. That's the main principle. Publication is just a concession that I give into because it's part of the culture and you can make a little bit of money and it doesn't seem to hurt anyone. But the script is not the artwork. You are not communing with or comprehending the work of art that I made if you're reading the script. I genuinely believe that the work of art is the performance that disappears at the end of the night. I think of published scripts as autopsy reports of things that were alive – or are alive at certain times – but on page they are dead. And partial.

RADOSAVLJEVIĆ: Is there anything else that can be said about your work's relationship with music?

SHAPLIN: I use a lot of underscoring – in almost all my shows there is sound running through the majority of the show, and looped sound. I pick really simple stuff, because I don't want to interfere with the text; the idea is that it's a bed that the text lays in. And sometimes I think that the looped music is a surrogate for audience's concentration. The loop is there to draw you in and to mesmerise and hypnotise the audience, and the text goes on top. It is a really cheap way of creating architecture, when you don't have sets and you don't have lights, and you don't have all the things in the theatre or in a cinema that are about inducing or imitating the dream state. The idea is that you go in there and the lights dim or something puts you into a dream state and ritualistically takes you out of the everyday and focuses your concentration.

RADOSAVLJEVIĆ: Talking of communicating with the audience, I have two questions. One: returning to that stylistic choice to present the way that you do – where did that come from? And two: what is it that you are giving the audience?

SHAPLIN: I acted periodically throughout my teenage years and when I first started writing for theatre, I wrote monologues. That must have influenced my writing in some profound way because I really conceived of all my early plays as largely demonstrative, just direct speaking to the audience. In *Victory at the Dirt Palace*, they are newscasters. *Pugilist*, they are in briefings, in preparation for a mission. *Switch Triptych*, they are all telephone operators sat at stations. Essentially, up until now, I have always been looking for ways to anchor the actor in a kind of non-naturalistic, non-fourth wall space.

I used to say that there is no setting in those plays. The setting is just the surface of the actors' bodies where the show essentially happens, and almost entirely on the surface of their face. And truthfully, I still don't know how to make people move on stage. It's so much simpler for me to stick the actors into the kind of patterns that you can write on a grid on a piece of paper. And when people move, it's very minimal and highly suggestive. It increases the intensity somehow, and then the thing isn't all diffused, and I'm not trying to create some sort of a fantasy space that then disappears. Everything is clean and simple that way.

The presentational style is a practical decision, and then it becomes a habit.

So what do I give the audience? Who are they? We used to say 'Fuck the audience' before we went on, as a way of meaning, 'Fuck them, they are not in charge'. And increasingly now I realise there is a double meaning there – the thing on stage is active, and the thing in the audience is passive and there's vibration on stage and there is matter in the audience. That was just a kind of a war cry. I guess I fantasise about unmooring the audience's cherished assumptions. I fantasise about being able to unhook certain dualities in people's minds and unhook people's presuppositions about progress or about the coherence of humanity or about capacity for change. Certainly the works are contrarian.

Probably the stillness of what we do does contribute to the sense of invulnerability and impenetrability of the ensemble – that we are more powerful than them, that we're more focused than them, that we have kind of a super-human connection between us. And because we work together without looking at each other, it looks like we're co-ordinated in some other way. I do think our intimacy is legible onstage. And most audience members don't realise that that's why they are enjoying themselves. Because they don't know that we're more intimate than the average company that they see, but it does register. Because most other theatre that you see a lot of the time has been made by people that were strangers to each other a month before you're seeing them. It's way different to look at people who have been working together for 12 years. It's just different. You're more co-ordinated. Our subjectivities are in communication. We're an intersubjective unit, a hive mind, when we're performing something that we've rehearsed.

RADOSAVLJEVIĆ: Tell me about the new partnership with Whit MacLaughlin and his ensemble New Paradise Laboratories (NLP). How did it come about and what is he bringing in terms of his ensemble way of working to the equation?

SHAPLIN: There is this impossible paradox here which is that on the one hand I'm very much aware that every play I write is the same. I just keep repeating myself. I'm just the same person. And there's some positive affirmation of that. Jeanie O'Hare[1] says that your artistic personality is established at the age of eight, and that really for an artist the journey is always backward to what you were at the age of eight to try and rekindle that energy. Because I have special knowledge I can look at my plays and say – look how they are all the same, look how every play has the same structure buried within it. But the audience doesn't necessarily know that. Well they do and they don't. I also feel totally imprisoned by that, and not willing to work with that. I don't want to make Riot Group shows every time. I don't want to always make the same show. I try and compel myself to write a new show every time.

The partnership with Pig Iron in 2004 definitely opened up for the first time for me the possibilities of a relationship between my language and more elaborate physical dramaturgy. Because Pig Iron is a Lecoq-trained company and they think about things physically and they have techniques and ways of thinking about the body and movement and motion that are analogous to the way I've come to think about language. And the dream is to bring those two things together, and those two things did come together. Also it was my first time writing for actors other than my own actors. And so I realised that I can write for other actors. I can meet an actor and see their work and then I can write for them. That opened up possibilities for me and a way to go towards something new.

New Paradise Laboratories is also based in Philadelphia and I saw their work and was very much taken with it. It's also largely about physical dramaturgy, but the subject matter and approach to theme couldn't be more different than Pig Iron. New Paradise Laboratories is much more inspired by sports. Certainly their work, is about an athlete's approach to what you're doing. Several people in their company come from sports backgrounds. I saw their piece in 2007 called

Batch, and it really detonated in my life – it was the most incredible piece of theatre I felt I've ever seen and I immediately wanted to work with the company.

The pieces fell into place, we got offered money to make a piece, and so me and Whit made a decision to work together – Riot Group and New Paradise Labs, with the general idea of me writing and him directing. And in the time since we decided to make that piece, he's stepped in and become an artistic associate of the Riot Group.

To put it really simply, up until *Pugilist Specialist* I was working as a writer and a designer and an actor in the ensemble. And there really was no director. I directed between those three roles, that's the only direction that a production got. After *Pugilist Specialist*, the demands to turn the company into an organisation that functioned meant that what I tried to do was step out of acting and just write and direct and try and run the company. And in the six years since I did that, I don't really know how to direct my own work. I think I do all right as an actor, and that's why in the new piece I'm returning to the ensemble as an actor. Now Whit stands in really as the director and it's the first time we had a director in the Riot Group, but we trust him in large part because he's become intimate with our way of working and with my plays and understands what we are after and refreshens and renews what we are after.

RADOSAVLJEVIĆ: Does he keep your aesthetic?

SHAPLIN: Yeah, he does. Whit believes that certain elements of the Riot Group staging are simply embedded in the text. The choice isn't really separate from the script. The Riot Group style of directing out, he is utilising in this new production of my play *Freedom Club* and he feels that he understands it, he understands why it works. But he also approaches it from a different angle. He gets to approach it fresh, it's not just a habit for him, it's not a default, it's something that he took the time to learn and has his own personal feelings about. It just means we can do what we are doing, but do it new. He also has his own approach to devising and developing physical dramaturgy and also textual dramaturgy. It's an extremely productive counterpoint for both of us. I think that our collaboration is influencing his work with NPL [New Paradise Laboratories] as much as the collaboration influences my writing.

Note

1 The RSC Dramaturg 2004–2012; currently Chair of Playwriting, Yale School of Drama.

150   *Working processes*

Bibliography

Kuharski, Allen J. (2005) 'Performance Review: "Pugilist Specialist"', *Theatre Journal*, 57(3): 524–5.

Soloski, Alexis (2004) 'Voice Choices: Operation: Quagmire: A Chilling Dramatization of the Ongoing US Military Fiascos', *The Village Voice*, 6–12 October, 49(40): 125.

Soloski, Alexis (2008) 'Theater: *Lear* on the Air', *The Village Voice*; 27 August–2 September: 37.

Soloski, Alexis (2011) '*Freedom Club* Takes Aim', *The Village Voice*, 12 January, available online at http://www.villagevoice.com/2011-01-12/theater/freedom-club-takes-aim/ (accessed 19 December 2012).

The Riot Group
http://www.theriotgroup.com/

14 Working together in Northern Ireland

Hanna Slättne (Tinderbox Theatre)

Barely a year after its conception in 1988, Belfast-based new writing theatre company Tinderbox received the ultimate endorsement – a donation cheque and a card from Samuel Beckett in support of their Festival of New Irish Playwriting (Hadfield and Henderson 1989: 3). Tinderbox was founded by actors Lalor Roddy and Tim Loane and producer Stephen Wright on the back of a successful run of a low budget Pinter double bill. This work created an audience demand for 'artistically dangerous' and 'challenging' theatre (Coyle 1991: 20), which Tinderbox set out to meet. The Festival of New Irish Playwriting which the company launched in 1989 continued annually until 2000, and Tinderbox's artistic vision too centred around new writing.

Artistic Director Michael Duke took the company over in 2003 with the intention of building on the company's existing reputation but also incorporating an emphasis on other forms of 'new work'. Mary Luckhurst notes that Duke's decision to hire Hanna Slättne as a full time dramaturg in 2004 was motivated by a desire to also facilitate collaboration between a number of Northern Irish theatre companies and artists 'to encourage innovative cross-art experiments, involving scripts, but not necessarily working on them through conventional development techniques' (Luckhurst 2010: 177). In 2010 Tinderbox successfully piloted a season of new work presented by a group of actors employed on long-term contracts, in the hope that this may lead to the creation of a more permanent ensemble.

Hanna Slättne was the founder member of the UK-based organisation the Dramaturgs' Network in 2001. Since 2004 she has run the dramaturgy strand of Tinderbox's activities and, in addition, she has provided wider support for writers at all levels in Northern Ireland, collaborating regularly with BBC Northern Ireland and Northern Ireland Screen, as well as a variety of regional theatre-makers. This interview, focusing on Tinderbox's ensemble experiment from the dramaturg's point of view, took place in January 2011 in Belfast.

Interview

RADOSAVLJEVIĆ: It might be useful to start with some background on Tinderbox Theatre company and how the ensemble project you recently had came about.

SLÄTTNE: For most of its lifespan Tinderbox has been a new writing company, and particularly so under the current Artistic Director Michael Duke. When he took over he had quite a strong vision of how to work with new writing so he requested to have the post of a dramaturg. This means that Tinderbox now has three very strong strands: productions, dramaturgy and outreach. Outreach has always been a big part of Tinderbox's work – creating exciting projects to engage with various groups, ages and races across Northern Ireland. We have been focussing on Northern Irish writers or writers working in Northern Ireland, because it's a region where new writing has been underdeveloped for historical reasons. But as well as developing new writing, the post of a dramaturg means that we work differently, it means that you can really spend time and focus on what it is that you are trying to do, and how you do it – which also led to the ensemble idea. Normally we do two to three productions a year.

There are two main factors that inform the idea of the ensemble: one is a strong wish to explore new ways of working here, to employ actors for longer, to create a collaborative artistic environment which hasn't really existed over a long period of time since the heydays of the Lyric. So that was one and the most important reason – to just expand the way people are working. The other one, which has come in lately, is financial. Northern Ireland has always had very little funding for the arts, much lower than any other region in the UK. We've been quite good at managing it, but you have to be very inventive and on the ball with that. Now that we are expecting more cuts, the Arts Council is looking for collaboration and new ways of working – and our idea of the ensemble fits quite well into that.

I shall talk about two different types of ensemble work that we've been doing so far at Tinderbox – a studio production and a full-scale production. The studio production is intended to test out new work without having to go through a whole funding cycle which takes so long that the writers get really frustrated. So we implemented the studio production which is really low budget: you rehearse for two weeks, you put it on for a week – to a professional standard but with very limited means. And then we have the full-scale production, with the normal budget.

There was another aspect which encouraged this idea of the ensemble – the fact that there is not a great habit of theatre-going in

Northern Ireland. So we wanted to create some events around theatre as well, and to have an ensemble presenting several pieces of work in a season was an idea of an event like that.

A few years back we did a Studio season. Tinderbox did a studio production called *The Virgin Father* by Jimmy McAleavey, and then there were three other young and emerging companies – a dance company called Assault, a fabulous physical theatre company called Red Lemon, and a very new company called Abandon. We just put our stuff together – we did a joint funding application, and did a season of work. That was very successful and encouraged us to think about the ensemble idea.

So the first ensemble project we did was the Studio Ensemble – the idea was to get three small scale productions performed by one ensemble. This just happened in the autumn 2010, it was called The True North Season. We had three writers who didn't have a brief – they were just writing what they wanted to write. They'd never read each other's work – it just so happened that they all resonated with each other, which was amazing actually, in a very positive way, they weren't similar at all. It was very much about contemporary Northern Ireland; it became very exciting as a thing in itself.

The idea was to have one design team. Starting a relationship with designer Ciaran Bagnall a few years back really fired this idea of an ensemble around one evolving set for the three plays, one crew, one set of actors who were working together for a longer time. That's the basis of the model.

Every actor was in two plays, so in the weeks when they were not in rehearsals they took on other tasks – they were helping with marketing or with costumes, or with our annual Young Writers' Programme 'Fireworks' – one of them took on directing one of the Young Writers' pieces and developing it using the rest of the cast. All of them felt part of the company.

RADOSAVLJEVIĆ: How many actors were part of the ensemble?

SLÄTTNE: We had six actors and one designer, stage manager, production manager, etc.

RADOSAVLJEVIĆ: Were the plays written for a particular number of actors, or did you cast them knowing what the plays were going to be?

SLÄTTNE: One writer took the brunt of having to accommodate a little bit. One play – a two-hander – was already written earlier in the year, and had been to America. So we started off with two female actors in the cast. Then we got a play we were very interested in, but that needed rewriting because it was so topical that events completely overshot the play – so it was a little bit of a blank canvas again when he sat down to rewrite the play in the new circumstances. Then we had the third writer coming on board, who just went away and developed his idea; and then we started to look at how, without changing meaning or changing the story, we could use the company as it was, or if we needed another actor. There were some discussions, but I feel that we were completely and utterly working with what the plays needed to do and what the plays needed to say, and that was the first priority.

RADOSAVLJEVIĆ: So you had one two-hander and . . .

SLÄTTNE: And two five-handers.

RADOSAVLJEVIĆ: How did you cast the ensemble? Were there specific qualities you were looking for?

SLÄTTNE: We were looking for an ensemble – people who were open-minded and willing to embrace this whole idea of doing other work as part of the ensemble and not have time off when they were not required. That was a key criterion.

RADOSAVLJEVIĆ: Were they all from Northern Ireland?

SLÄTTNE: We cast Northern Irish actors, particularly because the plays ended up being so much about Northern Ireland. One was set in a small town in the countryside; one was set in political circles and middle class families near Belfast; and one was a fictional play about two sisters, one of whom had become a politician and the other was of a working-class background. The tones and accents were very, very Northern Irish.

We cast some people who hadn't necessarily worked together before and we hadn't worked with quite a few of them either; but we had three directors, and the three directors had a say in the casting of their play. Not everyone got everything that they wanted, obviously, but I would say that we ended up with an absolutely fantastic ensemble cast. Mick keeps saying – we had the Studio Ensemble in order to learn as much as possible how to do an ensemble, and actually we didn't learn anything about how to manage the company, because the company was just so up for it, there was nothing to manage.

RADOSAVLJEVIĆ: What were the advantages that they saw in it?

SLÄTTNE: Because they were going from part to part, it wasn't so much about the individual parts, but I think it was actually about the company. It created a sense of the ownership of all three plays. Remember that they worked with three different directors – directors who work very, very differently, and that was very, very hard sometimes for some of the actors going from one play to the other; but because it wasn't so much about any individual play, it was actually about the support of the actors for each other through the different stages. It was a really tough gig for the actors. And they were fantastic at helping each other through those huge obstacles.

RADOSAVLJEVIĆ: How did you choose the directors?

SLÄTTNE: The play that had been to America earlier in the year came out of a co-production with Solas Nua. Because that was a co-production, we had two Northern Irish actors and the director was from America, Kathleen Akerley. Mick was directing one piece; and we had a young director, Des Kennedy, who we had been supporting and mentoring for a few years and we thought this would be a nice opportunity for him to be part of something bigger. The plays were called *Everything Between Us* by David Ireland which was the two-hander, *God's Country* by Colin Bell which was the one that had to be rewritten because of real life circumstances, and the third one was *The Cleanroom* by John McCann which came in at the end.

RADOSAVLJEVIĆ: How long were the actors contracted for?

SLÄTTNE: They were contracted for about 12 weeks whereas a normal studio contract would be for four to five weeks.

RADOSAVLJEVIĆ: Was there a financial challenge involved in terms of raising money? Did you have to talk your funders into this sort of project?

SLÄTTNE: Yes, it was very difficult. We had to start the project without having all the money, because we had so many funding applications out there about which we just had to go 'fingers crossed'. But to the funders, and to the Arts Council here, it was a very attractive idea.

RADOSAVLJEVIĆ: On what grounds?

SLÄTTNE: That it is quite efficient financially, but it is also interesting artistically. We produced three new plays for the price of one! There was a lot of publicity about it because it was a season, and it was relatively successful on those grounds. For me personally in my job, I've always wanted people from Scotland, England and Dublin, to come and see our work and our writers' work – which they very, very rarely do because we are where we are. But because we were able to present all three plays in one day at the end of the run, we actually got a lot of interest. A lot of people came from other theatres, so professionally for the writers that was brilliant, and for us too. It just created a sense of an event, and it was nearly completely sold out, you couldn't get a ticket for it towards the end of the run at all. It was really great to present new writing to full houses. People were queuing outside, and that happens very rarely out here.

RADOSAVLJEVIĆ: Did you have to have some sort of training built into the rehearsal period, some kind of ensemble-building process?

SLÄTTNE: I think Mick added that to his rehearsals. We didn't rehearse the plays one after the other. On the first day we had readthroughs of all plays, and then we started working on the first play the rest of that week, then the second play the following week, and after the first play again – trying to accommodate people's timetables, but also to get the sense of this being one project that we were doing. Mick is the Artistic Director of the company and the ensemble was his idea, so he built those things into his rehearsal time, whereas the other two directors came in as guest directors and did what they normally would do when rehearsing a new play.

RADOSAVLJEVIĆ: Are you aware of any other models that Mick might have been exploring, any influences or means of preparation in terms of how he was developing his ensemble idea?

SLÄTTNE: I think we kept talking between us. I don't remember looking at any models. We just tried to develop it based on our professional experience and the circumstances here. The other great thing about this was that we booked the actual theatre where this was going to happen, we rehearsed in the actual space – which never happens! And that was one of the key things. One of the learning points that we had was: I was the only dramaturg, and we hadn't set up enough how the company works with the visiting directors – how to work with the dramaturg, what it means to do new writing with Tinderbox. So for those nine, ten weeks, I was going from one project to the other, from one playwright's needs to another, and from one director's way of working to another, and that was a lot for one dramaturg. The next time what we will do differently is consider how we choose external people and how we introduce them to the way we work, and to our team.

RADOSAVLJEVIĆ: What does it mean to work with Tinderbox?

SLÄTTNE: Having a dramaturg on board for the whole process. For us it was quite new to have a visiting director as well, because normally it would be Mick, me and the writer working together from the start. What happened here was that two directors stepped into the process where there had been quite a lot of work done already on ideas and meaning and structure, and they had to continue that work and make it their own. As a new writing company we had two first time professional writers and one emerging writer in this group – they needed a lot of support and engagement and conversations. So stepping in as an outside director, especially if you were fairly new to new writing, was a very big step. Mick and I have worked together for seven years, we know what we do so well it can be hard to have someone step into that. We do place the writer and their ideas at the centre, and we have a very rigorous process – and I think a lot of people get taken aback by that.

RADOSAVLJEVIĆ: Rigorous in what sense?

SLÄTTNE: I would say textually and artistically. It was absolutely fascinating for me to go from one director to another because they work so differently and they prioritize very different things in rehearsals.

RADOSAVLJEVIĆ: Seeing all the work back to back on that final day, do you think that the audience was able to see all the work as Tinderbox work?

SLÄTTNE: Yes, I think they had a very strong Tinderbox feel, but you could also see different directing styles, which is so exciting. That was another thing for an audience to experience – we wanted to give them this set of actors and allow them to see how differently they work on different plays and to soak up the craft of acting and directing in different ways. Because when we put on one play, it all becomes so 'This is *the* play, and this is what Tinderbox *is*, and this is what these actors *do*' – and of course it isn't, it is just one play which is very different from the next, but by putting them all together, this becomes really apparent.

RADOSAVLJEVIĆ: What is the next phase of the ensemble?

SLÄTTNE: There are two things that are happening. One is to pursue this idea of how we work differently, and the other is to do a full-scale production ensemble. When the new theatre, the MAC, opens in 2012 – we want to do the same thing but on a bigger scale. Three new plays with an ensemble of actors – take what we've learnt from the Studio Ensemble there. But in the meantime, we are looking at ways of working differently in our other project The Total Theatre Ensemble. We are testing an idea of working as an ensemble across three disciplines, with three companies: Assault Events – a dance company, Theatre Abandon – a physical theatre company, and Tinderbox. We are going to get an ensemble of actors who can work across those three disciplines – movement, devising and new writing – to develop three pieces, again with dramaturgical input throughout, to see if we can gather an ensemble of actors who can be versatile in those ways, but also if it works for us as individual companies.

But even if we continue doing things separately, Tinderbox will still continue to collaborate with some of the individuals from those companies – it's that kind of a set up. A nice thing about this as well is that in these really financially tough times, there has always been a really strong ethos in Tinderbox with how Mick works and how I work – to support emerging artists in various ways. We're taking two companies that are not funded under our wing, so they don't disappear in this tough time ahead, and they can continue to work.

RADOSAVLJEVIĆ: That forms the next phase of the ensemble way of working – across disciplines.

SLÄTTNE: Which is that other aspect of really pushing how we work here. There is nothing new in this for people in England and Scotland – they've done these kinds of things before, but we haven't really to this extent, and this is where we want to go now and it is very exciting. I think we have some really good performers and theatre-makers in Northern Ireland at the moment, so it's just making sure that we all survive this crisis.

We are starting collaborations, discussions and projects that will probably go on for years across this group of people in between the work we all do in our individual companies. What we are hoping will come out of it is new kinds of performances and new ways of working for us and for our audience.

Bibliography

Coyle, Jane (1991) 'Tinderbox', *Theatre Ireland*, 25, Spring: 20–1.
Hadfield, Paul and Henderson, Linda (1989) 'Stage Business', *Theatre Ireland*, 20, September–December: 3–4.
Luckhurst, Mary (2010) 'Dramaturgy and Agendas of Change: Tinderbox and the Joint Sectoral Dramaturgy Project', *Contemporary Theatre Review*, 20(2): 173–84.
Mooney, Martin (2008) 'Tinderbox Theatre Company', available online at http://www.culturenorthernireland.org/article/900/tinderbox-theatre-company (accessed 19 December 2012).

Tinderbox Theatre Company
http://www.tinderbox.org.uk/

15 On writing and performance in an ensemble

Alexander Kelly (Third Angel) and
Chris Thorpe (Unlimited Theatre)

Third Angel and Unlimited Theatre were founded in Yorkshire in 1995 and 1997 respectively. Third Angel was formed by co-artistic directors Alexander Kelly and Rachael Walton, and Unlimited Theatre emerged from collaborative efforts of six University of Leeds graduates, three of whom remain with the company today: writer-performers Clare Duffy and Chris Thorpe, and artistic director-performer Jon Spooner. Both companies have experimented with cross-disciplinary collaborations and both have toured their work extensively around the world.

A *Los Angeles Times* review placed Unlimited Theatre's award-winning *Neutrino* (2001) in the tradition of 'such cerebral hits as Tom Stoppard's *Arcadia*, Michael Frayn's *Copenhagen* and Steve Martin's *Picasso at the Lapin Agile*'. However, unusually for a highbrow play, *Neutrino* was acclaimed by the same review as a 'lesson in theatre-making' for its staging (Miller 2005).

Meanwhile, Third Angel has secured a significant place in the contemporary annals of devised theatre. Heddon and Milling classify Third Angel as part of the 'fourth generation' of devising theatre companies, following in the footsteps of the respective previous generations of Forced Entertainment, Impact Theatre and the Living Theatre before them (Heddon and Milling 2006: 228). As another Yorkshire-based company, Forced Entertainment is in fact revealed in the interview that follows to be an important influence on both Third Angel and Unlimited Theatre.

While the two companies' work may appear distinct from the outset – Third Angel being more inclined towards the visual or live-art means of expression, as opposed to Unlimited Theatre's devising process oriented towards playtexts – recent years have led towards a number of collaborations between them. Chris Thorpe has collaborated with Third Angel on *Presumption* (2006), *The Expected Lifespan of Dreams* (2006), *Parts for Machines That Do Things* (2008) and *What I Heard About the World* (2012) – the latter one of which is also a collaboration with Portuguese company mala voadora. Third Angel has been part of Unlimited Theatre's *Mixtape Project* (2008–2010), which featured a number of other artists such as Action Hero, Stan's Café and Phil Kay. Alex Kelly was also credited as a designer on Unlimited Theatre's *Static* (2000), *Clean* (2000), *Neutrino* (2001) and *Tangle* (2006/2008). In addition to his ensemble work, Chris Thorpe has a successful career as an independent writer and performer.

This interview took place during the run of *What I Heard About the World* in February 2012 at the Soho Theatre in London.

Interview

RADOSAVLJEVIĆ: Let's start with your collaboration. What was it actually that made you want to work together?

THORPE: There's a historical reason and then there's an artistic reason. The historical reason is that Third Angel and Unlimited started at very similar times in two very proximate cities – Sheffield and Leeds. We were exposed to each other's work at various kinds of miniature festivals and got to know each other. Because of a two-year journey that Third Angel had before Unlimited had started – which is obviously not an issue now but when you're 19 or 20 those slight differences in age do seem more exaggerated – they seemed to me like people who were further along the path than us. I think that the two companies make work that is very different, but is located in the same stratum and the same area of British performance. I guess there was a very clear continuum in my head that went, for example: Forced Entertainment, who had been at it for a long time when we started, Third Angel, and Unlimited – within the same continuum but different stages in the journey.

RADOSAVLJEVIĆ: However, Unlimited placed a bit more emphasis on text?

THORPE: Unlimited was very much a devising and writing company – we made what we considered to be theatre, whereas I think Third Angel have always been a company who made theatre as part of their live art practice.

KELLY: For a long time we didn't call ourselves 'writers', and we thought about the task of 'writing down' as something that would happen after a show was made. Writing text was something that was done in the evening; it was not part of the process for the first couple of years – and we've moved towards bringing the emphasis on text earlier on in the process than we used to.

THORPE: Which is funny because Unlimited was very much the other way. We still talk about a rehearsal script – a rehearsal script is something that is very important for us to have. Occasionally we'll do a show where one of us will write a play, and we'll put it on – but the bulk of our work still comes from a devising process. The writing will be very much part of the devising process and will result, to a greater or lesser degree, in a rehearsal script – which has very much become a general rule over the years. What a rehearsal script means to us has changed in general over the years, but it has a very specific meaning according to project.

RADOSAVLJEVIĆ: That means that your respective rehearsal structures in your companies are different?

KELLY: I think so. In Third Angel, with certain projects, we will now look to have a finished text before the end of the making process. We think of the making process in three stages: an R&D stage, a devising stage, and a rehearsing stage.

RADOSAVLJEVIĆ: How long is each one of those stages?

KELLY: *What I Heard About the World* was 10 weeks in total. We had three weeks R&D early on in April 2010, a week showing a work-in-progress at PAZZ in Germany, and then we had a six-week making process up to opening it in Sheffield – and that was relatively luxurious.

RADOSAVLJEVIĆ: The making process was six weeks, and the rehearsal process?

KELLY: The rehearsal process for this was a little shorter than we had anticipated, it was about a week. I think we figured out what the show was with a week to go. And, of course, when you're rehearsing a devised show, because actually you're very familiar with a lot of the material and the building blocks of it, a week is actually enough if the material has been around for a while. If you throw everything out with only two weeks to go and then start devising it and rehearsing it in a fortnight, that's problematic.

RADOSAVLJEVIĆ: Do you usually organise the material?

KELLY: No, it varies actually. With *Presumption*, I was the outside eye. The project was led by Rachael, my co-director, and it was Rachael and Chris performing it, the three of us writing it, and in that first version me on the outside shaping and structuring, although that is a job that all three of us do. After that had opened, because we knew Rachael couldn't tour it, Rachael stepped out and re-directed it with Lucy Ellinson in it. I was only around for some of that process because I was teaching, but I imagine that that was a lot more like a traditional rehearsal process where you just re-rehearsed the show, didn't you?

THORPE: Yes, and the text was one element of the show that was very much about moving objects around the stage. It wasn't like rehearsing a play, because I think that one of the things that Third Angel's work does – at least the work that I've been involved with which is the more text-based end of things – the text is an element of the show that changes moment by moment or section by section according to what is needed. That's something that's carried through to *What I Heard About the World* – there's a lot of different kinds of text in the show. It's all about telling these stories, which are all the same type of story, albeit from different places, or different levels of humour, brutality, darkness, lightness. But there is a conscious effort to use the text as a tool in different ways to tell the stories in different ways. So there's scripted dialogue, there's a little bit of verbatim right at the start, there's first person narrative, there are lists . . .

RADOSAVLJEVIĆ: And when is the story decided on?

THORPE: The story of a show like this is the emotional narrative – and that's decided on probably just before that rehearsal period that Alex talks about, but it's decided on very instinctively at first. Interestingly, as a tiny little tangent, there's a show that me and Alex have talked about making for a long time, which is about the actual shape of the text on the page governing performance – which will be a new way of using text. We talked about a show where the text of the show was projected and the performers know the text and they perform it but the performance changes according to the font in which the text is projected. So, if and when we ever get round to persuading anyone apart from ourselves that that's a good idea – that will be a show in which the text is almost a character.

RADOSAVLJEVIĆ: How is the Unlimited rehearsal process different from the Third Angel process?

THORPE: Over the last eight years the Unlimited process and Third Angel process have kind of merged for me to the point that the commonality and the overlap between those two circles on the Venn diagram of those two companies has got bigger and bigger.

KELLY: And that's funny because Chris has done more work with us and I've also worked on a few Unlimited shows and my role increased from a set designer to a kind of sticking around more and sticking more of an oar into it. On my CV it says 'Something in between a Set Designer and a Dramaturg'.

THORPE: The two companies have grown up together and we've always been friends, and there's been a lot of cross-swapping of personnel over the years, but I don't know if those two rehearsal processes have merged in that way because of people bringing stuff from one company to another and vice versa, or because the two companies have been on a parallel track . . . I don't know how deliberate that is or whether that's a function of the two companies maturing and working in

different places. But the Unlimited process is still different and distinct from the Third Angel process in that we are very text-based, we
will spend a lot of time, much more time than Third Angel, with
John, Clare and myself sitting around a table interrogating the text
we're making.

KELLY: And that often happens before you've cast it as well.

THORPE: Yes. We don't necessarily devise in a room together anymore –
that very, very rarely happens. We sit at tables and we talk, and we
research, and we bring people in to speak to and we take things away
from those conversations, and we involve our designers and our composers at a very early stage – it's become a much less active and a
much more talkative process. Well, actually, that's not right, it's not
less active – the action has migrated into the language and the
dialogue.

RADOSAVLJEVIĆ: How long is that process of talking?

THORPE: It could be up to two months, over the course of a year, or 18
months. But that's actually pure time sitting around a table. With
Third Angel, we'll do a bit of devising, we'll play a game, we'll set a
task and we'll do that physically according to rules, and then go away
and write something. Unlimited, instead, would talk and analyse
research and then go away and write something in the same way. So
it's the same structure between doing stuff, writing, bringing it back,
but the stuff that is done is very different. And then a common thing
that both processes have – which doesn't necessarily happen in other
more traditional lines of performance – the text is not necessarily
ever owned by one person, there's that freedom to change.

RADOSAVLJEVIĆ: How did Unlimited come together?

THORPE: It was six people who met at university who didn't want to
necessarily do other people's work. When the time came that some
writing became necessary, it happened that Clare and me were the
people who came forward. In Clare's case, she had already shown a
very strong aptitude for doing it, and wanted to carry on doing it, and
in my case I kind of liked it and didn't think it was going to be as
arduous as the other people thought it was going to be. And then we
worked in various ways: sometimes Clare would pull in the script for
the project, sometimes I would. *Static*, in 1999, was a piece of writing
that I did – that was the first time that had happened with my writing
within Unlimited. I was the sole writer on that and that's the thing
that gave me the confidence to start writing outside of the company
as well. But I wouldn't have ever got to that position if I hadn't been
part of this company that actually knew that we wanted to make
work together. So it wasn't a company that accreted around one

writer or two writers, and it certainly wasn't a vehicle to produce the writing of anyone specific in the company. It came purely out of the desire and that trust in each other, and that desire to make work together.

RADOSAVLJEVIĆ: Yours was a degree in Theatre Studies?

THORPE: Yes, I did a degree in English Literature and Theatre Studies, which is a single honours degree at the University of Leeds. One of the major things that that course encouraged you to do, structurally but also ideologically, was to collaborate through year groups, and eventually with the MA and PhD groups. There was that real non-hierarchical, almost an insistence, that we were all creating work together. It was a total open forum, and that formed the ethos of the company because actually, part of the reason for starting Unlimited was that we'd had such a good time doing that that we couldn't imagine having as good a time doing anything else.

It's just three of us now: myself, Jon and Clare, with Jon heading it up as the artistic director, and we also have various other people who are very much company members in terms of the general managing. But as that core group of six has shrunk, the actual number of people in the company has expanded because the ethos is still the same – like I said earlier, it's about bringing people in and finding the artists that we want to collaborate with. A particular watershed moment was around 2000, when we realised that we were only making work with each other and we had been at it for three or four years. So, we put out a call for someone to collaborate with – and we ended up collaborating with Chris Goode on a project, and that kind of opened the floodgates, because out of that collaboration we made *Neutrino* – one of our defining projects. I wrote half of it and he wrote the other half, and there was a huge devised element to it.

So that kind of synthesised the writing and the devising. After that, first as a trickle and then as a flood, we built up this network of collaborators. Now we've got composers, designers, lighting designers, technicians, stage managers – and then as our subject areas increase, as things that we are obsessed with increase – we've got scientists, we've got space scientists. Unlimited run their own space agency, Unlimited Space Agency, which is dedicated to promoting space travel and technology for young people, and getting your satellite into orbit.

RADOSAVLJEVIĆ: And how did Third Angel come together as a company?

KELLY: Rachael and I met at university, we were in different years but we both did Theatre Studies at Lancaster. Then we went to Sheffield, because Rachael is from Sheffield originally, and I went and did a film course at Sheffield.

My mum and dad are both visual artists and my dad ran the foundation course at Walsall College of Art. So although I didn't do a fine
art course, I did a lot of time hanging around a foundation course as a
teenager. Early on it was assumed that we were from art school rather
than from a theatre course, I think.

The theatre course in Lancaster could be very practically oriented
if that's how you selected your options. In my second year I got to
make two devised pieces with Pete Brooks, of Impact Theatre and
latterly Insomniac, who taught there for three years. Those two devising processes had a big influence on me through Pete's approach to
making work.

In Sheffield, Rachael and I were both in the process of talking to
other people about setting up companies and making work, but those
conversations were stalling a little bit. There was a commission going
at Hull Time Based Arts for their festival called 'ROOT: Running Out
of Time' for something to do with civil liberties and civic pride, and
they were looking for durational work specifically. I was at film school
so I got access to a lot of video equipment and Rachael and I came up
with an idea for a show for this commission. We didn't get the commission but we really liked the idea, and we asked the Workstation in
Sheffield where my course was based if we could do it in their gallery
space. Because I'd been shortlisted for something else with the support
of Sheffield Independent Film who were also based there, they knew
who I was and that we weren't a couple of chancers. So we made that
piece called *Testcard* in the Workstation foyer gallery.

I don't know if it was ever a conscious decision, but Rachael and I
just always decided on what the space was as part of our job. We just
thought of it as one of the tools. Maybe that was to do with devising –
saying 'What is the space that facilitates what the performers are
doing? And what looks good in that sense?' – because we never had a
script to go to. And I had never understood the model in which the
actors get shown the model of the set on the first day of rehearsal. I
just find it weird, it feels to me like it's limiting some choices from the
beginning.

RADOSAVLJEVIĆ: And *Presumption* – being a piece which charts the life of
a romantic relationship through a metaphor of building a theatre set
on stage – is really a scripting of that space-making process in a way,
isn't it?

KELLY: Yes, absolutely. And in rehearsals these two processes ran in
parallel: writing this material for the couple, and playing the game of
building the set. For a long time we thought that playing the game
of building the set would unlock bits of the text, and it was pretty late

on that we did a run one Friday afternoon and thought 'This isn't working' and we had two weeks to go. And Rachael came in on the Monday and said 'Just change the power relationship, the text facilitates the bringing on of the furniture'. And we had half of the show by the end of that day. That's where the repeating of scenes comes from.

Once we knew what the rules were, we could build in the way the rules break down in the latter half of the show. So the making of the environment, how the performers interact with the environment, the tasks that they have to do, the visual job of the show has always been a part of what we think of our job as makers. We have worked with art directors sometimes and it's been really interesting working with mala voadora because Jose Capela, who's one of the artistic directors, is an architect. Their work is visually stunning, and you can draw a triangle or a third circle in the Venn diagram, because they work in some ways very similar to Third Angel in that they figure out what the task of the show is, but they also do a lot of talking beforehand the way that Unlimited do.

RADOSAVLJEVIĆ: You and Rachael are the core of Third Angel?

KELLY: Yes, we are jointly artistic directors. The way it works – and this has evolved over the years, it took us a while to understand that it's something that we were doing deliberately – is: one of us will initiate a project, and that person generally has the final say, but usually that person is in it, because we do originate projects that we want to perform. That's a slightly complex process sometimes because it means that the person who's the outside eye doesn't have the final say, but there is that trusted dialogue there that obviously involves some arguments and disagreements. If you're the outside eye, you have that authority because you can see what's going on and you can push for certain things, but in the end there is an instinct on the part of the person who originated the show.

But I also think that we both do slightly different jobs as the outside eye on different projects. So the ordering and shaping of the structure of a piece is more what I do when I'm the outside eye, and it's unusual for me to be in a piece with other performers. Whereas, with the solo performances, Rachael is very much there about getting the detail of the show for me, as a director really.

Then there are projects like *Story Map*, which is a durational spin off of *What I Heard About the World* – they're projects that get discovered in the making of something else, and take on a life of their own. It would be hard to say whether those pieces are 'directed' but they have a logic that is discovered in a task that makes sense with an audience.

RADOSAVLJEVIĆ: Chris mentioned earlier a genealogy which includes Forced Entertainment – how would you define them as part of your formative influences?

KELLY: Primarily in their existence as a company. Seeing Forced Entertainment was very important to me when I was a student at Lancaster. Rachael and I were both in *Dreams' Winter* in Manchester's Central Library. Just watching them operate as a company, as a collective – I think they were still called Forced Entertainment Theatre Co-operative then – just that sense of them as a group shaping that work, but with Tim kind of shaping it more from the outside, that made me certain I wanted to form my own company. I wanted to be a maker and have a company, not to be a jobbing director

THORPE: They are an influence in the sense that they prove that there is a future in it as well. Again, it's not necessarily an artistic influence, although you do see the influence of certain of their shows everywhere – all across the spectrum. But particularly coming from Leeds, from Sheffield, having that geographical proximity to them as a Sheffield company, they were the proof that you can work like that, whether or not you bought into and were inspired by their work. Some of their pieces are still some of the most effective things I've ever seen, but it's not so much about that, it's about the fact that they're there. It's about – to use a really shit analogy – seeing someone that has built a house that hasn't fallen down. It means that it gives you slightly more confidence to just get on with building a house and know that it's possible.

KELLY: They did it their own way and they set their own agenda and just stuck to it.

RADOSAVLJEVIĆ: When you started working with Chris did your process change in any way?

KELLY: It did a bit . . .

THORPE: I think there are a lot more set pieces in your work now, actually. I suppose there's a kind of strand of Third Angel's work of Alex or Rachael doing solo pieces, and they to me seem more structured and written, more about the text. The text has more influence and authority in them – things like *Class of '76* and *The Lad Lit Project*. But the company work, the kind of stuff that I'm involved in – *Parts for Machines That Do Things*, *Presumption* and *What I Heard About the World* – they've still got the elements that make Third Angel's work so distinctive, in that: there are parts that run to rules, there are parts that are different every night, there are parts where you occasionally don't know what to say. I'm not saying that I've had a massive influence on the company, or that I've changed Third Angel's ethos in any way; I think by the fact of working with someone who writes – in the way that I like to write – there's a lot more fixedness to the text when the text needs to be fixed, which weirdly increases the freedom when the text isn't fixed to be more unfixed.

KELLY: It's one very clear making tool that Chris gave us. With *The Lad Lit Project*, half of the text was pretty set by the time it opened, but it had been set by repetition, re-telling and a kind of live editing where Rachael would say 'You don't need to say that there because you already said that two sentences ago'.

Whereas in making *Parts for Machines*, that was the two of us talking a lot: Chris writing, me going and doing videos, making some models, getting a camera, and then spending the next morning talking, more writing, more finding tasks; literally sometimes saying 'Right, everyone get writing, we're all going to write for an hour. What are you going to write?', 'I'm going to write the thing the guy says during that meeting' – and then whatever you've got at the end of that hour you read it out, and sometimes it's four lines and sometimes it's loads, and sometimes amazingly, sometimes it's almost there. There's a section in *What I Heard About the World* that we call 'radio silence', which we tried in a couple of different ways up on our feet, and then in one of those movements where it was just 'Right, I'm going to write something', Chris came back after an hour with this text almost as it is in performance now. So the story was very familiar to us, but we didn't have the mechanism for telling it. And at some point in that hour, I don't know if it was the beginning or half way through, Chris had got this particular text device.

THORPE: Yes, I think that kind of sums it up. There's now an option, where there wasn't before, within devising time to just say 'Leave me alone for an hour, we've tried this out, we've been talking about this, we know what we want to say'. One of the options we have is for us to just go into the corner and come back and put a text on the table and say 'This is what I have interpreted as what we want to say' – and quite often that works.

KELLY: Which is a really nice extra thing for us to have as well as 'Right, I think I know how this works, I'm just going to improvise it, and then tell me what you think and then I'll improvise it again', or the reverse which is – 'I want you to improvise this'.

THORPE: Going back to what I was saying that writing has come into the Third Angel processes as a part of the actual making rather than as either a retrospective fixing of something or as an evening activity if you like, it's important to state this: It's not that there was a writer missing and therefore me coming in as a writer has moved it closer to playwriting because 'all that a good devising process needs to bring it together is a writer'. It's a change in the way that writing is viewed in the process. So it's brought writing closer to the process as a tool rather than as a solution – because it didn't need a solution. But the place of writing as a tool was a long way away; it was quite often retrospective, and now it's an immediate tool in the room, which is a brilliant development for me actually, as a playwright, because I get to spend 50 per cent of my time dynamically in a room with people, and the other part of my time that I spend writing for myself or writing a script for a cast, is enhanced by the fact that I don't have to do that all the time. And the writing in the devising process is enhanced by the skills you develop over the years – being very quickly and immediately able to suggest how people might talk to each other or how people might talk to an audience.

KELLY: It's recognising writing as an ongoing thing that doesn't have to be a constant process. It's something that is used when it is needed to be. For example, when we made a show called *Leave No Trace*, which we had an eight-week process for, four weeks into the process we realised actually that what we needed to do was go and write it down. And actually if we had got that tool of writing an hour a day, then we wouldn't have had to give the other performer the week off.

THORPE: It's almost like writing is seen sometimes as a separate skill which needs time. Obviously there are kinds of writing that need time, there are kinds of movement that need time, there are kinds of any strand of performance that need time, but I think that there's still a slight misunderstanding of what craft is in terms of writing, and how much time craft takes. It takes a long time to build up experience to be the kind of writer that you want to be, or to create the kind of text you want to create. You obviously have to be constantly creating, but actually in the moment when you've got a certain small way down the road of developing those skills, it doesn't take as long as people think. So I think that's one of the reasons why people quickly shut it out from devising processes a little too much.

Although, I say that, but I work with fucking devising companies all the time and I never encounter any prejudice against the written word or the process, it's just that it's still seen as something which maybe needs to be more considered and less spontaneous than being in the rehearsal room together, and I don't think it does actually.

KELLY: I think that there can be sometimes a slightly unhelpful feeling that you're obliged to keep everyone busy all the time –

THORPE: I think that's absolutely right. Because as you're developing a company dynamic, there's this feeling that no one can slack off at any point, where what it needs to be is that you realise that the points where something useful is happening might not involve everyone. And I think that leads to a lot of bad feeling, particularly in young companies. Not necessarily in deliberately making people feel bad, but that creation in a devising way has to be the constant effort of that number of people for the same number of hours when they're all in the room together. And, I think, it's a big watershed moment for companies when they realise that no, the spotlight of where the effort needs to be falls in different places at different times, and that is OK. It's not lazy to step out and say 'That's your job now', or it's not controlling to say to everyone on the other side of the coin 'This is something that I know that I can do so I will do this'.

KELLY: And it's not helpful for the person who's doing this bit of writing if everyone else is kind of hanging around thinking 'We need something to do, come on, get on with it'. We had a really useful breakthrough day on *Parts for Machines* where we had that kind of morning of talking, we got a shape and we understood the timeline of the plane crash that we were talking about, and we understood which voices we needed to hear within that. And Chris said 'I want to have a go at writing this particular voice' or whatever, and I said 'I want to go and look at model aeroplanes in a shop'. So I went out of the studio and left Chris writing and I bought some model planes, and Chris said 'What are you going to do with that?'. 'I'm going to make it; I'm going to sit here and make an Airfix kit next to you whilst you're writing'. And we videoed me making the plane. And anyone who had come in would have thought 'Oh, well Chris is writing a show, but Alex is dossing about . . .'. But, actually, the visual engine of the show was born that day, because I felt it was all right to go to a toy shop.

THORPE: You're right, that was a really good encapsulation of it.

RADOSAVLJEVIĆ: How has your playwriting changed as a result of starting to work with people like Third Angel?

THORPE: Third Angel has allowed me to expand, particularly influencing the stuff that I do on my own. They do this wonderful thing of never acting – Third Angel don't act. You will stand up occasionally and you will tell the audience 'I am being this person now' and you would say words that that person would say, but for the most part when you are speaking to the audience you are a version of you speaking to the audience, and that's really influenced the way that I write. I can't really say that it's influenced the version of Robin Hood that I wrote last year for the Latitude Festival, that was iambic pentameter and a very different kind of thing, or the plays that I have written that have been about character. But what I think of as being possible to call a play has changed to much more encompass that idea that it is enough, if you're careful and you put in the work, to stand in front of people and talk.

Bibliography

Byrne, John (2011) 'How do I balance the interactive elements of site-specific performance and the scripted or planned aspects?', *The Stage*, 29 September.

Govan, Emma, Nicholson, Helen and Normington, Katie (2007) *Making a Performance: Devising Histories and Contemporary Practices*, London: Routledge.

Heddon, Deirdre and Milling, Jane (2006) *Devising Performance: A Critical History*, Basingstoke: Palgrave Macmillan.

Kelly, Alexander (2000) 'Third Angel: Class of '76', in A. Heathfield (ed.) *Small Acts: Performance, the Millennium and the Marking of Time*, London: Black Dog Publishing.

Miller, Daryl H. (2005) 'Chance encounter of the witty kind', *Los Angeles Times*, 11 February, available online at http://articles.latimes.com/2005/feb/11/entertainment/et-neutrino11 (accessed 19 December 2012).

Stanier, Philip (2010) 'The Distance Covered: Third Angel's *9 Billion Miles From Home*', in Alex Mermikides and Jackie Smart (eds) *Devising in Process*, Basingstoke: Palgrave Macmillan.

Third Angel
http://www.thirdangel.co.uk/home.php

Unlimited Theatre
http://www.unlimited.org.uk/home/

Part III
Ensemble and the audience

16 Sharing the experience of imagination

Mike Alfreds (Shared Experience, Method and Madness)

Mike Alfreds has run theatre companies in the US, Israel and the UK, as well as freelancing as a theatre director and teacher around the world. In 1975 he founded Shared Experience, which he ran until 1987. He was Associate Director at the National Theatre in 1985 and 1987–1988. In 1991 he took over the Cambridge Theatre Company, renaming it Method and Madness, and ran it until 1999. Since then, he has directed at Shakespeare's Globe, the RSC and internationally, as well as giving frequent workshops, masterclasses and seminars. Having discovered his love of theatre at the age of 10, Mike Alfreds has devoted more than 60 years of his life to it.

Alfreds is an actors' director. Sheila Hancock believed him to be 'the perfect director to coax a performance out of [her]', while Ian McKellen described him as 'one of the three best directors in the country' (Benedict 1996). In a Foreword to Alfreds' 2007 book *Different Every Night*, actress Pam Ferris notes not only the sense of freedom and personal growth an actor derives from Alfreds' approach, but chiefly 'the pursuit of excellence' that characterises his career journey (Alfreds 2007: xii).

Observing him in rehearsals in the mid-1980s, David Allen was struck by Alfreds' directorial style which was more akin to a 'coach', 'prompting from the side-lines' rather than 'working for results' (Allen 1986: 328). His ultimate aim as director is summarised as being about creating a 'world which has the soul and essence of the original play' (1986: 321), though it should be added that the same applies when he works on adapting prose.

In addition to his directorial creations and adaptations of novels, Alfreds has also made his own translations. In 2011, Alfreds translated Pierre de Marivaux's *The Surprise of Love*, which was directed by one of his past collaborators, Laurence Boswell, at Bath Theatre Royal. In addition to multiple BTA and TMA awards in the 1980s and 1990s for his productions of the classics, Alfreds' productions of Philip Osment's new plays were nominated for the Writer's Guild Awards three times, and awarded in 1993. His second book about theatre-making, *Story-Theatre*, is due to be published by Nick Hern.

This interview took place in November 2011 in London.

Interview

RADOSAVLJEVIĆ: It might be interesting to start with your own back-ground – how did you get into theatre?

ALFREDS: By the time I was 18 I had seen a huge amount of London thea-tre and read hundreds of plays. I acted at school and with a local ama-teur group. But at some point, I decided that I wanted to direct and, when I happened to move to the States, I trained as a director at Carnegie Mellon – or Carnegie Institute of Technology as it was called then. It had a very good theatre department with an intensive training programme for directors. Directors had to study everything: acting, voice, movement, make-up, playwriting, theatre history, thea-tre literature, design, lighting, stage management as well as directing. This was 1957–1960 – I graduated over fifty years ago!

We worked very long hours, we had endless projects. For our cos-tume design, we had to sit for hours in the library, tracing in minute detail examples of costumes and identifying them – a different period every week. We had to write long essays on comedy, tragedy, melo-drama and farce. As well as our actual physical productions, we had to direct a play on paper – a huge document with appropriate essays on the playwright, the play and its cultural frame and environment – design the sets and costumes and create a complete prompt book with meticulous blocking and sound and light cues. We had three acting teachers who taught in very different styles. One was an advocate of the then highly fashionable Method, which of course exerted the greatest influence on us. One was very old fashioned – she had starred in Eugene O'Neill's *Desire Under the Elms* in the 1920s. Her approach was all about blocking: we used to have to do these terribly compli-cated turns – you couldn't just walk upstage, you had to move in S-curves so that as much of your face was kept visible to the audi-ence. The third acting teacher was very pragmatic. He taught stage fights, a little bit of blocking, a little bit of motivation, a little bit of style, and slept with most of the co-eds.

We created and saw a lot of theatre – every two weeks we saw a triple-bill of one-act plays. Our work was very strongly analysed and criticised after performance. You were confronted by your directing

class and almost all the faculty throwing questions at you: 'Why did
you do it like that?', 'Why was the door there?', 'Why did you have a
door?', 'Were you meant to be indoors or out?'. And you had to justify
yourself in a very precise way.

I had directed quite a bit beforehand in a semi-professional way and
my instinct was pretty good. I can see that now. But there was a period
while I was studying when all my instinct died. I was determined to be
a very dutiful student, trying to follow all that we had been taught in
class. My shows were very correct but they didn't fly. And then suddenly – and much to my relief – some time later, my instinct returned,
hugely strengthened and supported by all this knowledge. And that
knowledge has stood me in good stead throughout my whole career.
I've a great deal to thank Carnegie Mellon for.

RADOSAVLJEVIĆ: When you finished your training, did you come back to
the UK?

ALFREDS: Not immediately, I worked in America for a while. I was
Artistic Director of a couple of provincial theatres. And then I felt
the urge to come back to England. Very interesting things seemed to
be happening here. In the 1950s the Royal Court had opened, there
were a lot of new plays and it all sounded much more exciting than
New York theatre, which by then was being overrun by musicals to
the detriment of drama, let alone new writing. I came back to the
UK and had the most horrible time. I couldn't get work. I had already
done about 40 productions, I'd trained and got a degree, I'd run two
theatres and it was as if I'd dropped off the Moon. At 28 I felt passé,
and there were about three years when I didn't work. I was very
depressed and totally discouraged. It was a very establishment, very
Oxbridge-dominated scene, and I became very bitter and twisted
about the whole thing.

However, a friend of mine was teaching at LAMDA and he passed
on to me a class he couldn't take. They liked what I did and I ended
up teaching at LAMDA steadily for five years. Teaching taught me
so much and formed part of how I think and work now. When I
started teaching, a lot of things that hadn't been clear to me when
I left Carnegie – Method confusions about objectives, actions and the
like – suddenly became absolutely obvious. In those three years when
I hadn't been working, my theatre brain – my unconscious – had been
free to quietly work things out.

One of the students happened to be an Israeli actress. Her husband
was an influential director who ran one of the best alternative companies in Tel Aviv. He invited me to do a production. It was a huge
success and I got flooded with offers. I am a totally non-devout Jew,

but I thought 'Well, maybe God's telling me to go and check out my Jewishness', and so I worked in Israel for five years. I had my own company in Jerusalem. The theatre was called the Khan. It was a sort of cave – a wonderful space. And I also freelanced in Haifa and Tel Aviv. What was brilliant for me was that they had very long rehearsal periods. In my very early days of wanting to be a director, I had started to read descriptions of the productions of Vakhtangov and Stanislavsky and Meyerhold – and it seemed like another world. They rehearsed for a year, they had the sets ready on Day One, they improvised, they worked all night long – you couldn't conceive of these wonderful dream conditions in the UK or the USA. Suddenly in Israel I had three or four months to do a show. Because of my teaching I'd already started to build quite an elaborate rehearsal process for myself, and so I was able to expand that, and I really made use of those months. I did some very good work and developed more and more of the process with which I now do my work here. So when I came back to England and founded Shared Experience, I had a lot of knowledge and skill and experience – and rehearsal methods.

Shared Experience was founded in 1975. And I ran it till 1987 – I did 13 years, then Nancy Meckler took it over when I went to the National Theatre.

RADOSAVLJEVIĆ: So you founded Shared Experience with the intention of working in this particular way?

ALFREDS: I had given myself a very clear brief. I'd been thinking about it so much, I kept going to the theatre and asking myself 'Why is theatre so boring? Most of the time it's awful. Why on earth are we all sitting here?'. This was back in the 1970s. 'Maybe theatre is dead but it just won't lie down'. And then I thought 'No, no, theatre has been going for 2,500 years. Why should it die now?'. And I literally made lists of what theatre had that nothing else had. There were two critical points. One was a cliché – 'It's live'. And the other was – 'The actors transform themselves into other people'. From those two facts I built my idea of the sort of theatre I wanted to explore: If the theatre is live, what does that mean? If it *is* live what's the point of staging something and telling the actors to do it the same way every night? Because if it's live one should be doing the opposite: allowing every night to be genuinely alive, open ended, spontaneous – like life! – and true to the moment.

You see, blocking imprisons the actor. It literally puts a block on them. Pre-rehearsing every move is a superficial and empty security. It's much better to have an inner security of 'I understand my character, my character's needs, my character's relationships, my character's use of space, my character's attitude to life'. Actors should be free to create afresh and truthfully every night, spontaneously, depending on the audience, on themselves and what they are discovering about the role. And nothing should be hidden – especially this wonderful phenomenon of actors transforming themselves.

So my brief to myself with Shared Experience was that shows had to live in the moment, the actor had to be free, and you had to see the actors transforming – they didn't go off and hide in the wings. They stayed on stage the whole time and transformed into different characters in front of the audience. What's more: the actor is the only element that makes the theatre live. The actor is the life of the theatre. Not the director, not the designers, not the lighting, not the playwright. The actor is what makes theatre theatre. And for my money the playwright provides material for the actor. Not: the actor serves the play.

At Shared Experience, the actors would work with nothing in an empty space – they wouldn't have costumes, there'd be no make up, set, props, there would be no musical instruments – nothing but the actors. There would be constant white light on both them and the audience; we'd all be in the same space.

RADOSAVLJEVIĆ: A bit Brechtian?

ALFREDS: Yes, a lot of people say it's very Brechtian, but it wasn't at all distancing or alienating. Quite the contrary. The actor says 'Hello, I'm an actor. Once upon a time' – and transforms into a character and we're in another time and place. Then the actor says 'And that's what happens to that character' – and we come back to our reality. It was very thrilling, and it was, I suppose, very revelatory for the audience. The actors had to learn all sorts of new skills. And the idea of an ensemble became an essential part of the vision.

Actors have to work together. Because if I'm live – I'm only alive because of my relationship with you. If we are playing a scene, I've got to play off what you give me. If I know what you are going to do before you do it, there can be no spontaneity, no surprise, no emotional truth, only warmed-up virtual reality from some time in the distant rehearsal past. The actors have to play off each other and they can't cling to past results. If they had a laugh last night which they desperately want to happen again tonight, you've got to say 'Well, you may not get it tonight, it doesn't matter, you'll get a laugh somewhere else'.

RADOSAVLJEVIĆ: How did you put the company together?

ALFREDS: A lot of students who had trained and built a language with me at LAMDA had, during the five years I'd been in Israel, started their own careers. I contacted those students that I'd really enjoyed working with and said to them 'Shall we form a company?'. That was the nucleus of the company. I started off with six actors, and I worked with relatively few over the 13 years. Some people would go for a while and new people would come in, and the original ones would come back; there was always a flow of people. But they had to be actors who were totally committed to working this way, and to touring – we toured endlessly, it was very hard work. They had to have good bodies, they had to have good voices, they had to play in different styles and find the truth of every style we played in. Everything had to be – not realistic, but truthful – and played with absolute immediacy. They had to be daring and generous and emotionally open.

RADOSAVLJEVIĆ: How did you train them physically?

ALFREDS: The Laban efforts I found very useful because they connected the inside and the outside. I love the whole principle that if I move in a certain way – and I believe in this more and more – that every gesture I make has some sort of an inner feeling, some emotion connected with it. We're holistic, our body, mind and feelings are totally interconnected. Our emotions are actually in our bodies, in our muscles. If I strongly point my finger at you – immediately I feel accusatory. I have no reason to, but the physicality evokes that particular sensation. The body is a repository of our feelings and memories. I started off very much influenced by the Method which was always working on the principle of 'inside-out'– which was a total distortion of Stanislavsky. Now I know you can also work from the outside in. Both are valid – this way, you don't limit yourself.

I did a lot of Laban, I did a certain amount of Michael Chekhov's work, and then I worked with brilliant movement and voice teachers whom I learnt a lot from. More recently I've done circuit training with the actors. That was extraordinary!

I'm a great believer in the body as a means of reaching the imagination and releasing spontaneous truth. If you want actors to do heightened work, they really have to have a way of accessing large feelings and huge physicality. So I developed a rehearsal process described in my book *Different Every Night*. The process is very detailed and complex. But when the actors get to performance, they feel utterly confident, because they know so much – they know and inhabit a world, they are layered with thoughts about the character, feelings, attitudes. If something goes wrong, they'll deal with it, they'll know how what to do. So, actually, nothing can go wrong for them. Because they are being true to the moment, not trying to cling to something that happened several weeks ago and no longer has much relevance!

The problem for actors is that they are always being asked for results, and if you're working out everything in advance, you're totally destroying any chance of tapping into your real creativity. So performances can be very efficient and very clever – the actors know what they are doing in a slick, efficient way, they know how to get my laugh, etc. – but that's very empty for me. I find that sort of acting (and that's most of the acting I see) completely stillborn.

The ensemble side of the work is quite simply about working together, genuinely together, which means being generous, open, knowing when to lead and when to follow, trusting yourself and your partners and going with whatever happens.

RADOSAVLJEVIĆ: I want to return to Shared Experience for a bit – how long were the rehearsal processes?

ALFREDS: They were long, twelve weeks or more – as long as I could get. And then we would go on tour and we would keep rehearsing and changing things while touring. So you could say a show was almost nine months of constant work, clarification, elaboration, detail, refining things, making the conventions we were using consistent.

RADOSAVLJEVIĆ: Did you feel supported when you founded the company in terms of funding?

ALFREDS: Oh, it was a good time then! There was a tremendously positive feeling in the air. There was money. The Arts Council wanted to support people and funded us generously. Then you even had the right to fail! The first five, six, seven years of the company were joyful. All parties involved were satisfied. The actors were pretty well paid and doing good work and being rapturously received so they were happy, the audiences and the venues were happy with the shows, and the Arts Council were happy because we were doing good shows and getting good audiences. It was, for a while, a little glimpse of perfection! I may be looking back with somewhat rose-tinted glasses, but I do remember that period being an incredibly joyful time for me. It's never been *quite* the same since.

RADOSAVLJEVIĆ: What were the most significant productions from that period?

ALFREDS: At the start of it I said 'Well, if I want to explore new ways of working I don't want to do a play – a play might lock us in old habits'. So we started out with storytelling. I'd had a little experience in Israel with *A Thousand and One Nights* – *The Arabian Nights*. So we started working with that rich material and ended up having three evenings of totally different stories – and each evening was in a totally different style. In addition, we did two shows for schools as well. So we had a repertoire of five shows. We'd just walk into a space and say 'Once upon a time . . .'.

The first show was very sexy, voluptuous, and the language very ornate and the actors extremely athletic; the second one was like a slapstick, shaggy dog story – which we did in a very confined space, the actors could only move within the width of the five standing together; then we did a series of tragic stories about people on a caravan to a mythical city to seek salvation, telling their stories on the way.

What was wonderful was that because we had time, and I was really very meticulous, we were able to work on techniques and skills that you would only dream about doing. I remember in my early years as a director, I'd go into rehearsals thinking 'Oh, we're going to do this, that and the other'. And suddenly it would be the dress rehearsal and I hadn't touched one of those wonderful things I told the actors on the first day of rehearsal. I'd never got round to them – we'd just been dealing with getting to understand each other on a very basic level. But with time, I could take a group of actors, and with each show we could go further and really work on very complicated skills.

Of course, there are problems with ensembles: people get tired, people get too familiar with each other, you have to encourage them to give each other distance. I had to learn that about myself too. In my enthusiasm, I was often far too much on top of the actors. I had to learn to step back and give them space. And I must say, the actors were wonderful. Off their own bat, they would come into a theatre early, discuss how last night's show had gone and, in the light of that, talk about how they should approach that evening's performance.

With an ensemble you've got the problem of relationships. When people are working intensely and intimately over a long period, there is inevitable wear and tear. You don't have to go to the pub for a drink every night if you don't want to. And you don't have to love each other – as long as you respect each other's work. On the whole, they worked amazingly, but there have been times when they got – justifiably – exhausted. And then they'd start to pick on each other's irritating little habits. And on me and mine!

RADOSAVLJEVIĆ: How long were you running the Cambridge Theatre Company?

ALFREDS: Nine years. Cambridge Theatre Company was what they call a middle-scale company, touring mainly to small towns, very provincial, very conventional. I set off with great hopes, and I had some nine, ten years of frustration. Nothing quite worked. The things I wanted to do, the audience didn't really want. They wanted very short shows that were nice and simple – with nice costumes and nice sets. But within that I did some good work. I had a marvellous collaboration with a playwright called Philip Osment, whom I'd worked with when he was an actor. He wrote some fine, fine plays for us. And I invited David Glass and Neil Bartlett to co-direct with me. I had been feeling stale and I wanted to see theatre through the eyes of some other directors I admired.

After the first four years, we had problems with the Cambridge local authorities, so, with the blessings of the Arts Council, our main funder, we moved to London, found a wonderful home with a beautiful rehearsal space and changed the name to Method and Madness. The first year was terrific. I could get back to having an ensemble again. I had four actors and we did three plays. I adapted a Thomas Hardy novel *Jude the Obscure*, we did *Private Lives* and Philip Osment wrote a play for the actors. It was a very good year – tough for them but they were very talented actors, very attractive.

RADOSAVLJEVIĆ: Who were the actors?

ALFREDS: Geraldine Alexander, Abigail Thaw, Simon Robson and Martin Marquez. It was the mid-1990s. I won a best director award for the three shows and the productions got nominated for awards. I thought 'Yes, I can really have an ensemble!'. I got so carried away that the next thing I did was to plan a three-year project. I managed to get 10 very courageous actors to commit themselves for that length of time. We planned to build a repertoire of five shows. We got the Arts Council blessing. And it was a disaster, because the venues didn't want the repertoire. They didn't want to co-operate with any new way of doing things. Our shows were accused of being too intellectual, too serious and too long. We struggled for 20 months and then we just weren't earning any money, weren't getting enough bookings, and we had to disband the company. Nobody wanted ensembles. The whole idea of companies and ensembles was dying.

Theatre is a most inefficient business these days. Many productions mean a group of people who probably don't know each other, have never worked together before and have no shared language, trying to create a complex phenomenon, a performance, in far too short a time. That's why so often everyone is cutting corners to get the show on at what looks like a presentable level. If theatre practitioners were surgeons, people would be dying in their hundreds on the operating table. And if we were engineers, bridges would be crashing down around us. To this day if I say 'What's your action?', and there are five people in the room, there'll be five different ideas of what an 'action' is. Or an 'objective'.

RADOSAVLJEVIĆ: Your work has often entailed adaptation?

ALFREDS: Yes, I do a lot of adaptations, because I find that a wonderful source for discovering new forms. Non-dramatic material, perversely, forces you to invent ways of working, and that can be very exciting – and refreshing. So it's exactly this: here's an empty space, here are the actors, how are we going to do this? Are we going to tell you about it, demonstrate it, act it out, live it? It demands that you look at all the possibilities for what would be the best way to make this piece of text work. Depending on the nature of the language and how the story is constructed, you say 'How can I take those literary devices and find equivalent theatrical forms for them in order to be true to both the spirit and word of the story?'.

What I do now with a novel is to trim it down to a reasonable length – I won't make any major decisions – I'll remove what clearly isn't necessary: repetitions, bits of plot that wander away from the main line. Then I'll work with the actors, and gradually we'll shrink it. What I try to do is not cut – but compress, distil the text. So instead of hacking the text to pieces, you reduce it like a good sauce, you retain the essence. It's a slower process, but this way you keep much more of the writer's unique voice.

The challenge for a production is to find a suitable physical, visual and aural three-dimensional world that will bring to life most appropriately the world of the language. So the form of the show was always what the content of the story and the language of the story dictated.

RADOSAVLJEVIĆ: And that's also a means of engaging the audience with the rules of the game.

ALFREDS: Yes, That's another big obsession of mine – the rules of the game, the conventions of this unique world we're creating. For me, that's what the rehearsals are about – discovering what the rules are for this particular game we're going to play. If it's football we can't use the rules for cricket or tennis for golf. I'm absolutely rigorous about conventions. If we're talking to the audience, how are we talking to the audience, why are we talking to the audience? Should the other character/actors know or acknowledge that someone is talking to the audience? And if so, why and how? Endlessly questioning our choices.

In *Bleak House*, we had six black chairs and we decided we were not going to turn them into objects, they would only be things to sit on. They could also be horses or carriages, or benches; put two together and this could be a bed, but they were always things to sit on. We decided on this because the story was so rich and so serious that we didn't want to distract the audience with whatever inventiveness or 'clever ideas' would have occurred if we had started to transform the chairs into what else was needed. It felt too cute or gimmicky. Also, chairs couldn't have been transformed into every prop that the story mentioned – so we would have ended up with a dissatisfying, messy mixture of some things being mimed and some being suggested by the way we handled the chairs. The objects that we needed to show were mimed very naturalistically. You try to create an artistic world with its own consistent rules and truths. And you need time to find the form. In order to be free you have to prepare. There's no freedom without discipline!

What I love about this sort of theatre is that, if you really work at it, you can make the audience see almost anything for themselves. With *Bleak House*, we just had those six black folding chairs, and we worked on a flat floor. But there are scenes where someone at the top of a staircase is talking to someone else at the bottom. And we found techniques for that illusion. We had to explore the physicality of how you do that. Often it wasn't at all what you'd do in real life. But the audiences really believed they were seeing someone on a staircase.

We worked in constant white light, no cues at all – and audiences were convinced we had a rich and complicated light plot – they swore they saw candlelight, gaslight, firelight, chandeliers, fog and so on. What they were doing was imagining worlds of their own; they saw their own show.

This leads me to what I haven't talked about yet that is so important – why live theatre can be so rich and fulfilling for the audience. If you keep things open, work on what is essentially an empty space, you allow the audience to create their own performance, imagine their own show. The audience becomes creative. Most productions I see, the audience are shown everything – this is what it looks like and this is how you've got to react, this is what it's about, cry now, laugh here. Whereas I'm not going to tell the audience how to behave or what to think or what the play is about – it's up to them. Nor will we show them a complete picture. We will give them the best we can of what we've understood from the material; we will suggest and let them create and see their own images and make their own interpretations. So every member of the audience sees the performance through their own personal frame of reference. Theatre is essentially metaphoric.

When I first started *Bleak House*, I asked myself 'How shall I do it?' – because it has so many strands and layers: it's very political, very satirical, it's also a thriller, a mystery story with a detective, it's also very comic. And there's the sentimental, very emotionally-felt story of a young girl growing up and finding her identity. It's also a savage attack on the iniquities of the law – a lot of the story is about people getting caught up in law cases which go on unresolved for generations, while people die waiting for money that never arrives. And you think 'Well, I could do a Kafkaesque production – very expressionistic. Or I could do the show in a sort of caricatured manner. Or I could do it as a piece of noir'. But I concluded any such choice would be reductive and we had to do everything that's in the novel to the best of our ability. What was gratifying is that people would come to me after the show and say 'Oh, what a wonderful thriller', and then somebody would say 'Oh, it was so funny, I haven't laughed like that for ages . . . ', and then somebody would say 'God, it's so politically right on now', and somebody else would say 'It's like Kafka, isn't it'. And a French woman, funnily enough, came up to me and said 'Thank you so much for allowing me to see my own show!'.

We called the company Shared Experience, because that was exactly what we did – we shared the experience of our imagination with our audiences. We suggested and evoked, and they ran with the suggestions and the evocations.

References

Alfreds, Mike (2007) *Different Every Night: Freeing the Actor*, London: Nick Hern Books.

Allen, David (1986) 'Exploring the Limitless Depths: Mike Alfreds Directs Chekhov', *New Theatre Quarterly*, 2(8): 320–35.

Benedict, David (1996) 'Alfreds' way: More method, less madness', *The Independent*, 29 May, available online at http://www.independent.co.uk/arts-entertainment/alfreds-way-more-method-less-madness-1349648.html (accessed 19 December 2012).

Shared Experience
http://www.sharedexperience.org.uk/company.html

17 An interactive ensemble

Greg Allen (The Neo-Futurists)

'Few theatrical works offer so much, so fast, with such theatrical intensity' (2010: 27). Such is Justin Maxwell's view on The Neo-Futurists' show *Too Much Light Makes the Baby Go Blind* – which has been running in Chicago continuously since 1988. The deeply aleatoric nature of the piece means that its content is never the same, even if its game-like conventions remain in place. Audience members roll the dice to determine their admission fee, and on their way in they are given a name-tag with a randomly derived name as well as that evening's menu of 30 plays which will all, ideally, be performed within the next strictly timed 60 minutes. The audience will determine the running order – and partly the success of the '30 plays in 60 minutes' challenge – by shouting out numbers as soon as each previous piece is finished. Meanwhile, the 30 numbers, hung on a clothesline above the stage, will be removed one by one as they are called. At the end, the audience will roll the dice to decide how many new plays need to be written for next week's show and they may even be consulted on which pieces should be replaced. If the house has sold out for the night, pizzas are ordered in and shared by all after the show.

The format, loosely inspired by the Italian Futurists, was conceived by Greg Allen, although the 'icky parts', as Maxwell calls them, such as the celebration of 'war, industry and fascism', were left out of the equation. In fact, Allen's initial political motivation was to run the company entirely based on consensus voting as the best way 'to buck Uncle Sam's capitalist system and create art' (in Love 2008: 30). Over the years, Allen has prefaced each show with a continuously changing manifesto, and in 2005 he published 'Greg Allen's 25 Rules for Creating Good Theater' – featuring also a 26th rule which calls for the breaking of rules (Allen 2005). These rules have also attracted the interest of Information Architects and online experience designers (Ojanen 2008).

Richard Schechner and Augusto Boal are cited as major theoretical influences too, leading Maxwell to conclude that the secret of The

Neo-Futurists' success is contained in the fact that '[they] are drawing on complex aesthetic traditions that have been shaping non-narrative art and theatre for nearly a hundred years' (Maxwell 2010: 27). Fundamentally, however, their work – which is epitomised by *Too Much Light . . .* but not restricted to it – is characterised by its ability to appeal to an ever-youthful audience. When The Neo-Futurists started a New York branch of the show in 1995, it was seen by the *American Theatre* journal as 'a staple late-night diet for hip, young audiences with attention-deficit disorders' (*American Theatre* 1997). Similarly, Maxwell argues that the show appeals to the Generation X's 'heavily mediated culture of indeterminacy'. Thanks to The Neo-Futurists' rejection of mimesis, character and illusion, the audience are given an opportunity to get to know and build relationships with the real performers – even if both the cast and the audience are constantly regenerating through the addition of new members. This familiarity, apparently, 'creates an environment where the audience is just as committed to a successful performance as the performers' (Maxwell 2010: 27).

The Neo-Futurists' main strength as an ensemble, therefore, is an ability to build and maintain a community. And the way they seem to do this is by fostering interaction.

The interview with Greg Allen took place in the company's base in Chicago – The Neo-Futurarium – in April 2012.

Interview

ALLEN: I went to Oberlin College, which was the first integrated co-ed college in America – it has a long history of liberal politics. I really got into theatre about half way through Oberlin. Before that I was a photographer and a filmmaker and a bit of a writer. So I came to theatre very late – my artistic existence was in the darkroom until then. The idea of being on stage in the light was pretty far from me. I got interested in theatre from the literature side of things, reading Beckett and Pinter and Albee.

I was accepted for a semester on a London programme, where I got to see 60 shows in London and Stratford, and that was very influential. When I returned I pursued playwriting and directing as well as performing. I graduated in 1984 and moved to Boston without any belief that I could continue in theatre.

RADOSAVLJEVIĆ: What exactly was influential for you in London?

ALLEN: I was always much more non-narratively driven, much more interested in experimental work. I wasn't terribly interested in straightforward, fourth wall theatre. I really sought out the fringe stuff from the big shots: from Royal Court to some of the more experimental shows at the National and the RSC, to lots of pub theatre and whatnot.

Not only did we get to see amazing shows but we also got to speak with amazing people. I got to see the Anthony Sher version of *King Lear* up in Stratford, the famous production with Michael Gambon, whom I didn't know at the time. *King Lear* has always been my bible so to speak, I've always held it as a kind of touchstone for my work. That was the production which set up Lear and the Fool as a comic duo: the straight man and the clown, and their relationship was the heart of the production. In the mock trial scene where Lear symbolically tries his daughters in the hovel, Gambon took a knife and stabbed Goneril who was represented by a pillow. But in that production he stabbed through the pillow and killed the Fool. So the Fool's famous line 'And I'll go to bed at noon' made total sense to me for the first time. That choice totally blew me away. To see really alternative views of theatre at such a high level was something I had never experienced before. I got to talk to Patrick Stewart, Judi Dench, Daniel Day Lewis. Everyone I talked to later became really famous! It wasn't just one production – the National's production of *The Good Soldier Schweik* with thirty-foot puppets, or *The Revenger's Tragedy* with Anthony Sher done in the round, was spectacular theatre.

RADOSAVLJEVIĆ: So eventually you got to Boston.

ALLEN: I moved to Boston saying 'OK, well, that was fun, theatre's done!', because you can't make a living in theatre in the States. But I found that I was still interested in it, and, since there was no theatre in Boston to speak of, I enrolled at the National Theatre Institute at the Eugene O'Neill Theatre Center in Waterford, Connecticut. They had a pre-professional training program for 14 weeks. I went there as a director, but during that time we studied everything from Peking Opera to jazz dance, playwriting to directing to costume design, I mean – everything. Even though I had entered as a director, I was very much encouraged as a playwright, and also as a performer. They said 'You have to decide which one you want to do'. And I was like 'Well, no, fuck that. I'm just going to be a theatre artist, I'm just going to do everything'.

I grew up near Chicago, a northern suburb, and hadn't thought that I would really come back. Not the happiest of upbringings in that I found the culture of the North Shore of Chicago very oppressive. But after the O'Neill I felt that I should go back home to Chicago to deal with my upbringing, and also, because this was the mid-1980s, it was the place to do theatre. Steppenwolf and Wisdom

Bridge and Remains and the Organic were all established new companies that were doing interesting work. So I moved back to Chicago in 1986 and started volunteering for these bigger companies doing backstage work. I was literary manager for the Organic, I was assistant casting director for Wisdom Bridge. In Chicago I took classes as well – I was taking a devising class at the Organic.

RADOSAVLJEVIĆ: Was it called 'devising' at the time?

ALLEN: It's a good question – it wasn't called 'devising'. It was 'production creation' or something like that – 'performance creation'.

The Organic was a long-time theatre company that had basically come to the end of its run by the end of the 1980s. It was big in the 1960s and 1970s under the direction of Stuart Gordon. He then went on to Hollywood to direct such infamous films as *Re-Animator*. He became this Hollywood guru – which is pretty funny! But he was famous for bringing sci-fi to the stage in the 1960s. Joe Mantegna and *Bleacher Bums* came out of the Organic too. So Organic had this kind of experimental history. I was in a show at the Organic and assistant directed shows at Wisdom Bridge and Remains, and then ultimately made a connection to someone at Stage Left who offered me the chance to create an off-night or late-night show. Stage Left was a little dinky storefront theatre, but basically a more politically-minded theatre company. And they'd been around maybe half a dozen years at that point.

When I was at the Organic taking these classes, I was very frustrated by trying to write the great American play with ten characters and three acts. So I latched on to this really short form. I was writing scenarios for theatre – three a day on a single sheet of paper – for months, and I also integrated Italian Futurist ideas. At Oberlin I discovered the Italian Futurists through Phil Auslander – who is a fairly big theoretician nowadays – he had a one-semester placement at Oberlin when our theatre history professor was gone. I was really turned on by the Futurists' fiery rhetoric and the idea of throwing everything out the window. The dynamism and the body madness and synthesis and simultaneity – all these different ideas were very inspiring. This short sensibility combined with my own beliefs in non-illusory theatre all came together.

During all that time – from London, through the end of Oberlin, through the O'Neill – I had been developing this performance theory of Neo-Futurism, although it wasn't called that at the time. So when I was offered the possibility to direct something off-night or late-night at Stage Left I said 'Well, what about this idea? This Futurist idea?'. I had heard that some cities have late night theatre, which didn't exist in Chicago at that time. So I opened *Too Much Light Makes the Baby Go Blind* as a late night show on 2 December 1988.

I was 26. In rehearsal I preached my beliefs in what theatre should be to my ensemble of friends and people who had auditioned, and came up with the idea of presenting '30 Plays in 60 Minutes'.

RADOSAVLJEVIĆ: Originally you wrote the whole script?

ALLEN: I did originally for the stage reading, but when I got my company together I said 'OK, we're going to be called The Neo-Futurists and we're going to write plays individually and bring them in'. We actually opened the show with some original Italian Futurist plays as well, or adaptations of them.

RADOSAVLJEVIĆ: So did the whole formula that you are using now come about at the same time, or did it evolve over time?

ALLEN: Really, I put it all together by opening night. The only thing that's changed, believe it or not, is we originally performed off a set list of plays that I would put together before the show. We did that for about two months until I realised: 'Why don't we just perform them in random order?!'. And then I invented the menu concept and the clothesline. That was in early 1989.

RADOSAVLJEVIĆ: What's the significance of the name-tags that the audience are given on their way in?

ALLEN: I was thinking about that the other day. To me it's an Ellis Island effect. When immigrants came to America, they would all get funnelled through Ellis Island in New York. They would come in with names that the people filling out documents had no idea how to spell. So they would horribly distort your name and make you 'Jane Wilson' or something. So I liked the idea that the audience would be assigned a new identity, a new start, when they came to the theatre. The name-taggers always wore headphones with blasting music so they couldn't actually hear what your name was. Also it was a nice task-orientated element that fit in with the aesthetic of the show. The original idea was that the people with the headphones tried as hard as possible to write down what they heard when you answered 'What's your name?', and just task-orientated-wise they had to put down the word that they heard in the song or what they made out of your name. So you get this nonsense name on your name-tag. It's devolved to become just silly names that the people give to you.

In the early days, we also brought the audience directly onto the stage before they'd sit in the audience – we would bring them out onstage and interview them as they came in before we let them sit in the audience.

RADOSAVLJEVIĆ: One by one?

ALLEN: Well, we would bring out up to five – it depended on how many interviewers we had – but we would interview them one by one.

We had a microphone so the audience could hear what we were saying. It was a way of also breaking down that separation of who's performer and who's audience. When we moved to The Neo-Futurarium that element had to go away. We were at Stage Left for about a year and a half, and we were at Live Bait for about two years, and then we moved here. So we went from 75–78 seats in each of those theatres to 150 seats. We tried to do it here, and it just took too long to get 150 people in – it just slowed things down way too much.

RADOSAVLJEVIĆ: Casting the ensemble members, did you look for a particular type of performer who was able to improvise, or did you look for a particular set of skills?

ALLEN: Never improvisers. We've never been improvise-orientated at all. I was just looking for interesting people basically, because, especially in the original ensemble, it wasn't necessary to have people with a theatre background. We had a singer in a rock band, we had an actor, we had someone who was a writer primarily, someone who was a performance artist. It was basically people at the beginning of their theatre career.

RADOSAVLJEVIĆ: Did they have to be able to write?

ALLEN: It's funny because in that original ensemble there was one guy who never wrote a single play, which is basically unheard of now. Now everybody writes and that's part of the job – although some people are more prolific than others.

RADOSAVLJEVIĆ: How did you select them? Did you have auditions?

ALLEN: I pulled in a couple of friends: I asked Karen Christopher and I asked my friend Robin MacDuffie to be part of the company. But I did have auditions. The auditioners were a bunch of people I'd never met before and there were some people I knew. I talked about the theory of Neo-Futurism and we worked together. I think, we used the Surrealist 'Exquisite Corpse' concept, and I said 'here's your script, explore it in sound and motion'. I did some exercises and tried to figure out what these people were like and what they could do.

RADOSAVLJEVIĆ: Would you say that there was some characteristic that they all had?

ALLEN: I guess what I was looking for was people who could be down to earth onstage. I wasn't looking for actors – I was looking for people who could express themselves very directly and honestly onstage.

RADOSAVLJEVIĆ: And in those early days were all the plays pre-written before they were rehearsed or were they ever devised together?

ALLEN: At that point we would rehearse every night, and we were performing only two days a week: Friday and Saturday, late night at 11:30. So there was some group devising involved where I'd give exercises and we would create something out of that, and we'd say 'Oh, this is cool, let's put that in the show'. The rest of the time it was the way it is now – where you write something and bring it in – though it wasn't as formalised a system as it is now. I was very much the direc- tor – I directed all the pieces, made the menu and put them in order.

RADOSAVLJEVIĆ: How did the rehearsal process unfold?

ALLEN: Early on we just agreed that we would premiere 10 new plays per week. But we were still using the rolling of the dice admission scheme, and it was just a dollar times what you rolled: so one to six dollars – which was much more pure and beautiful. Now it's nine dollars plus the roll. Then I came up with the idea of: why doesn't the audience roll the dice to determine the number of new plays each week – so we shifted over to two to 12 new plays every week. That also made us more random, and the random idea of the clothesline and the menu also made the show much more organic. We would rehearse just as we would do now: propose new plays, figure out what's going into the show, rehearse those plays. Early on we used to rehearse four times a week, then three times a week, then two times a week, and then by the time we left Stage Left, it was just once a week, which is what it is now.

We start on Tuesdays, at seven o'clock and go to like 10 or 11. We each bring in individual scripts, we share our titles at the beginning of rehearsal, then we distribute scripts to whomever we want to be in the piece. We read the plays going around in a circle until all the plays are read. Then we go around the circle again and each nominate a play to go into the show that is not written by us. You have to nominate someone else's play, and someone else has to champion your play for it to get into the show. If we need, say, nine plays this week, we go around the circle, each person getting to nominate a play until we have, say, seven. Then we go down the list of remaining plays, we dis- cuss all of them so every proposal gets feedback, and then we come up with some system for picking the last couple of plays. But at the end of that process we've got the nine titles that are going into the show. The way it is now is that the author of the play is then responsible for directing that play, and casting it. The leadership goes back to them, and we work through the play on its feet. In most cases the author is usually the central person in the play. Because there's this non-illusory element that runs throughout Neo-Futurism where we're always tell- ing the truth, it's hard to write plays completely from someone else's perspective. So then we stage all of them, the technician comes in, we do lights and sound, and we figure out who is to bring in the props that week. We get here Friday two hours before the show – hopefully everyone's memorised their lines by then. We run through those new plays, we rehearse them a couple of times with tech. We rehearse some of the old plays that still need a brush up. We do the show. The next night we get here an hour and a half before the show, discuss how the show went the night before, discuss all the plays by going through the menu, rehearse everything else we need to, and do the show. Sunday night we get here an hour ahead of time, everyone gives notes on how everything went the night before, we run anything we need to, do the show, and then by Sunday night two audience members will have rolled the onstage die, so we know what the total of the two rolls is and how many new plays we need to create for the next week.

RADOSAVLJEVIĆ: Are you still involved?

ALLEN: I'm now out of the ensemble. I'm doing other things, I've got lots of other projects I'm writing. I performed until the end of 2011.

RADOSAVLJEVIĆ: But are you involved in those meetings?

ALLEN: I'm not. The show really runs itself. I also have a company in New York, called the New York Neo-Futurists, I'm very hands off with them. I go out and train their new ensemble members periodically.

RADOSAVLJEVIĆ: Do you have to train the ensemble members in this form of short writing?

ALLEN: Well, now it's trial by fire. I teach three different kinds of Neo-Futurism Workshops: masterclass, collaborative creation, and site-specific. A lot of the students would go through these classes so that helps with finding new ensemble members. Nowadays newly cast ensemble members just come in and observe the show for a week, and then they're in. The thing is, now it's been going so long that there's a history, and we have published books of our plays, and people have also been able to see the show up and running. So it's not like starting from scratch, like in New York, or like it was here originally. When I start a company I do an intensive workshop or residency for at least two weeks. I teach Neo-Futurist residencies around the country, and a little bit abroad, where I work with 12–15 students for a couple of weeks – teaching them the Neo-Futurist methodology and then having them create their own work. By the end we have a show – not quite as elaborate as this one obviously – but a production where we put together a collection of short plays that we've created.

RADOSAVLJEVIĆ: They are very young – how many different generations of cast have you had?

ALLEN: I've lost track of how many generations we've had. What we do usually is: when we lose somebody from the ensemble or a couple of people, then we have auditions. And we've had auditions every year and a half to two years for 24 years, so I don't know what that comes out to. I think all together we have had about 65 Chicago Neo-Futurists. Phil Ridarelli, who's still an ensemble member, joined us in

1989 – he has come and gone since then a couple of times, but he's still part of the ensemble.

Usually, at any given performance, about half of the ensemble is performing – because the other half has to be able to tour, or are doing other shows with other companies. How many people were in the ensemble last night? Seven?

RADOSAVLJEVIĆ: Yes, that's right.

ALLEN: I think we have 12 in the ensemble right now. Four of them are brand new, six months old, so things turn over – just like the show itself turns over. I mean, it's a young person's show. It's a young audience. It's a young sensibility in terms of performing every week, every Friday and Saturday, until one o'clock in the morning . . .

It's interesting, because once it took off I was like 'I wonder how long I'm gonna be doing this?'. I was wondering if the audience would get older with me. But instead the audience has stayed the same age and I've just gotten older.

RADOSAVLJEVIĆ: How has the content changed over the years? How is the young person's sensibility different now from what you had at the beginning?

ALLEN: At the beginning it was a fairly angry show. It was very much 'Stick it to the man!'. I would come out as this MC and give a manifesto at the top of every show about: 'Get out of your seats and take part in the world' and 'Don't be voyeurs!'. So I remember it being fairly angry for a year or so, and slowly, I think, it's gotten more predictable, and more set in its ways. There're certain styles that people have latched onto. In terms of the writing it's hard to characterise it as going one direction or another – it's so individually based that each individual Neo-Futurist comes in and they have a certain style or a certain voice that they add to the show. Whenever we're casting, we're always looking for what we don't have. We'll cast someone who is primarily a clown or a mime, we'll cast someone who is primarily a writer or a performance artist or politically active or a poet. I forgot to mention that – when we first started there was always a strong poetry background to a number of the performers. The Poetry Slam started in Chicago, so we've had a couple of Poetry Slam performers in the show, as well as debate people. We occasionally had a couple of people with a background in improv, but very few actually.

RADOSAVLJEVIĆ: But there was always this idea of having 30 pieces in an hour so everything had to be really short?

ALLEN: Always, for *Too Much Light*. A year into *Too Much Light* was the first time we did another full length show. I did a piece based on *King Lear* called *Leary* with Karen Christopher and two other Neo-Futurists.

RADOSAVLJEVIĆ: And what form did that take?

ALLEN: That was very much a performance art piece that was resonating off of *King Lear*. I don't remember if there was actually any text from *King Lear* but it was kind of a deconstruction. I took a lot of text from lots of different authors – Edward Lear, Timothy Leary, Henry Rollins, Georg Buchner – telling the story of Lear through totally other means.

RADOSAVLJEVIĆ: And it was a full evening performance?

ALLEN: Yeah, it was an hour and a half. But I called that performance art. And then I did another solo piece called *Nothing*, and we did a piece called *09/09/90*, which was based on the news. We set the title before September 9, 1990, where we said 'Whatever's in the newspaper on that day we're going to write a show based on that and then perform it'. That had the format of short pieces too but often people get the mistaken sense that all of our work is short and broken up into tiny parts.

RADOSAVLJEVIĆ: In what way was *Leary* manifesting the principles of Neo-Futurism?

ALLEN: We were very much ourselves even though we were representing the characters of Lear, Cordelia, Reagan – as we called Regan; he was called 'Reagan the Fool'. So it was kind of a conglomerate – it wasn't at all a narrative throughline.

RADOSAVLJEVIĆ: Which year did you move to The Neo-Futurarium?

ALLEN: I think 1992, so this is our 20th year here.

RADOSAVLJEVIĆ: And how did you end up here?

ALLEN: Theatre Oobleck is my favourite theatre in Chicago. Also a total ensemble who devise their own work with playwrights and then use the ensemble to embellish the work. They'd found this space and held it for a year but they had always been itinerant before then – and after that actually – and they found holding down a space was just too much for them. After a year they were going to give up their lease so I said 'I think we'll take it'. I pitched it to my ensemble saying 'You know, we could have our own space for the same cost that we're already paying for a late night space twice a week'. So we went for it. It was a risky proposition, but not too risky – doubling our seating capacity, and ten times the space. So we moved in here, I redesigned the theatre to be lengthwise – which was what we had at Stage Left – a shallow wide space which was very conducive for the clothesline, and nobody in the audience is more than ten feet away.

RADOSAVLJEVIĆ: What did you go on to do when you started to develop your personal career?

ALLEN: I devised and directed about 28 shows here for The Neo-Futurists. My show that just closed was called *The Strange and Terrible True*

Tale of Pinnochio (The Wooden Boy) as told by Frankenstein's Monster (the Wretched Creature). That was my 28th production for the company. I did a show with Theatre Oobleck called *The Complete Lost Works of Samuel Beckett as Found In An Envelope (partially burned) In A Dustbin in Paris Labeled 'Never to be performed. Never. Ever. EVER! Or I'll Sue! I'LL SUE FROM THE GRAVE!!!'*. It was a hit at Edinburgh about 10 years ago, and then went on for a three month UK tour. It's had eleven different international productions.

RADOSAVLJEVIĆ: It's really interesting that you actually cited the RSC as one of the formative influences, considering that your work is very rooted in the alternative, avant-garde practices.

ALLEN: But even then, I think, the English sensibility is so much more experimental than American. Most of what we do is very straightforward, narrative, realism-based in America and just seeing these alternative takes on the classics really opened my eyes to what you can do even with a known work. One of the early shows I directed here was *The Revenger's Tragedy*. We did *The Neo-Futurist Revenger's Tragedy* where all of the actors were up against the back wall with their name and all the names of their characters written on the chalk board behind them. When a character would die, they'd slash it off the chalk board. We had one wig for the whole show, so they kept throwing it around to whoever needed the wig, and also I put an Interlocutor onstage to answer questions from the audience at any given time. The Interlocutor would decipher what's going on, give plot synopsis. So it was a production with footnotes onstage, very self-conscious, very self-aware.

RADOSAVLJEVIĆ: So the blackboard is really part of the performance space?

ALLEN: It has gotten to be that way. It was put up for a show that one of our ensemble members, David Kodeski, did a long time ago and we really latched onto it and liked it. Back at Stage Left when we opened, one of the things we did was give the audience chalk at the beginning of the show and say 'Design our set'. So before the show, the audience would be drawing all the stuff on the back wall in chalk because it was just a blank wall, and then we would perform in front of their drawings. That was really cool, I liked that a lot.

RADOSAVLJEVIĆ: So it's become a bit less interactive than it was at the beginning?

ALLEN: In some ways it has – in that the initial framework around the show has become less interactive. I think it was much more interactive early on. Even the individual plays were much more dependent on the audience being there and taking part or responding. We try to keep a certain balance and a certain voice of interaction in the show, still. Just the number calling keeps it pretty alive.

RADOSAVLJEVIĆ: It is actually interesting that your audiences are very willing to interact.

ALLEN: Our audiences have become so willing to interact that often when we are doing other shows here their instinct is to jump up and take part. I did a production of *70 Scenes of Halloween* at one point, where there was an actress knocking on a door saying 'Let me in, let me in', and one of the audience members jumped up and opened the door! And it was like 'Thanks, can you close the door?'. It's part of the culture of coming to a Neo-Futurist show, knowing that you're going to be an active participant.

RADOSAVLJEVIĆ: Have you been associated with other ensembles at any point in your career?

ALLEN: I've done recurring work with Oobleck, with the Splinter Group which was a Beckett focused company, or just on my own. My magnum opus was *Strange Interlude* at the Goodman downtown, the biggest theatre in Chicago. *Strange Interlude* is Eugene O'Neill's nine-act, seven-hour show, 350 pages long.

RADOSAVLJEVIĆ: Very opposite to the form you've developed here!

ALLEN: Yes, that's the great thing! And yet still very Neo-Futurist: interactive, self-conscious, the actors were very much themselves presenting the show. We got hecklers, we had people standing up and screaming at the stage during the show, which was pretty funny. Other people thought they were an audience plant, and I was like 'No, these people are genuinely very pissed at what I was doing to their beautiful play'. And it got standing ovations every night.

Bibliography

Allen, Greg (2005) 'Greg Allen's 25 Rules for Creating Good Theater', available online at http://jhorna.wordpress.com/2007/11/24/greg-allens-25-rules-for-creating-good-theatre/ (accessed 19 December 2012).

American Theatre (1997) 'Too Many Plays', *American Theatre*, 14(4): 5.

Love, Bret (2008) 'New Visions in Artistic Direction', *Stage Directions*, 21(5): 30–1.

Maxwell, Justin (2010) 'Welcome to Your Neo-Future', *American Theatre*, 27(2): 25–7.

Ojanen, Karri (2008) 'User Experience Design is About Creating Good Theatre', *Threeminds*, 12 November, http://threeminds.organic.com/2008/11/user_experience_design_is_abou.html (accessed 19 December 2012).

Orel, Gwen (2005) 'Critic's Pick: *Too Much Light Makes the Baby Go Blind*', *Backstage*, 8–14 December, 46(49): 42.

The Neo-Futurists
http://www.neofuturists.org

18 'Creating safe emergencies'

Phelim McDermott (Improbable)

In 2002, a production of *Shockheaded Peter* received four Olivier nominations and the Award for Best Entertainment. It was revived several times following its initial West End and Broadway runs, but its co-creator Phelim McDermott summed up its greatest achievement as follows: 'it's in the West End, and yet you can't really say who wrote it' (in Logan 2003).

Improbable was founded in 1996 by actors Phelim McDermott and Lee Simpson, producer Nick Sweeting and designer Julian Crouch. The three artists had previously collaborated on a number of regional shows, and in the same year, at the West Yorkshire Playhouse in Leeds, McDermott and Crouch conceived *Shockheaded Peter*, together with a cast of actors and the cult band The Tiger Lilies.

Collaboration, liveness and playfulness are held up as the key values of the company's way of working and are often registered by critics as their distinguishing feature. Evans notes that 'Improbable Theatre is interested in a partnership with every person present' in a way which combines Brechtian 'respect for the audience' and a tendency to 'court' them 'as playmates' (Evans 2004: 317). Meanwhile, tracing the company's 'performative DNA' to 'the specifically British sense of cerebral silliness of music hall and Monty Python', Remshardt concludes that by watching an Improbable show 'the audience has attended not merely theatre but theatre-in-the-making' (Remshardt 2002: 29).

Since 2005, Improbable has introduced another strand to their work which could be described as cultural activism. These events, known as Devoted and Disgruntled, have run at least once every year, giving all interested parties an opportunity to engage in a conference-like discussion about theatre over a weekend. Though they might have sometimes led to an impression of a 'constant fractious rub between idealism and pragmatism' (Trueman 2011: 11), the Devoted and Disgruntled meetings have also reconnected with the ancient function of theatre as a civic forum – placing the responsibility for theatre's survival in a shared space between the theatre-makers and the audience.

An intense interest in collectivism eventually drew McDermott to Philip Glass' opera about Ghandi *Satyagraha*, partly prompted by an open invitation from the English National Opera (ENO) in 2004. Following an encounter between McDermott, Crouch and Glass – which Glass experienced as a moment of instant recognition (Cote 2008: 22) – Improbable went on to create another transatlantic success. *Satyagraha* premiered at the ENO in 2007 and transferred to the co-producing Metropolitan Opera in New York a year later. Respective revivals of the piece were staged in 2010 and 2011.

This interview took place in July 2011 in London.

Interview

MCDERMOTT: The ensemble is a hot topic for me. Sometimes I am frustrated about how people talk about the ensemble. Very often people have an idea that it just means having a group of actors for a certain amount of time. And I think that's a surface level idea of what an ensemble is or potentially could be. We haven't necessarily had the same group of actors, but at the start of the process, even if it's a short process, most of the work that I've done over the years has been about ensemble and how to work together to create something where the group mind has an identity and a voice of its own (rather than me as the director saying what to do, or even having a collaboration in the sense of a group of people all competing to find out what the best idea is). Very often a devising process or a collaboration process isn't necessarily ensemble, because sometimes my experience within those processes has been that the people who have the loudest voices, who can argue for the best idea, carry that idea through. And that's not really what I think good ensemble is.

This issue – how to collaborate and what it really means – is a lifetime practice. Our journey, working with Open Space, has informed that practice where the role of the facilitator is to be totally present in the moment and invisible. The idea that as a director you put yourself out of a job has been part of our work for years and years.

RADOSAVLJEVIĆ: How have you managed the notion of leadership of the company as a team of Artistic Directors?

MCDERMOTT: It's been a challenge because as artists you grow and you change, but I think understanding something about the journey around Open Space and understanding something about how organisations work has been essential to the idea of reinventing what the company is. If a company stays together more than seven, eight years, it has to go through a cycle of rebirth in some way. We had a process seven or eight years ago when we reconfigured and came out at the other side, and I think at the moment we are going through a similar rebirth. It's very hard to continue the growth of a company if you hang on too much to its identity or its sense of self – your ego has to go through some kind of humiliation process if you're going to come through to the other side. Or it stops and becomes something else. And there's a big lesson in the Open Space practice, because it's a set of principles and a set of values about understanding that we are not in control. There's a self-organising principle happening, and a lot of the time the creation of shows, the creative process is about a conversation with that. And if you try and hang onto your own side of the conversation too strongly, life and other people's impulses will work to reorganise you.

RADOSAVLJEVIĆ: Can you describe how Open Space works? And how is it used in Devoted and Disgruntled?

MCDERMOTT: Devoted and Disgruntled uses Open Space, but that set of principles and that way of working was originally created to work in business, corporate contexts. It's been used by activists, there is a strand of it called Practice for Peace. The guy who created it, Harrison Owen, says he doesn't necessarily know why and how, but whenever you Open Space somewhere, peace breaks out. I was drawn to it because I read his book about it. There were certain things in it that I realised were describing what we already did and we'd been trying to do in our creative process. The politics of theatre, the things that are frustrating around management and producing, I'd seen as very difficult to deal with as an artist. And I saw that this process, which was a rehearsal room process, could also deal with these other challenges. So stepping into that, starting that journey and then going back into the creative process was really exciting.

RADOSAVLJEVIĆ: How does Open Space work? What are the main principles?

MCDERMOTT: You can describe it very simply and say: it's about putting the whole agenda up on the wall from the people who turn up, creating a market place, and just going to work. It's basically: get all the issues out, and work on the issues that you care about. But there's a series of four principles. It's like a big improvisation game. Harrison says 'They are descriptive not prescriptive'. They are not rules, they are only describing what happens in life anyway, it's just we're very skilful in getting in the way of those things. The principles are:

- *Whoever Comes Are the Right People* – So you don't worry about who you think should be there but isn't, it's the people who care about that issue. It works on the bigger scale if they come to the Open Space, but it also works on the principle of the sessions that people call. It may be 50 people that turn up, it may be two people, or it might be one person – they are the right people to be working on this issue, because they care about it. So you don't have the issue of someone in the room saying 'Oh, we shouldn't be talking about this'.

- *Whatever Happens Is the Only Thing That Could Have* – You don't talk about what should have happened: 'If only we'd done this, if only we had this', you check into the reality of what the situation is and you work from there. All these things can be applied to an acting company and to audiences: whoever in the audience comes are the right people, you don't worry about who should have come. The reality of the situation: 'We've got this much funding, we have this many performers, we only have this space to work in', and so on.

- *Whenever It Starts Is the Right Time* – There may be a clock that says 'Timetable – we should work on this at this time'. That's not how creativity works, it has its own timetable and our sense of our own clock, our own body clock, our own being has a timetable which is more seasonal – it has a growth and it has a falling off, if we can follow this more, then we'll be more creative and stop when we need to stop, start when the time is right. If it says 'The show starts at 7:30' – if you're in Italy, it doesn't necessarily mean that: the show starts when it starts, whenever it starts is the right time.

- *If It's Over, It's Over* – So if you have an issue, and in 15 minutes you've dealt with it, you don't keep working just because it says the session is an hour and a half. You stop. That's the four principles.

There's now a new principle which has only happened in the last month, which is *Wherever It Happens It's the Right Place*, which refers to how there's work that might happen during that time and in that venue, but it doesn't stop at that, it goes out into the world and the work continues. It's not place- or event-specific – Open Space happens everywhere and anywhere.

There's one law, and the law is *The Law of Two Feet*, the law of mobility which means, you don't stay anywhere if you are not learning or contributing, and if you are not happy about where you are – you must leave and go where your time is being used well. If someone is boring you or you are frustrated, or you have an idea, you move, so the whole system keeps moving like a big hive. And also, you can go outside: Open Space is life.

Harrison says a great thing: 'The good news about Open Space is: it works, and the bad news is: it works'. Because it really reveals what's happening. So for an organisation that's a top down organisation it's really challenging. If the people at the top want to continue believing they're in control and if they have an agenda they want to push through, they may find that something else is emerging. I feel that all those things relate very much to our experience as a company in devising and creating an ensemble. Because ideally the best shows are the ones where you held the space and actually there have been things that emerged and nobody had an idea of where they came from. Very hard to go 'Who actually had that idea?', which is fantastic because everyone is surprised. That's when true ensemble comes about. In that place, it's not 'me', 'you, 'good idea', 'bad idea', it transcends that and goes deeper than that. I could put six people on stage and go 'Follow each other, follow your signals and see what's happening', and you can see it: if one person goes 'We should all do this' and everyone does – it's got no energy, no life. But if something happens *between* people in the space – it's got an amazing energy, and it leads people into the unknown and into the place where they are more vulnerable, so they are more awake, they are more present on stage and something happens that's never happened before, and no one came up with the idea.

I was listening to the poet David Whyte and he was talking about the Romantic poets – Keats, etc. – and he said they talked about two different kinds of imagination: the first imagination and the second imagination. The imagination where you come up with a new idea or a clever idea, is actually what they would call the second imagination, and the first imagination is the creation of an image within oneself, which holds the space for these other things to come through – which I think again is what ensemble is amongst people. It's the holding of an image together in which new things are given birth or are midwifed, which could never have happened if those people had not come together.

RADOSAVLJEVIĆ: Is this holding of an image together where the director has their own role to play?

MCDERMOTT: They have their own role to play in maybe saying 'Here's an intention, we don't know what it is yet, but together let's create an image that we feel within ourselves that can lead us somewhere'.

I think shows where there is a sense of a shared image between and within people have the effect that's beyond individuals or the sum total of individuals.

RADOSAVLJEVIĆ: How does that work in rehearsal?

MCDERMOTT: Sometimes it does and sometimes it doesn't. Very often it would be like fishing. The things that are in the air that the show might be about are talked about or maybe improvised, or there might be a moment where suddenly someone catches something and they do something and everybody's following! You don't wait, you just go with that impulse, you feel the impulse – and that's a learnt thing. I would say, Improbable as a company have learnt how to do that. And if we bring people in, that's what we are training people to do. It's more like sports training than it is 'Now we work on this bit of the text'.

RADOSAVLJEVIĆ: Could you summarise what your training of the new members consists of?

MCDERMOTT: No, because it's different every time. That's the interesting thing – there's a set of skills and tools that we might have taken from different practices. They were heavily influenced by the work of Michael Chekhov in the beginning and the research that I did in that, reading his work and finding my own way to teach it, working with atmospheres, working with psychological gestures. That work then combined with Keith Johnstone's work *Impro* and improvisation games. A big influence has been a guy called Arnold Mindell who was the subject of a show we did called *Coma* – about working with people in extreme and comatose states near death. He invented Process Work, which is a psychotherapeutic forum work, applied in lots of different contexts.

RADOSAVLJEVIĆ: How does that work?

MCDERMOTT: Lots of different ways. I did an intensive training in Portland, Oregon. There is a four-year – sometimes five-year – training in the practices of Process Work. It's a way of following the dreaming – using dreams, body symptoms, relationship conflicts, all these things that are the secondary signals of the world as opposed to the primary signals, primary processes.

So in working on a show, we say 'OK, we are going to work on this show and it's about this' and we set off – and then lots of things happen that are secondary things that aren't in our plan. Rather than ignoring those and trying to push them out, we would pick them up and use them. On a simple level, we might have a day's rehearsal and someone might have an accident on the way to rehearsal, or they might arrive late because something has happened, or someone might interrupt the rehearsal. Instead of ignoring that, we would pick that up and use it. We'd say 'OK, what does that signal mean?', and we'd represent it in different ways, try and find a mythical story underneath it.

Very often in a process there will be synchronicities that happen that are like little signals. For instance, I did some work on a show called *Beauty and the Beast* recently with two performers – one is a burlesque performer and the other is a guy called Matt Fraser who is a thalidomide and an actor who is active in disability rights. We're working on their show *Beauty and the Beast*, and we are looking at shadow play. Julie says 'Oh, I brought this shadow puppetry thing from France' – and it's little puppetry cells with pictures from fairy-tales which you put in a little box and they make shadow play. And in one of them there's a picture of a crow, and it's got this little pink thing in its beak, and then we looked out of the window and we saw a black crow and it had a pink feather in its mouth, and we went 'Oh, that's like something that we've been talking about. That's weird'. Now, there's something in that. A quality or a signal, that could be unfolded. And it might be unfolded into a way of playing, it might be unfolded into a character, it might be unfolded into a strategy of how we work: 'What is the message of the crow and the pink feather? What is this thing, this dark thing connected to death that's got this soft beautiful pink thing? It's paradoxical – and maybe the show needs that quality?'. The story of the *Beauty and the Beast* is in this crow and the feather. Very often those things get you to go 'Oh, yes, that's interesting, now let's get back to work'. And we would try, if possible, to pick those things up more.

I think the practice of the ensemble is to find out what the group's secondary content is. As the director, I may sit down and say 'I think that this play is about this', and I have a concept of what the show is about and it's a very intellectual concept. But actually the group discovers that in the process of putting on *Hamlet* or *Macbeth* something else is being dreamt up in the group that's got nothing to do with it, and these strange things – there's gold in them.

RADOSAVLJEVIĆ: How long are your rehearsal processes?

MCDERMOTT: Usually six weeks if we are lucky. But often we'd have a pre-period where we get together and work for say a week, and then another week, and then we'll have an intensive rehearsal. Very often the show won't be put together until the very last week. But we'll work on shared skills, shared ways of working, working with space, with improvisation games – and in a way it would be training people up so they can put a show on really fast.

RADOSAVLJEVIĆ: Can you discern any particular stages in rehearsal?

MCDERMOTT: There is the stage at the beginning when everyone goes 'Hurray, this is how I always wanted to work – it's marvellous!'. And then there's the stage when people realise we mean what we say and we genuinely aren't going to fix things until much later than other people. And that's very often a slightly painful process. People sometimes fall in love with us and then fall out of love with us. Because in this process of people taking responsibility for themselves there comes a point where they say 'Yes, but what do I do', and we say 'Well, you have to decide what you do – it's your decision'. And it will be different today from tomorrow. Sometimes we've done shows where it's not set at all. We did A *Midsummer Night's Dream* and the scenes were not set. So they could play them any way they wanted – differently each night. That's a challenge if one person goes 'I'm not playing'. This is the difficulty in the ensemble. Because ensemble is a thing which actually exists only because people believe in it. And if one person says 'It's not going to work', they'll be right. Because it will drop to the level at which the limitation of the belief is. That's the challenge of this process – the idea that what might be happening between people is more interesting than what you can do on your own. Some people just find the vulnerability in that very difficult. And then some people have a breakthrough.

RADOSAVLJEVIĆ: I understand that the main principle here is going with unanticipated circumstances, but how do you deal with situations that might jeopardise the show itself – what happens if you have people dropping out?

MCDERMOTT: In a way, the company are trained up to deal with that more than other companies would be. In a way the process is almost a process which ensures that accidents will happen, hopefully. And hopefully the audience are a surprise and you're creating a space in which things can unfold that haven't unfolded before. Sometimes that works in amazing, surprising ways – *Shockheaded Peter*, for instance. We hadn't finished the show before the first night in front of an audience, and lots of accidents happened and then they ended up being in the show.

Creating safe emergencies is an exciting thing, and it's a thing that theatre can do better than anything else. Better than film, because the film's finished – it's quite hard for a film to change its reaction in response to the audience's reaction, unless you go through a process where you keep editing once you've shown the film. Similarly the TV has very crude means of buttons. But this very simple thing that theatre is, has a very sophisticated system of feedback – which works on the simple levels of words and what we see, but also on much more intuitive levels of atmosphere, the collective mind – and the collective conversation that happens can bring forth things from performers that they'd never known they could do.

That is why I think that theatre, if it becomes more like itself, will be a more and more important thing as the world changes. I'm interested in this potential with the Open Space – that these four simple principles and a law create an incredibly sophisticated system. Which is what we see in nature, too. The things that happen in nature that self-organise, operate on very simple rules, but they become very sophisticated. A flock of starlings, or birds organising themselves, for example. There's a very simple system that creates that, and the simpler and more elegant that system is, the more sophisticated it can be. It's not about creating a system which can get as complicated as it possibly can in order to control things – which I think is generally how our management and organisation systems work. It's about how we can engage with the unknown on incredibly sophisticated levels, and it involves giving up something.

RADOSAVLJEVIĆ: As a leader with that sort of a leadership style, how do you deal with the stresses of the unanticipated results?

MCDERMOTT: This is what I've learnt from Process Work and from what we call the World Work as the group process. It's interesting because it relates to Michael Chekhov and his work with atmospheres. Let's say the atmosphere is what exists in the space between us (and the atmospheres of different places have a profound effect on us). As an actor in a rehearsal process – I could in my imagination create this café on stage with all the intuitive signals I give off by imaging the atmosphere of this.

Something that I learnt from World Work is that the atmosphere of a space in relation to people and organisations is created by the roles that are in the space. For instance, if you walk into a church, Michael Chekhov would say there's an atmosphere in that space that will have an effect on you, almost like the gas in the air, you'll feel it on your skin. But that atmosphere is created by the roles present – so it might be the priest, it might be the people who are religious, who are praying, but then if you go on a more profound level, if you look at that crowd of people, within that crowd of people there will be the role of the person who is deeply devout, there will be the person who doesn't believe in God, there will be a young child who doesn't know what this thing means. Also in World Work they talk about 'ghost roles' – so ghost roles would be the things that are spoken about but not present. A ghost role might be God, a ghost role might be the dead in the church, the ancestors, the children. If you are working on an issue in World Work, let's say racism, one of the ghost roles very often is the 'racist' because it's talked about but – where is the racist? In World Work you embody those roles and bring them in, and a shift in atmosphere happens when you bring those roles in. In a creative process, while creating a show, one of the ghost roles often is the audience. 'What are the audience going to think?'. They're in the rehearsal room present, but unspoken. The critics, the ghost role of the people who have given you the money to do this show, the ghost role of your last show – these are all present. So if an atmosphere becomes difficult or oppressive, one of the ways to shift or relieve that is to embody those roles and bring them in and say 'OK, what does this role want to say?'. The role of the critic might have something to say about the last show you did and this show: 'I hope it's going to be better than your last show'. If you represent them in the space, this can shift an atmosphere.

I had a moment with a chorus in the process of putting on *Satyagraha*. It's an opera about Ghandi and 'satyagraha' is his way of changing the world through the force of love and the force of truth – 'truth-force' it means. In his conflict with the British Empire, he was actually saying to the people 'In order for this to change, we have to use this force, which is what's between us' – ensemble again! This is interesting, because in the process of putting on a show, you have to address this in some way. First time I worked at the ENO, first time I worked on an opera, so I went 'I know, I'll have a day with the chorus. I'll get them working well as an ensemble and it will be great. I'll get to know them and they'll enjoy it'. They came in, and there were more than 40 people there. They were all: arms crossed – and it was a really tense situation; at that time, people were being laid off at the company because of the cuts. So I thought 'I can't go with the plan I had, I have to address this. I need to say what's going on here in the room. There are some roles here creating this atmosphere so I'm going to speak them'. And I said 'If you feel an affinity with this role, come and join me'. In World Work, you are encouraged to switch and fill the other side. And I stood in different parts of the room saying 'Why are we working on this when we could be working on this incredibly difficult music', and 'Who is this guy, I don't know anything about him' – I put these different roles and different voices on, and then I put one in the space where I said 'I don't even want to be here, I want to go home now'. And 25 people came and filled this role in! Basically I was trying to fill out how they were dreamt up to be in this role 'Who is this direc-tor?'. It ended up with me and one guy in the interaction where I was saying 'I want to try and get to know you, how can I do that?', 'Well, if you wanted to get to know us you could have had a drink in a pub with us', 'Are you asking me to come for a drink in the pub?', 'Yeah, I'm asking you to come for a drink in the pub' – and underneath this process there was something trying to happen about meeting. I had a production meeting, and I walked out thinking 'I'll see if they are waiting in the pub for me', and they were like 'Is he really gonna turn up in the pub?'. And there were two or three people there and we talked, and they ended up being my closest allies in supporting this thing through into something that they were ultimately very proud of and cared about and were working on as an ensemble. But to be brave enough to do that, I've only learnt that through a continual practice of going 'I have to say this', and finding the way to do it.

RADOSAVLJEVIĆ: There is also something about being able to be aware of it going on at that moment in time. Because most of the time one becomes aware of things with hindsight.

MCDERMOTT: That's why I say it's like fishing. Because it's relaxed but very awake, so that you are ready to go and grab it.

RADOSAVLJEVIĆ: And it's about trusting your intuition.

MCDERMOTT: Yes. And trusting the bit of oneself that's connected to the dreaming, that's underneath things. And trusting that if you follow that path, which is an unknown path – it's a path of crumbs and you have to pick up the crumbs – the footing will appear for you. And it does. If you've done it enough times, it's hard to ignore it. Because you have to be true to yourself. Improbable's journey has been about trying to walk that path more congruently, more and more. And new versions of it have come up.

RADOSAVLJEVIĆ: I was just going to ask you to go back to the beginning of Improbable's journey and what your respective backgrounds have been in terms of training, how you met and started working with each other?

MCDERMOTT: The person I worked with first was Lee Simpson. He's one of the Comedy Store players, so he works as an improviser. When we had no money or funding, basically what paid our measly bits of food was doing improvisation gigs above pubs – doing comedy gigs to pave the way. That's one of the interesting throughlines. It's still there and I still do the Comedy Store now and again with Lee, and it's interesting because it's a crucible. There's people there who are not that interested in theatre, who turn up and go 'Make us laugh'.

RADOSAVLJEVIĆ: So this was early 1980s?

MCDERMOTT: Early 1980s, mid-1980s. I went to Middlesex Polytechnic and I did a Performing Arts degree in Dance, Drama and Music. But there was a sensibility on that course around having an agency in creating your own work – which I think I would never have had if I'd gone to Drama School. I left college in 1985, and I had my own company when I left, with a woman called Julia Bardsley. It was called Dereck Dereck. It existed for about two or three years and then she became a freelance director and started working in reps. I went on a course with Keith Johnstone and that's how I met Lee.

The shows that we made with Dereck Dereck were very good. We would spend a year working out what they were going to be, and then we would do them. It was a sense of no surprise. Working with Keith, I began to discover 'failing' and that the route to a continued practice and to heartful practice was actually learning how to fail very well. To fail elegantly and with style, so that you were led into places that were outside your comfort zone – and then to discover that two, three failures is a stepping stone to something totally new that you didn't imagine. That was a big life-changing thing for me, and something I still struggle with. Because if you have a success then you go 'Ah, that's the way to do it!'. But as soon as you say 'That's the way you do it', it's over – because you'll be tripped up again. Life has this way of disagreeing with that.

I also had a relationship with different people through books. Michael Chekhov – I just read his books and had my own intuition about how to do it. Arny Mindell and Process Work – I read his books and then ended up meeting him, and the same with the Open Space journey. So there's a kind of imaginative relationship through books, where I found a practice within myself before I've learnt it from the person.

Through doing improv shows and beginning to direct rep shows, I met Julian who was working as a maker. He'd been working with Welfare State – and they have a kind of lineage with Bread and Puppet and Peter Schumann. There was a shared thing about the process of making and improvising around making with Julian and his design work that connected up there.

RADOSAVLJEVIĆ: How did Improbable come about? What was your first project?

MCDERMOTT: We worked in rep first – we did shows, directing, designing. *Shockheaded Peter* was actually the end of that period. Improbable was formed because, having been working in the rep, I was a bit frustrated about wanting to do some work that was more from us, more personal; we wanted to put together a smaller-scale show that was devised. So the Arts Council said 'You need to form a company', and we went 'Oh, OK . . .'. We'd just done this show called *Improbable Tales*, which was an improvised play – big scale, and it had a big set that flew in and out. The stage manager on the book discovered there was no script, so he had to make narrative decisions. It was the first show he'd ever called, and he had to decide which set to fly in, following the story. As the ensemble goes, it was very interesting because it spread to involve the technician. And he had to watch the story and go 'I'll bring in the cave' or 'I'll bring in the forest, or the palace'. And sometimes we'd go 'Oh, OK', and sometimes we'd go 'Oi, get rid of that'. The technicians had lots of props backstage and you'd come off-stage and they'd offer you props. The technicians were dramaturgically involved as much as the performers were. It was really exciting, and it caused lots of trouble for the following shows where they had to go back to just doing what they were told.

RADOSAVLJEVIĆ: Did the Improbable methodology, if there is such a thing, occur before Improbable?

MCDERMOTT: Yes. Because we'd been improvising, making different kinds of shows, I'd been exploring how to do theatre with text. I'd been using different methods where I would get the other actors to dub, so they would read the text and be up in the space. Then I read a book by a guy called Jeremy Whelan – *Instant Acting*, which was very interesting because it almost looked like a book that people in the UK would ignore because it looked like cheating. It was a process were you recorded text and then played it back and the actors moved in the space, and then you re-recorded and played it back, re-recorded – and it was basically a way of actors learning text without ever sitting down and learning their lines. It really broke and undermined this thing where a performer would sit at home, learn their lines, and decide how they were going to say them. They discovered how they were doing the text in the crucible of the ensemble – in response to this actor, in response to this atmosphere. That was really exciting for me because it was a radical way of working and a radical way of getting actors to work. I'd been playing with that in the repertory shows, and we did that on three or four shows. So that became a way of working with text that supported the ensemble to happen. Because as a director, if they did something brilliant, instead of saying 'That's great, keep it', I'd rather go 'OK, do it again and do it differently', trusting that the next time they did it, they would do something even more brilliant. Or if it was good, it would stick around, without the director saying 'That bit's good, keep that'. All your instinct as a director is to go 'If there's something good, hang on to it'. And if you don't do it congruently and trust the process, people go 'What's going on here?', and they don't trust you.

There was a show that Lee and I were in – a production of a comedy based around *A Midsummer Night's Dream*. The group of people that were put together weren't mainstream performers, some of them were stand up comedians, some of them were improvisers, but it was a motley bunch of people. We performed it at Nottingham. Some of it had real Shakespeare, and although it was improvisation and fun and jokes, there were bits of it where they really did *Midsummer Night's Dream*. They didn't necessarily do Shakespeare well, but the spirit of it was extraordinary. In Nottingham we had this great wave of response, audiences went crazy for it, and we were asked to take it to the West End. In the process of taking it to the West End a discussion happened higher up that certain people in the ensemble should be replaced by people who are better at Shakespeare. So in this process when we took it into the West End, the standard of the acting went up – it actually got better, but the quality of the show and the quality of the ensemble went down.

I think it's the primary duty of the ensemble or the creators, or the holders of the space for an ensemble, to look after the spirit, and if it hasn't got that, it isn't an ensemble. It doesn't matter how good the actors are.

RADOSAVLJEVIĆ: Do you have a sense of where Improbable will go next?

MCDERMOTT: I think there is a sense of Improbable finding out how it opens up more to other people coming in and connecting to those shared sensibilities, so it becomes more like an Open Space event. We've been doing associate projects, so we've been mentoring other performers on their own journey to creativity. This *Beauty and the Beast* project will be an associate project. And we are trying to open space for them to learn, be with us, benefit from a relationship with us but not appropriate them, so that if they then want to go off and do their own projects, and take their own journey somewhere else, they can do that.

The other thing is being open to the fact that it might be over. So 'When it's over, it's over' – one of the principles. At certain times we hang on to a story of how a company is, and it may be that the company itself finds a new story. Or you go 'That company's life has finished', in the process of, for instance, funding bodies giving money to companies. That process is quite brutal. One of the reasons it's brutal is because I don't think we have models of how to do that elegantly so that it's not a disaster. We don't have models of how people who work their way up to running big companies step aside to become elders and mentors to leave space for other people to come in.

That's also part of our journey and the enquiry that we are on. Because as a company that's been around for quite a while, we have to find ways to do that. And how you do that consciously rather than it happening to you – that's a big question.

RADOSAVLJEVIĆ: Is there any way you would try and define your ensemble using a metaphor?

MCDERMOTT: I think the Open Space journey is interesting because the metaphor of opening space as a process and as a practice has become more and more important. Space is a thing that different pedagogues have talked about in different ways: Peter Brook's 'empty space', [Viola] Spolin's use of 'space games', Lecoq and space. That is interesting in theatre because it can be a metaphor, but actually it's a tangible thing. Spolin talks about theatre being a space where you make the invisible visible.

I know what it feels like when space is closing down. I feel separate from people, I feel the skin on me looks disconnected from other people. As a company, recognising when space is closing down and when space is opening up is really important, because when space is open you are in a space of possibility and you are in a space of agency and responsibility. You could take any meeting, any rehearsal room, and say 'Is the space open or is the space closed?', and I just think that's such a valuable metaphor to even ask that question. And in the process of asking questions, are we continuing to ask questions that open space? If the company isn't asking those questions any more, and it seems the question's been answered and there isn't another one to ask, then that's the end.

References

Cote, David (2008) 'Puppet Regime', *Opera News*, 72(10): 22–5.
Evans, Lise (2004) 'The Hanging Man Review', *Theatre Journal*; 56(2): 317–19.
Logan, Brian (2003) 'We Got It Wrong? Great!', *The Guardian*, 28 May.
Remshardt, Ralf (2002) 'Touring the "Insulted and the Injured": Theater der Welt in Köln, Bonn, Düsseldorf, and Duisburg, 2002', *Western European Stages*, 14(3): 25–32.
Trueman, Matt (2011) 'The Wisdom of the Crowd', *The Stage*, 17 February: 10–11.

Improbable
http://www.improbable.co.uk/content.asp?p_id=2

19 The dramaturgy of long-term cross-cultural collaboration

Peter Eckersall (Not Yet It's Difficult)

Formerly working as an actor, Peter Eckersall is Associate Professor in Theatre Studies at the University of Melbourne and resident dramaturg for the performance company Not Yet It's Difficult (NYID) which he co-founded with artistic director David Pledger and lighting designer Paul Jackson in 1995. Eckersall has frequently written about NYID, summarising its work as a relationship between arts practice and cultural activism (Eckersall 2010: 202). The company utilises text, corporeality and technology in making performances which are rarely shown in theatres. Another aspect of NYID's aesthetic and methodological operation is its concern with intercultural collaboration. They have made work with the Japanese company Gekidan Kaitaisha and the Korean company Wuturi. Pledger and Eckersall had originally met through their shared interest in the work of Suzuki Tadashi, which has deeply influenced the work of NYID too. Bree Hadley notes that the company are, however, successful in resisting potential dogmatism by deploying an 'inflected Suzuki Method' which provides 'an intriguing way of disrupting the integrity of this system while enhancing the effects of its discipline, staging it with humour and intelligence' (Hadley 2007: 117).

The corporeality and physical rigour of NYID's work is its most often reported feature, though the company is ambivalent about using the term 'physical theatre' as a descriptor (Eckersall 2002: 15). At the same time, the works are often intended to engage the audience intellectually.

Eckersall's academic expertise is in the area of contemporary Japanese theatre and performance, and it partly informs this interview which took place in April 2011 in Belfast.

Interview

ECKERSALL: In the Australian context there's not a long history of ensemble work, and there is no longer a repertory system of theatre that often supported the work of ensembles in the past. There was a historical model of touring companies mainly from England and travelling around for six months or so, working in rep. Later, the arrival of the Australian theatre scene after the 1960s was also initially ensemble-based. The reason I'm giving a certain kind of history is because, to an extent, ensembles in the Australian context, however they are defined, evolve from and sometimes seek to resist this history.

In the late 1960s, in Melbourne there was a company called The Australian Performing Group (APG) who were at various times an ensemble, and they were also a kind of Marxist-Leftist workers' collective very much involved in debating questions of authority and power within theatre and society. For a period they tried, somewhat utopianly, to have a theatre company where every role was equal and everybody was multi-skilling. So that put an interesting model of what the ensemble means into the contemporary Australian theatre scene. Out of that also grew the notion of the avant-garde ensemble which was not so much politically motivated, although the avant-garde ensemble really owes its direction to the arrival of the political ensemble because they both used the same spaces.

So, at the end of that period of the 1960s and 1970s, a number of avant-garde ensembles evolved, which are the history of what we now call 'the contemporary theatre movement'. They were based on the notion of a small group of people training in a particular process that was very often physically or psycho-physically based, influenced by international trends, and then producing works usually under the influence of one particular leader who was a director, writer and performance maker. Very often I think these ensembles were associated with notions of journeys and searching and trying to reformulate theatre practices through the experience of training. A number of those groups transformed into quite long-lasting theatre companies.

For example, in the 1980s there was an influential company called Anthill. Under the artistic director, Jean Pierre Mignon, they did radical adaptations of European classics and had an ensemble of actors, many of whom didn't come from conventional theatre training institutions but came out of a collection of university programmes. Renato Cuocolo's IRAA Theatre is one of the most long-lasting; a company working between Australia and Italy, founded in 1978 and active in Australia from the mid-1980s.

Theatre-in-education, a movement popular in the 1980s, was very often ensemble-based in the sense that you had a group of people who were employed to work together over a year to produce works, but they were not necessarily wedded to the artistic idea of an ensemble.

In some cases those companies ended up producing high levels of artistic work because of the fact that they had a de facto ensemble, and in several instances visionary directors came into those companies and transformed them. Most significantly, in recent times, the company Back to Back, a Geelong-based company that was established around 25 years ago to work with actors with intellectual disability. They're an ensemble that has been headed by Bruce Gladwin for more than 10 years now, and they've made very important artworks that are now touring the world.

Many of the ensembles of the 1970s and 1980s didn't survive in forms that we conventionally understand ensembles to be, because the funding situation was reduced, and as we moved into the 1990s, we had almost a contradictory trend where the ensemble system was breaking up and many of those people who had been working in big or medium tier level ensemble companies in the 1980s were no longer funded on that basis, so they became independent producers. At the same time in the 1990s we had a very strong rise of small to medium sized theatre companies operating on the basis of production funding, so in many instances these companies – like NYID – didn't seek to become large companies with large infrastructure.

NYID is an ensemble to the extent that three people set it up: there's an artistic director, David Pledger, and a technical design and production manager, Paul Jackson, and myself as the dramaturg. We began doing research and development led by Pledger, working with a group of actors for the first five or six years of the company's life. We never formalised an ensemble, but when we made our shows, if those actors were available, they were often cast – they had skills that we needed because we were developing, like many ensembles, a very specific active vocabulary that was for NYID part-physically based and part to do with the way that actors were working in the relationship to media. So it meant that for that period of time we had a shared vocabulary that we developed as an ensemble-like company, although if you applied the definition of the ensemble of the 1980s where actors were employed for 52 weeks of the year, it didn't exist. These actors were actors who trained with us and were employed on projects – as we all were for a period of time.

RADOSAVLJEVIĆ: How did the three of you come together?

ECKERSALL: David and I are the same generation and I think we initially met through common friends in the theatre, but we both shared an interest in Asian performance forms. David and I were both doing Masters in Asian Studies. We were both interested in the work of Suzuki Tadashi, and then later I started a PhD in Japanese Theatre, and David was performing and training with Suzuki Tadashi. We spent two years, before formalising the company, working three times a week in various spaces that we could access for little money. Melbourne – still to a degree – is distinguished by the fact that you can actually access space reasonably cheaply; this is in dramatic contrast to Sydney – which is why a lot of contemporary theatre companies in Australia start in Melbourne. It's much less so now because real estate's more expensive everywhere, but then we could do deals with people. I think that this is an interesting aspect of Melbourne performance culture. You could talk about the ensemble-like nature of Melbourne performance culture in the sense that there is a historical legacy of people doing deals, and that still exists to some degree and is a very productive aspect of our culture. You could argue that it goes back to the fundamental social-collective Marxist idea of the APG, even though nobody is espousing those kinds of ideas anymore. But, it's amazing that even the mainstream theatres do those kinds of deals with people.

RADOSAVLJEVIĆ: What would be the main binding tissue for your ensemble?

ECKERSALL: Ideas, and the desire to communicate ideas through a performative form. The quality of the ideas I think too. We're not desperately committed to one form of training or performance. In that sense we're not like an avant-garde ensemble where they're rigorously, year after year, 'digging the same ditch'.

RADOSAVLJEVIĆ: What are the kinds of ideas you dealt with recently?

ECKERSALL: We began with David Pledger's focus on the idea of exploring a physical sensibility for Australian space. We took as our basis Suzuki Tadashi's practice, the contemporary Japanese body training for actors, which has of course been designed for a company that has various ideas about space, culture, history and Japan, and then we said 'Well, what are the conditions in Australia that are completely different?'.

It's a vast, flat land; there is a physical performance vocabulary in indigenous populations and many other conditions. Our first performance was called *Taking Tiger Mountain by Strategy*. It was a re-working of a cultural revolutionary opera from Beijing from the time of the cultural revolution in China, when Chairman Mao's wife, Jiang Qing, who was a former Beijing opera singer, was given the task of creating seven model operas which were going to be the only plays being performed in the whole of China during the cultural revolution. Each would be ideologically pure in spirit and tone and yet would be entertaining for the masses. We're political theatre-makers and we always want to express a relationship to the political. Making theatre in that period, in 1995, we were identifying various aspects of propaganda that existed in the political domain of our culture, and we brought those references into a kind of basic mapping of the cultural revolutionary play.

We had done three years of physical training and we had a young company of incredibly fit, multi-racial cast, skilled in dance, martial arts, acting and sport. Our early works were about the technologies of the body, the politics of the body, and the authoritarian gestures of the body, because of how that related to contemporary political life.

Our third show was called *The Austral/Asian Post-Cartoon: Sports Edition* which was a very large piece based on Australia's relationship to sport. We became notorious with it because we had a Vietnamese actor in the company who was a very skilled martial artist and we staged a very realistic fight. We had no seats – it was like a sporting arena; the audience were following us around, and we were using very early cameras, simultaneously broadcasting onto televisual screens. We staged a beating of the Vietnamese actor based on a real life incident, and because we had such good physical performers it was incredibly realistic and it was quite shocking – we gave the audience no warning. And then we reconstructed the same thing as a martial arts exercise. That show really put us on the map.

We made a series of adaptations of plays developed by Pledger: Franz Kafka's *The Trial*, in a show called *K* which we did several versions of – one in Australia, one in Korea with Korean actors, a kind of bilingual and intercultural partnership. We did a long-term development with a company called Gekidan Kaitaisha from Japan called *The Journey to Confusion Project*, which was about interculturalism and bodies in an age of globalisation. More recently we've done a show called *Blowback*, which was about a fictional occupation of Australia by the American armed forces staged as a television soap opera, and which I've written about in Jen Harvie and Andy Lavender's *Making Contemporary Theatre*.

More recently, Pledger's tended to make dance physical performance pieces that have actually gone back to the early work of the physical training. Over the years he has articulated a system of training he calls 'Body Listening' which is about actors locating a physical understanding of spatial dynamics into their practice. We did a show called *Apoliticaldance* – it was a hard-edged show about bodies loosely based on Beckett's *The Unnamable*, which is a short story about bodies in hell. That was quite an abstract show, and David abstracted it further with another collaboration with Korean artists.

RADOSAVLJEVIĆ: When you work with other artists – like the Korean collaboration – do you have to train them up in the way that you work?

ECKERSALL: I guess over the years NYID's developed a philosophy of
collaboration that informs our company's practice, and that's very
much written into our mission statements. In Australia, because the
national touring scene is small, a lot of small to medium companies
have made their name in Europe or Asia – the idea of touring is quite
normal to our companies. NYID wanted to try and develop a way of
working that was a little bit more long-term and a little bit more
collaborative. In other words, taking the fundamental philosophy of
the artistic director – the idea of the body in space – if you locate
that philosophically into a touring model: you've got a body in a
touring space that's only there for three days. It's a post-modern
ambient body.

There's an irony in that theatre is supposed to be grounded in
cultural experience and yet most of the time the most significant
artists are flying. So we started to explore ways of working within the
realities of contemporary life. A lot of the people in our company have
families, they don't want to be on the road for endless amounts of
time. The way that we resolved it was to collaborate: so we make
shows with people, and we often work with them more than once.
David has been working in Korea for close on 20 years and has worked
with some of the performers many times. I have been working in Japan
for a long time. So, there's a vocabulary that we have begun to understand in various ways – the dramaturgy of long-term collaboration.

The Gekidan Kaitaisha project had two artistic directors: one from
Japan (Shinjin Shimizu) and one from Australia (David Pledger) –
and that was much more difficult to resolve as an ensemble practice.
'Gekidan' means theatre, and 'Kaitaisha' is the word for deconstruction – 'Kaitai' means to pull apart. So they have this very postmodern
name – they're absolutely deconstructive in their practice. But they
also trace their lineage to the 'originary' moments of Butoh, particularly the 'ankoku' – the dark soul Butoh of Tatsumi Hijikata, the really
profound disassemblage of the body in a kind of very dark visionary
performance style. Kaitaisha are an ensemble and they're also an
interesting case in this because they have a group of people who they
have been working with for years – who train every week and who do
the same repetitive practices under the leadership of an artistic director. When they make a show they essentially put together elements
from their performance vocabulary in different ways. Only over a
longer time-frame do they develop new performance vocabularies.
They're truly avant-garde in this sense. It was the first experience of

this kind of intercultural collaboration for both groups. We worked over three years and we produced a performance that was kind of a journey to confusion – as we called it. We were aiming to theorise this as a 'politics of difference' kind of moment.

RADOSAVLJEVIĆ: How long is your rehearsal process usually?

ECKERSALL: The rehearsal processes vary but they are never short. In our early days we worked in the evenings or on the weekends. But for many years we've paid people for their work and that means that we work within a more industrial context for Australian artists involving actors' equity and agreed working conditions. So, we're not like a Japanese ensemble company where working conditions are not as clearly industrialised.

We've developed a process for a lot of our work that involves a series of phases. The process begins with the artistic director posing themes and ideas for the performance. Then there'll be a research and development phase where as much as possible we bring performers and crew together in a one- or two-week reading and discussion process. As a dramaturg, I tend to do a lot of my work there. We bring in a lot of perspectives to reflect on the theme of the show under development. We do a lot of interactive work drawing material from what people are saying around the table, and we document this process. Then we tend to break and there is a period of writing. Typically, most of our work is actually written by the artistic director from the material in the devising process. Then we come back and, depending on the situation, we try and get another creative development period where we work on the floor. We go into a more traditional rehearsal process later on. So, it's a gradual process, and very often we're thinking about, planning and putting in place funding for that next stage. Sometimes works only go to a certain stage. But we never work in that really highly structured way where you've only got three weeks to produce a show from beginning to end.

RADOSAVLJEVIĆ: What would you say your main role as a dramaturg is in a process like that?

ECKERSALL: The most important things that I do are curatorial practices in the research phase, and also a critical reflexivity around the piece when it's made. I'm one of the members of the company who work to produce a kind of dramaturgical response to the work in development. I work sometimes as a performance dramaturg in the sense that I'll be there watching runs and giving feedback, and I've done that quite a lot. And often I'll write about the work and do interviews with people. I see that work of creating the discourse around the work as dramaturgical as well.

RADOSAVLJEVIĆ: How many core members are there at NYID at the moment?

ECKERSALL: Three. The general manager is not in the core team. We used to have a strong idea of that but now it's a little bit more fluid.

RADOSAVLJEVIĆ: How many performers are there in the pool of performers that you work with?

ECKERSALL: About 10 or 12. Associated artists, there's about 15 at the moment, I think. We have some sound artists, media artists and some musicians now because our latest project is called *AMPERS&ND*. It is a collaboration between NYID, Wuturi from Korea and the Elision Ensemble, which is a contemporary music ensemble based in the UK. We did the first stage of that in Hellerau in Germany recently.

RADOSAVLJEVIĆ: This is the project you are currently developing?

ECKERSALL: I am more connected to another project called *The Meaning of Malaysia*. A couple of years ago NYID made an art installation project in a house about the meaning of home. It was installed in a suburban house and it was a walk-through experience for the audience, where each room was designed according to a particular, theatrical sensibility. We're now working with Instant Café Theatre in Kuala Lumpur. They set up a house in the suburbs, called Chai House, as a centre for people to come together and have play readings and discuss ideas. We've done two stages of this project together where we collaborate with local artists – visual and sound artists, writers and performers – and the project will be a house that explores the meaning of Malaysia.

RADOSAVLJEVIĆ: That's interesting because some ensembles define themselves in terms of the space that they work in.

ECKERSALL: We don't have a home base. But the question of space is very important – the space of a project. We did a project once in central Australia that was about taking the experience of working in a studio space for three years to the desert. So space remains crucial to the practice, but we don't have a space as such. In fact most of our work has been made outside of theatres, in car parks or in church halls – and when we've made it in theatres we've either made it iconically in a proscenium arch, or we've gutted the theatre and turned it into something else.

There's an argument that says that it's much harder for ensembles to exist in our time, economically and politically. As a scholar I work in contemporary Japanese performance. I wrote a book about the 1960s–1990s and there was a lot of ensemble activity in the 1960s in Japan, which created a whole new set of theatre practices. It's interesting to think about what's happened to that idea of an ensemble – a lot of ensembles have ended, but then others are continually coming up: companies like Chelfitsch for example, working principally under the directorship of an auteur. They apply a particular methodology to their practice and their performances have a continuity of theatrical vocabulary. But at the other end of the spectrum there have been a number of artists who have worked in ensembles for many years and have broken out of that way of working. There was a critique of ensembles in Japan after the gassing in the subway by the Aum Shinrikyo cult in 1995. People began to see how ensemble theatres could be seen to have cult-like practices. They were often removed from the wider community. Some Butoh companies were like Buddhist retreats where 'disciples' would wake up at 3:00 in the morning and be vegetarian and shave their head. In one company, disciples changed their name to a variation of the leader's name. Training with Suzuki Tadashi was also quite authoritarian. There was a critique of that kind of ensemble system after the Aum. Kawamura Takeshi, who had a company called Daisan Erotica, spoke about how Japanese companies should reconsider their situation. For him it was a case of just not being able to work like that anymore. The cult-like conditions of production had become too problematic.

RADOSAVLJEVIĆ: But that is changing in Japan?

ECKERSALL: There's a contradiction here and an interesting problem for contemporary performance. The 1960s practices often showed us that the production of something radically new came out of an experience of an immense suppression of individualism and a simultaneous commitment to strong discipline-based processes that were very often absolute. Grotowski is a classic example of this, Butoh is another example and Suzuki training. A lot of Western actor training – the psycho-physical training system that I did when I was at drama school, for example – is cult-like. You're given a set of parameters that are not readily known, they have to be internalised, they have to be understood through the body, and you never understand them ultimately. There's a certain politics to that work that on one level is very exciting and produces new things, breakthroughs happen. On another level it is profoundly authoritarian. I think that that mentality has broken down to a large degree. Economically people can't afford to live like that anymore, where they commit to their art in such extreme ways. So the question is: how do ensembles exist in the twenty-first century?

RADOSAVLJEVIĆ: Exactly!

ECKERSALL: And what do they look like? They don't look like the 1960s practices. And who's in them now? Do they enable, as often happened in those days, the person who had no actor training at all to wander in and be transformed through this experience? We're working in so many different ways now; very few people spend their whole life working within one company structure anymore. Actors, designers, directors, dramaturgs – we all become much more adaptable. And that idea that you dig that ditch over and over again, which is a very profound and historical practice in the arts, has much lessened. So in a sense maybe the artworks themselves become shallower and more lateral in the ways that they proliferate?

The other thing that is really important here is that when ensemble practices in the 1960s and 1970s were prominent, the national theatre culture was also very strong and people didn't travel as much. It's often said in Australia that to go to Europe was so far and so expensive, we would read *TDR* and try to imagine these practices. So, at drama school in the late 1970s for example, it was kind of compulsory to study Grotowski and Artaud, but all of this was through books or articles from *TDR* or through somebody who had gone there once and come back. But now, my students go to New York for their holidays to see The Wooster Group, so the kind of critical, artistic and theatrical vocabulary that they have is so much more vast and intimate. And people get bored more quickly. That's also a challenge.

Ensembles in the first decade of the twenty-first century reflect other trends in contemporary society and in the arts – they are more porous and flexible than in earlier times and have replaced the idea of depth with collaboration and lateral expansion. There is an economic aspect of the artist as a sole trader and artistic production as a commodity that undermines the notion of the collective, but there is also a greater diversity of practices and generosity that comes from a kind of global presence. The ensemble as a quasi-religious unit has been transformed by forces of plurality and secularity; meanwhile, artistic relationships take place in a much more diversified cultural and aesthetic scene and transform much more quickly. They are less formal and the life of ensembles seem to be shorter. At the same time, the sense that ensembles are spaces of interaction and invention are features of work that have spread to become more the norm than exception.

References

Eckersall, Peter (2002) 'On physical theatre: A roundtable discussion from "Not Yet It's Difficult" with Peter Eckersall, Paul Jackson, David Pledger, Greg Ulfan', *Australasian Drama Studies*, 41, October: 15–27.

Eckersall, Peter (2010) 'Not Yet It's Difficult – *Blowback* (2004) – Unmaking *Blowback* – a visceral process for a political theatre', in Jen Harvie and Andy Lavender (eds) *Making Contemporary Theatre: International Rehearsal Processes*, Manchester: Manchester University Press.

Hadley, Bree (2007) 'Dis/identification in contemporary physical performance: NYID's scenes of the beginning from the end', *Australasian Drama Studies*, 50, April: 111–22.

Not Yet It's Difficult
http://www.notyet.com.au/

20 Ensemble as a tool of civic engagement

Katarina Pejović and Boris Bakal (Shadow Casters)

Founded in Zagreb in 2001 by actor-director Boris Bakal, dramaturg Katarina Pejović and a group of artists, the company Shadow Casters (Bacači Sjenki) has successfully and seamlessly combined international collaboration, theatre-making, urban intermedia projects, activisim, pedagogical work, video art and curation into a coherent single body of work. Very often their projects maintain continuity over a number of years, resulting in multiple series of public events and performance creations which they call 'time sculptures' (Rogošić 2008: 56). Stemming from a cycle of inter-disciplinary workshops and urban voyages, originally held between 2001 and 2003 in Zagreb, Ljubljana, Bologna, New York and several other cities, the Shadow Casters' projects have evolved into a multi-pronged exploration of the individual and collective identity, globalisation and the politics of public space. Between 2004 and 2008 they developed a trilogy of pieces *Process City* based on Franz Kafka's *The Trial*, and between 2010 and 2011 – in co-production with partners from Sarajevo, Zagreb and Belgrade – they created a trilogy of interactive pieces *On Togetherness*.

In 2007 they presented a documentary installation called *Vitić Dances*, a summary of a four-year project involving activism to save from complete neglect and ruin a skyscraper, designed by an internationally renowned Croatian architect Ivan Vitić, by restoring the community spirit among the skyscraper's tenants. A full-length documentary film of the same name is due for completion in 2013. This project was more widely known as *Man is Space* and has involved public debates as well as site-specific performances. Marjanić recalls one such street dance event which was intended to 'strengthen fragile city spots through an investigation of the relationship between dance and architecture' (Marjanić n.d.: 188, my translation). The notion of fragility characterises their entire dramaturgical approach, as explained by Bakal in the interview below.

Višnja Rogošić describes Shadow Casters as an 'open membership performance group' and interprets their 'multi-phase' creative methodology as a means of 'emphasizing their socially involved position' (Rogošić 2008: 56). In writing about the interactive piece *Ex-pozicija* (which forms the middle part of the *Process City* trilogy), Rogošić explores the company's form of authorship which treats the director and the dramaturg as 'co-ordinators, translators and navigators' (2008: 57) and the audience members themselves as co-authors.

Shadow Casters have received numerous awards in and outside of Croatia, including CEC ArtsLink Award in 2003 for *Shadow Casters* project at The Kitchen, New York, the BITEF Festival Awards in 2007 and 2009 for *Process City*, and an award at the MESS Festival in Sarajevo in 2008.

The interview was conducted in Cluj, Romania, in December 2010 and Zagreb, Croatia, in November 2011, and was translated from Croatian by Duška Radosavljević.

Interview

RADOSAVLJEVIĆ: How would you define yourselves as an ensemble?

PEJOVIĆ: We are a rowing pair, without a coxswain. And what we are running is – a platform. Formally and legally Shadow Casters are an artistic organisation, but we call ourselves an 'artistic platform' so that we can explain the fluidity of our work both to those people we work with on a project-by-project basis and to the world outside.

RADOSAVLJEVIĆ: What was the background of your collaboration?

BAKAL: We have known each other for a very long time – nearly 25 years. The cultural territory of the Balkans where you and Katarina and I are from, used to be called Yugoslavia. This cultural scene used to be very well integrated, with lots of mutual familiarity among artists, particularly in the 1980s when 'only the sky was the limit'. People made some crazy work all around the place – sometimes together, sometimes in our individual cities: Zagreb, Ljubljana, Belgrade, Sarajevo. That is when Katarina and I first met; even though we weren't working together at the time, we knew of each other.

PEJOVIĆ: At the time – between 1984 and 1989 – I used to live between Belgrade and Ljubljana. In Belgrade I had a professional life as a dramaturg. I worked for TV and theatre, I wrote various texts – mainly critical and theoretical – I wrote plays, but the collaboration with the Neue Slowenicshe Kunst (NSK) was actually what I was really interested in. Thanks to a very fortunate circumstance, I met their dramaturg Eda Čufer and we immediately understood each other and began collaborating.

Meanwhile in Zagreb, Boris was making a kind of work that was linked to what the NSK was doing in spirit and through some shared genealogies, but it was still entirely independent. Simply, the spirit of the time was entirely in sync with the genius of that generation – I can say that now, from this perspective. Had someone offered me to live anywhere else in the world at that moment, I don't think I would have dreamed of accepting. Because Belgrade had this whole New Wave scene with some amazing people who were friends of mine, and it was the same in Zagreb and it was the same in Ljubljana. So we were really at the right place at the right time.

BAKAL: This is important to know: our encounter, which happened 15 years later, took place in Vienna. Why do I underline this? Because the 1980s did not anticipate the break-up of that cultural scene. I don't mean 'political scene' – we all know what happened politically. But the cultural scene also entirely disintegrated in those ten or twelve years: contacts were lost, and at some point during the disintegration both Katarina and I left that place, each in our own direction: me in the direction of Austria, France, Belgium, Italy, and Katarina...

PEJOVIĆ: America, Slovenia, Holland; and then various individual projects in various European locations. We didn't know where we would end up, and somehow we had very similar journeys, but both of those departures were prompted by the war. We didn't have to leave, we chose to leave. Boris was in a more complicated situation because he received call up papers for the army. To be a male in 1991 in any of the former Yugoslav republics was not a very enviable position. However, I wanted to leave, I chose that; and the encounter in Vienna was perhaps the first of a series of synchronicities which we have continuously and conceptually dealt with through the work of Shadow Casters. It was accidental, it could be referred to as such, but that accident was a bit too purposeful to categorise it that way. I had just started on my project which would involve eight women artists and one man artist from Holland, Germany and Austria. Meanwhile Boris came to Vienna for a meeting about a project called *Hotel Europa* which he was doing in Bologna and which was a very complex European project based on a text by Goran Stefanovski and taking place in multiple European locations. He came for a meeting about that project, and we happened to be in the same place at the same time.

RADOSAVLJEVIĆ: You are a dramaturg, and you, Boris, are an actor?

BAKAL: I graduated in Acting in 1981, but already then I was planning to do my own authorial projects. In 1984, I made *Stolpnik* which became a big hit. I played it in an apartment – in a private space which, through theatrical gesture, was transformed into a public space. This was on for three years 1984–1987, and people from the whole of Yugoslavia and beyond came to this private apartment – my apartment – to see this performance.

RADOSAVLJEVIĆ: That is important to emphasise especially in relation to the dominant form of theatre in this part of the world, which was dramatic theatre. This means that you probably fit into some more alternative, avant-garde genealogy?

BAKAL: We have continued something that existed in this part of the world in parallel. In Zagreb, our precursor was Kugla Glumište[1] which existed since the early-to-mid-1970s until the mid-1980s. But both Katarina and I have also worked in official institutions, on projects which were very mainstream, and in that process we were refining our craft and trying out what it was that we did *not* want to do.

PEJOVIĆ: I am actually the child of BITEF. Literally speaking. I attended the first show of the first BITEF in 1967 when I was five years old – a Kathakali performance. Then I watched Luca Ronconi's *Orlando Furioso*. The first more comprehensive but still entirely wondrous memory I have is of *Einstein on the Beach*. I saw that when I was 14 – I was endlessly spellbound and possessed by it. But I didn't yet know then that the profession of a dramaturg existed. I found that out a year later when I met Borka Pavićević, who was a dramaturg connected to the BITEF Festival as well as the theatre Atelje 212. I started working at BITEF when I was 17, and since that festival, which took place in the year 1979, I did some eight or nine consecutive years.

The first professional engagement I had was during my first year at the Drama Academy when I assisted Roberto Ciulli on *The Decameron* at the Atelje 212. He wrote the text with his dramaturg Helmut Schäfer based on Boccacio. Despite it being on in an institutional theatre – that work was very different from everything that was going on in theatres in Belgrade at the time and for a long time afterwards. I did a project with Borka Pavićević at the Pivara,[2] and for three years I worked with Ljubiša Ristić[3] – on his two megalomaniac musical theatre shows at the Sava Centre, *The Secret of the Black Hand* and *Carmina Burana*. In between those two shows we did a one-off festival called Godotfest. Ristić invited to this festival *Hinkemann* by the Scipion Nasice Sisters Theatre – which was the theatre fraction of the Neue Slowenische Kunst. My collaboration with Ljubljana started then, as did my regular trips, which continued until the war. The war was a big cut, a moment of discontinuity. I stopped doing theatre, and Boris too – he made a programmatic decision to stop.

BAKAL: I concluded that art was absolutely insufficient at that moment in time as a means of any kind of response to the challenges of the then emerging postmodern-political structure of the world, and to what I would actually call 'ethical cleansing'. I don't believe in 'ethnic cleansing'; I think it is a highly debatable term because it presupposes an easily definable *ad hoc* existence of ethnicity per se – which I disagree with. In the end we always talk about evil – the perpetrator and the victim, and in order to get to those terms, one has to deal with ethical cleansing first. Having realised that art could not respond to this, I started doing politics – humanitarian work and some kind of ethical work, which seemed important to me at the time. There was literally a year during which I thought that I would never get back into theatre or film or the intermedial projects I was doing – without any regret at all – because I was already in a different place. And I have to admit that that was terribly nourishing. That act of giving up on art and the change of perspective that went with it later became the very stamp of all my work and the work that Katarina and I have been doing. That change of perspective is actually a dislocation from a secure position that artists wish to have – a secure position in relation to the work itself, in relation to the theme, the text or the narrative. This is what we keep doing – we constantly dislocate ourselves from that position and create a certain unease, a sense of risk. We often use the term 'high-risk dramaturgy' in relation to our work. And from within that silence, from within the artistic hiding and from the place of contemplation about – the very theatrical concept of – 'here and now', Katarina and I met somewhere as if in mid-air above some trampoline, and we began our first project.

All our projects, even the theatre ones, are always intermedial. They are never just theatre or just conceptual art, just site-specific or just activism – they are always inter-laced. I am engaged in an investigation of what I currently call in its new phase – the notion of 'fragility'. Contrary to the artist-control freak, the artist who works with 'fragility' – the fragility of realty, for example – actually has greater control over the process. This flexibility makes it possible to work from the 'here and now', from what is actually happening, rather than working with the notions of 'as if' or 'potential reality' or some kind of 'illusion'.

RADOSAVLJEVIĆ: What was the first project of Shadow Casters?

BAKAL: The very name Shadow Casters comes from Marcel Duchamp, from a phase where he was making some moving objects which cast a shadow. It seemed to us that that name which actually meant all and nothing – everything has a shadow, wherever there is light, there is a shadow – was a unifying principle for everything we wanted to do.

That first project was also a matrix of discovery of a kind of shared methodology and what would become an ongoing engagement with the notion of private and public space – and more specifically the injection of the private into the public and the public into the private – through a narrative that threaded through different cities. We started off in Zagreb, and then Bologna, and then . . .

PEJOVIĆ: Graz, Ljubljana, Belgrade, New York. That's where another one of our shared interests also came together, and that's the notion of mapping a city – i.e. the reading of a city through a narrative. Therefore we have two kinds of mapping – public and private – the interface of which is a narrative.

BAKAL: When we speak about a narrative which filters or emanates through text – for us everything is text. Every situation, every event is text – it is read out, it writes itself, every place, every site and locus is a text because it carries a meaning that has been written into it. Our first project was about reading the text from within the matrix of the private and public space.

RADOSAVLJEVIĆ: What did the project look like?

PEJOVIĆ: Practically speaking, it was quite complex, because it took place in two phases, with a year in between. The first phase lasted for 15 days. We had an intensive workshop with a group of people we assembled via an open international Internet call. In addition to performers and fine artists, we also had writers, photographers, historians of art, architects and so on. Some of those people were from that city; some had never before been in the city.

The workshop consisted of a set of sessions which were either process-oriented or thematic. It is very important to say this: the group was subdivided into two, by their designated abode. Each subgroup lived in a particular part of the city for a week, and then they swapped. One of the more important instructions was for them not to discuss their accommodation across the groups in the course of the first week. Why? Because we put them up in two very extreme parts of the city – in terms of class and location. At one end we would have a villa or a fantastic luxury apartment; and at the other end, we would have a flat in a working class estate. So on route to our point of assembly they would have a totally different kind of experience of the city. This applied even to the people who ordinarily lived in the city – they had to have the experience of the group.

BAKAL: They also had to be foreigners in their own city. That was the idea – to arrive at a new viewpoint through collective alienation, through the creation of two organisms. That's the kind of narrative that people often neglect – for example, you have a group of people working in a particular theatre, and one person comes from across the road, and another person is travelling from some new part of town, using 25 different kinds of transportation, but it goes without saying that we are all having to work together at the same time on the same thing for two hours. And that is what leads to misunderstandings. So we took that 'misunderstanding' and placed it in the very centre of action.

The whole time they were all working in parallel on various kinds of techniques – intermediality, hypertext, urban hypertext, city tagging. The city was treated as a map of different kinds of content which were hypertextually layered one over the other.

PEJOVIĆ: The performance techniques were also complemented by a video-making workshop which was also designed to teach perception and to raise awareness of different points of view. They learnt some filmmaking, framing, composition, editing, and the basics of creating a web page.

At the *Shadow Casters Workshop Presentation* which was a public presentation, people would come into some public space and take a seat in the auditorium – in Ljubljana it was the Modern Gallery, in Zagreb, the Internet Centre, in Bologna it was the Cineteca, and in New York, The Kitchen.

After Boris and I made a brief introduction, we would ask for a number of volunteers who would help us navigate the page.

BAKAL: There was a big screen from which the webpage was navigable and visible to the whole of the auditorium.

PEJOVIĆ: We required the number of volunteers which was equivalent to the number of our workshop participants. The volunteers didn't know that aside from navigating the page, they actually volunteered to step into the performance. At the end of the webpage navigation, which would lead the volunteer through a maze of a personal journey through the city, an instruction would appear on the screen prompting the volunteer to leave the presentation space and go outside to meet someone. After some hesitation, the volunteer would get up and leave, and at the same time as he/she left the building, a video projection would commence in the auditorium – equivalent in some way to what was going to happen outside to the volunteer.

What happened outside was a one-to-one journey, led by the person whose route he/she had previously chosen in the Internet navigation. It was particularly important to us that if those people were the citizens of that city, they had an opportunity to discover its previously-unnoticed aspects – to discover the known in the unknown and the unknown in the known. By the end of the presentation, the audience who stayed behind would eventually realise that, because they didn't want to do anything but to just sit there and watch – they may well have seen all the videos – but they hadn't had the exclusive experience.

BAKAL: As with all our projects, I think it's evident that we are dealing with the notion of personal intervention into the real space-time structure of meaning. That's why I say that the *Shadow Casters Workshop* was a gamut of methodologies which allowed us to explore which directions we would be moving in in the following 10 years. And that's what happened.

PEJOVIĆ: The second phase reassembled the same team that worked with us a year before and added into the mix a number of local professionals – forming a big network of collaborators who proceeded to work together for two months on the creation of a new system. In Zagreb, we created 68 points in the city which were all interconnected into various narratives. It was a kind of system that people could enter at several points around the city. Audience members went on these travels on their own, led by different kinds of instructions which took the form of written messages or non-verbal signs, or the form of an encounter with someone, but those travels were not linear. At every point they had to make choices – left-right, onwards-backwards, up-down, yellow-red.

BAKAL: That was a very important principle – raising awareness of the fact that we are always making decisions and that those decisions have their consequences.

PEJOVIĆ: Even when it seems to us that we have no choice, meaning: I'm sitting in a car, I'm totally stuck in a traffic jam, I can't do anything – I still have a choice. I have a choice to take this calmly and think about other things, or to be angry and irritated and so on.

We had six or seven big narratives and those narratives intersected at particular points. So you could either stay within your story or enter another one. The way it often happens in life – someone enters someone else's story, as we say.

BAKAL: The scheme was relatively simple and relatively complex – mathematical. Those 60–70 points around the city were either private apartments, or restaurants, courtyards, museums, institutions. We tried to remind people of some places they don't remember any more, and to create opportunities for some non-places, i.e. the places that people visit but only because of their function, such as the railways station, supermarkets, etc. Every narrative lasted around an hour and a half or two hours, so it would take around 15–16 hours if someone wanted to go through the whole system.

PEJOVIĆ: At one of the points at, let's say, 3pm, you'd receive an envelope from a waiter in a café. He gives you a choice of two and you pick one

which says 'Come to the Sava Bridge at 10pm'. The signs we used
included ones that already existed in the city – ranging from graffiti
and street stencils which would acquire a different level of readability
within that context, to some new artworks made by our collaborators,
such as a video projection onto the waters of the Sava River, which
was visible from the Sava Bridge.

BAKAL: In Zagreb we ran a competition for the best story of those who
passed through the system...

PEJOVIĆ: ... And the winner could come to New York with us.

BAKAL: Another one won a foreign language course and the third one
won a shoe voucher – because he had to walk so much around town,
so he could buy new shoes!

RADOSAVLJEVIĆ. And the next project was *Process in Progress?*

PEJOVIĆ: That's right. The third part of the trilogy.

RADOSAVLJEVIĆ: Which, unlike the aforementioned one, is based on a
specific text.

PEJOVIĆ: On Kafka's *The Trial*. I think that that novel is paradigmatic for
the time in which we live – which is repressive in some less visible and
less readable ways compared to some other more obviously repressive
times – the position of an individual in today's 'developed' societies is
very similar to the position of Josef K, in fact. That's one of the reasons –
it's topical. And the other reason is that all of Kafka – and that novel
in particular – has had the same interpretation throughout the twentieth and even the twenty-first century: a deadly serious metaphor of a
dark world within which an innocent individual is caught up, a prede-
cessor of absurdism, etc. In the novel itself, Kafka very clearly demon-
strates that Josef K contributes to his fate to a considerable extent,
because he makes wrong decisions at wrong times. Instead of waiting
patiently with his uncle at the solicitor's office – he goes to have a cud-
dle with the maid; when he should be modest – he is arrogant; when he
should be focused – he is distracted; when he should be engaged – he is
facile, etc. Kafka himself says that Josef K is a product of bad habits.
The notion of Josef K as an innocent victim is wrong in our view. The
whole idea therefore came not out of a desire to challenge various honourable literary critics who interpret Kafka in this way – and thanks to
whom we have inherited the term 'Kafkaesque' as denominator for
something dark, absurd, for a sense of being trapped – but a desire to
provide a different perspective on this problem.

RADOSAVLJEVIĆ: And you had the idea from the outset that this should
be a trilogy?

PEJOVIĆ: We did have the idea that it should be a trilogy, but we hadn't
determined from the start what would be the constituent parts of the

trilogy. We commenced a kind of deconstruction of the given material. Chronologically we worked backwards, third part first, but in terms of the overall structure, we were thinking in a linear way. We started off with the text itself: Boris made an extraordinary adaptation of the entire novel, very pregnant with meaning, but concise and compact. The show is only 70 minutes long. It proved to be very successful with younger audiences who have an a priori resistance towards Kafka and classical literature in general. So when they see the show they always say 'We understood it all, we got it, and it's so dynamic'. In terms of staging, it is a performance that respects the classic relationship between the performers and the audience. In addition to the three protagonists – two actors and one actress, all of whom take it in turns to play Josef K – the show's fourth protagonist is the video projection, which is at the same time a continuous analysis of the juxtaposition between the wide angle and the close up. The close up provides a different kind of information to the one available in the wide angle of the stage, and this represents a kind of homage to Orson Welles and his own *The Trial*.

The second part, *Ex-Position*, was inspired by a particular moment in the novel itself, the parable called 'Before the Law' which is told by the Priest in his encounter with Josef K in the cathedral. This also provided a structural basis for *Ex-Position*. And finally, the first part *Vacation from History* represents a further focusing in on the detail, which doesn't necessarily mean a loss of connection with the original source, but a focus on a smaller entity, which is a short story *A Dream* (*Ein Traum*) written by Kafka and featuring Josef K as a protagonist. This was written before *The Trial* and in the form of a simple record of a dream. It opens 'Josef K dreamt' and this is followed by the account of the dream which takes place in a graveyard and leads to Josef K's recognition of his own grave.

BAKAL: While working on the adaptation, I read all of the existing adaptations in mainstream cinema and theatre – from Bergman's via Weiss' to Orson Welles' – and didn't find that anyone was really dealing with the main substance of the work itself, but with an interpretation of it.

It seemed to me that the a priori rhizomatic structure of Kafka's work was actually two-fold: in terms of its style, but also in terms of the fact that it is unfinished, that it is like a deck of cards. You can pull out the cards one by one and form new meanings; you can play a new round with it. So I said 'Max Brod played out his own round – why do we still, a hundred years after Kafka's death, have to play Brod's round, which is in any case quite selective?'. He had even excluded some chapters which were finished. He remained within his own kind of linearity, which was just his own – regardless of how much love he had brought into the project as a close friend of Franz Kafka's. I felt we needed a new one.

The second thing was the problem of interpretation. At one point I noticed that the reader is literally imprisoned in the story with the text itself; the text is a cage, which Kafka had erected around the reader – and this is what gives us this sense of being trapped. And then we have that encounter between the Priest and Josef K in the cathedral, which leads to absolutely nothing, other than the fact that many philosophers then wrote about it. Benjamin wrote about it, Agamben wrote about it, Horkheimer, I think even Adorno mentioned it somewhere – so there are masses of other texts which this story had produced, but within the novel itself, it is inconsequential. Nothing changes within the story as a result of it. It forms a kind of a tract which I simply cut out of our adaptation and used it as a thesis for the second part of the trilogy – Ex-Position. At the point at which the Priest starts telling that story in our adaptation, Josef K interrupts him and says 'Excuse me, are we at the main entrance now?'. Something that had produced so much meaning afterwards – in our view, simply went over his head. And that is paradigmatic, because he misses the point of everything.

Just like it happens to all of us on a daily basis: we miss the point of things, the loves of our lives walk past us, our chances to become rich, or honest or honourable or good simply pass us by without us noticing, or not as the case may be. This creates a certain Taoist approach to the work. By the way, we found that Franz Kafka was indeed fantastically knowledgeable about Taoism and that he possessed all the works on Taoism that had been translated into German by then. So a certain Taoist, Buddhist, and Eastern philosophy and the view of the world based on interconnectedness, is discernable within this work. And this cast a new light on our reading of this text.

RADOSAVLJEVIĆ: So having explored the city in the previous project, you returned to the theatre for that final part of the trilogy, and then again came out of it.

PEJOVIĆ: Yes, that was an outing into the theatre. But now we are doing a whole new trilogy in the theatre – On Togetherness. In ZKM[4] in Zagreb we made Explicit Contents, in Atelje 212 in Belgrade we made (R)evolution Masterclass, and the third part Male Female / Female Male (MFFM) is a co-production with the Zagreb &TD Theatre and the Sarajevo festival MESS – so we have a mixed Zagreb and Sarajevo team. The third part actually consists of a double bill – meaning that we have a trilogy consisting of four shows, I call it a 'threeandahalfology'. One half of the double bill is male and the other female. This means the first has a male-only cast and the second female-only, and each show is for single-sex audience. For single-cell organisms. We are trying to explore the male-female question under laboratory-like conditions.

The actors improvise practically everything in the entire trilogy. In *Explicit Contents*, the performance begins in the theatre hall, but after five minutes the audience is divided into six groups, each led by a pair of actors to different spaces in the building otherwise inaccessible to the audience. The Belgrade performance too is also a hardcore improvisation. We deliberately called it *Masterclass* because we are really treating it as a kind of masterclass – inviting the audience to conduct a personal revolution. We are using the original etymological meaning of the term 'revolution' – not a sudden reversal, the brutal cut, the coup – but the meaning of turning 360 degrees around one's own axis. So first of all, it's a process, second it presupposes work on the self, and thirdly it implies a certain change of perspective and a return to the same physical point which is no longer the same point of view.

We concluded that, for us, that is a relevant perspective on revolution. We are not interested in revolution as a big ideological and political question, but in exactly what every individual can do with their own sense of responsibility about themselves first of all, and then about the world around themselves – in terms of a series of micro-revolutions. Six actors are working on this with 120 members of the audience in two hours, improvising throughout. They have an overall structure – a set of segments and they know the sequence of those segments. They have big school-style blackboards where this sequence is outlined. The audience is sitting facing each other, always surrounded by the others – you can't hide. The audience votes for six out of twelve topics, which we found to be generally relevant for this moment in time, like: health, education, parenthood, sex, faith, death, ecology, tolerance, etc. Then members of the audience pick at random an actor who will be doing each segment – the actors have to be ready to play any of the segments on any of the themes. And that creates a certain positive kind of tension. In this show, everyone is going through a big masterclass. We asked the actors that, as 'the ignorant schoolmasters', they open themselves up to the possibility that in every moment of time they could also learn or understand something from the audience. That is of course very difficult. The show has caused confusion because it is unlike anything previously done in Belgrade and does not belong to the local institutional theatre aesthetic.

RADOSAVLJEVIĆ: What was the departure point for the project about togetherness as a whole?

PEJOVIĆ: It was a desire to explore the question of togetherness from three different standpoints. *Explicit Contents* – as the first part of the trilogy – deals with the theatre community as a pseudo-community: a community of polite strangers whose elbows rub against each other. In some way they occupy a non-space. This happens far too often unfortunately, even though theatre is the most direct and the most live of all media – which constitutes its own specific magic and in turn prevents it from going out of fashion or becoming archaic. Only we have to defend it from the domination of the bourgeois model which has permeated our culture and which does not allow theatre to be anything else. What we consider classical theatre nowadays has only been going for three or four out of 25 centuries! For centuries theatre took place in the streets, at public squares, in private houses, in churches, in open fields, on sea shores. It was all 'site-specific' then.

Explicit Contents started in 2009 with a competition we launched to look for the 'biggest problem'. For a week we were based in the Vladimir Nazor Gallery in Zagreb, where we were receiving candidates. We had lots of candidates, drawn from a very broad range of audience – and each of them was given an opportunity to give an account of their problem in front of a panel of judges. All of the panel members in the end gave their votes and we chose six problems which between them covered the sorts of aspects that seemed vital to them but also to us – although we didn't have the right to vote. Subsequently, we made an Exhibition of Problems. Those six problems or six themes contained within the problems eventually formed the basis for the aforementioned inner structure of *Explicit Contents*. But this only emerged during the rehearsals for the show – yet another synchronicity.

We decided to start the whole project with the show's opening. The premiere was thus going to be literally the first encounter between us as the project's initiators, the actors who would work on the project, and the audience. Three hundred people turned up and filled the big auditorium of ZKM. Boris came out and I later joined him, to explain that the show did not exist. The actors who were invited to work on the project knew that the show was not going to take place. They knew that they hadn't made anything, but they didn't have a clue as to what was going on, and this created suspense . . .

RADOSAVLJEVIĆ: And the audience had bought tickets for the show?

PEJOVIĆ: Yes, yes, yes, of course – they bought the tickets for the premiere. But the show did not exist. So we explained to them that we had run the Competition for Problems and they could see the Exhibition of

Problems in the foyer on their way in. And we explained that this was by no means a provocation of any kind. We had no desire to cause anger, but that in the time that followed we in fact wanted to talk to the audience about the kind of show they wanted to see. They could decide how long this was going to be because we had anyway laid out some post-show drinks, and we could conclude straightaway if they wanted to. They had all come with some kind of an idea as to what they expected to see, whether they knew our work or not, and we wanted to know what this was.

At first, some of the audience members reacted indignantly of course, with aggressive questioning, but then gradually they began to participate and became constructive. We were writing up all the suggestions on a whiteboard. Some audience members came on the stage and wrote on the whiteboard themselves, and a certain form was starting to emerge. After about an hour and a half we sensed that that was it, and we invited the audience to come back in two-months' time, by when we would have worked with the twelve actors to create a show on the basis of their suggestions. We wanted them to be present at that occasion which we were going to call 'the premiere of the first reprise'. But what was very nice was that a lot of them did come to the post-show drinks reception serving red wine and big batches of homemade bread with olives and rosemary.

People were breaking bread, drinking wine, and still discussing the 'show' – what did and did not happen, what else they could have said, what other ideas they had – this went on till 3:00 in the morning. They actually threw us out of the theatre at 11:30, but a few groups of people stayed behind and went for more drinks, and a considerable number of people we had never met before, continued to participate in this discussion. Afterwards they wrote to us, and this is how we ended up with a kind of community around the show. For some three or four weeks we worked intensively with the actors. Gradually, a structure emerged around those six problems and because there were twelve of them, we ended up with six pairs of actors, but the basic idea remained that the show didn't exist and that people were coming together in order to create it with us.

This is what that looked like: you come and buy a ticket, the actors are walking around the foyer and every audience member receives a colour sticker. The audience then divides into six groups according to the colour of their stickers on their way into the auditorium – so if you had come with a partner you would most certainly be separated so that you joined different groups. They will have heard a series of instructions read by Boris and myself in which we basically say that the show doesn't exist and that in the next hour and a half it will be made by them with their guides. Then the acting pairs arrive, each in a distinct performance style, they meet their group and take them to a variety of locations inside the theatre – from the roof terrace to the cellar, including changing rooms, green rooms, rehearsal rooms, etc. – but the point is that the entire theatre building is utilised. The actual auditorium is empty for about an hour and a half, but after that time everyone comes together again on the stage. Every group performs their own bit, which they will have prepared, and that is what forms the 'action' of the piece: a small music number, or a choreography or even a dramatic moment – but what is important is the 'counter-action' which takes place simultaneously during the previous hour and a half. Everyone performs their bit but one of the actors co-ordinates all of the six groups, all of the 144 people or however many it was that could fit on the stage of ZKM. In the end they all walk up to the proscenium and take a bow in front of the empty auditorium, and the sound person cues the applause.

   As for the third part of the trilogy – the double-bill *Male Female / Female Male* (MFFM) – it had as its focus the question of community contained in the elementary relationship between the two sexes.

BAKAL: Or two kinds of energy.

PEJOVIĆ: This was crystalised through two questions: the question of pleasure and the question of reproduction. On the one hand they are existential, on the other, they are political. And Boris's idea of segregating the audience ended up becoming an incredible social experiment. This situation opened up many possibilities and questions on what we understand by the male question, the female question, the question of relations between them, and the notion of stereotypes, which proved to be very fruitful and provocative. When the audience was confronted with stereotypes, they also had an opportunity in that space-time encounter to consider why those stereotypes are the way that they are.

BAKAL: That is connected to something that I used to say in the 1990s – whatever people do, whatever they have done throughout their history – their actions are always a response to some fundamental questions. Whether the question is well heard, whether the response is desirable – it is adequate to a particular social dynamic which was dominant in that particular moment and the way it was being read at the time. Those were the parameters within which we were exploring community too. So we asked some questions and monitored how the questions were being answered. What is also very important about all three parts of the trilogy is that they were all encounters – all those people who go through the system of the show can really meet each other and talk to each other. In some of them, they literally find out the names of the people they are with, and in *(R)evolution Masterclass* and *MFFM*, you are constantly within view of another audience member, you are constantly in contact and there is no hidden part you can play, so as Katarina says: you are no longer 'polite strangers'. Instead, the bland notion of audience transforms into people who make discoveries for themselves and for each other.

PEJOVIĆ: MFFM is one big polygon for an examination of cultural differences within a society which is liberal to a certain extent, but still deeply patriarchal. In this society there is a great quantity of women, especially in urban environments, who are emancipated. They have no problems being public personalities, they have no problems expressing their opinions and attitudes, but despite this, public discourse is not something that is very present in this society. Public discourse does not even have the important function that it had at the twilight of socialism, for example in the late 1980s. This kind of theatre piece allows people to start to talk about things, not from an ideological position, but from the position of one's self – so in any role other than their given role.

RADOSAVLJEVIĆ: And this of course is very important also in terms of civic duty, which is insufficiently defined in this part of the world.

PEJOVIĆ: What is important to note is that the sense of togetherness in the former socialist countries is terribly distorted, because the whole notion of collectivism was ideologically branded. It was highly formalised ideologically. Following the change of system in 1989, the idea of togetherness was totally swept under the carpet, and now, 20 years later, they are all in a terrible situation in fact. Because they have no tools to create togetherness and togetherness is reduced to some very primitive forms such as football supporters, or fan clubs of a particular turbo folk star, groups congregated around marginal activities. Those are the kinds of communities in existence today but without true togetherness on a bigger level.

   We attempted to investigate various aspects of what it is that a community can achieve – in which ways it can be created, and in which ways it can transcend the kind of preconceptions that exist here in this part of the world in relation to any kind of collectivity. It seems that in Croatia and in the West Balkans we have somehow skipped the whole period of individualisation which has characterised the history of the West for at least a century now. We have arrived at a point now where community is in crisis because of the insistence on individualism and on the individual as the basic cell of

society, but at the same time the society is not being created because
the individual always stands in opposition to something, and shapes
his/her own existence through opposition to something. On the one
hand, that is something which contributes towards the destruction of
community in the West, and on the other neoliberal capitalism is
constantly pushing people to enter the system within some kind of
isolated point of view as consumer-machines. Neoliberal capitalism
cannot tolerate any kind of community other than the collection of
individuals who express their individuality through how they con-
sume products of the industry of desire. But in our region we have
actually had to skip the organic development of this. We went from
the tradition of socialism directly into its total negation and an
enforced adoption of the consequences of neoliberal capitalism. In
any case, the result is similar – there is no tangible community, no
functional community, no productive or active community – in any
sense. People have no sense that there is any kind of a communication channel through which they can act or influence what is going
in their lives. The apathy and fatalism, which is generally recognised
as characteristic of this place, is also a consequence of this.

Notes

1 An interdisciplinary art group founded in 1975 with the intention of reinventing theatre as 'an urban ritual' and a 'social situation' (http://www.avantgarde-
  museum.com/kolekcija/ht/autor.php?lang=en&autor=165#inf, accessed 20 July
  2011).
2 Pivara (Brewery) was an independent avant-garde venue founded by dramaturg
  Borka Pavićević in the 1980s. Since 2004, Pavićević has been running the
  award-winning Centre for Cultural Decontamination.
3 One of the most experimental Yugoslav theatre directors. In 1977 he formed a
  supranational Yugoslav theatre company named with the acronym KPGT –
  using the first letter for the word 'theatre' in each of the four Yugoslav languages
  (Croatian, Serbian, Slovenian and Macedonian). He also created various site-
  specific theatre experiences, including one on a raft on the lake Palić.
4 Zagrebačko kazalište mladih (Ze-Ka-eM) – The Zagreb Youth Theatre. http://
  www.zekaem.hr/.

Bibliography

Araneo, Margaret (2008) 'The Croatian Centre of ITI'S Third Annual Showcase
  Croatia: 17–21 October 2007', *Slavic and East European Performance*, 28(2): 55–65.
Bauer, Una, 'Maieutics & synchronicity. Boris Bakal, Shadow Casters', *Frakcija*,
  33–4 (Winter 2004–2006): 76–91.

Marjanić, Suzana (n.d.) 'Zagreb kao poligon akcija, akcija-objekata i performansa: kolažna retrospekcija o urbanim akcijama, interakcijama i reakcijama', *Up & Underground Art Dossier*, 11/12: 171–94, available online at http://www. up-underground.com/brojevi/11-12/10/ (accessed 19 December 2012).

Rogošić, Višnja (2008) 'Vraćanje prostora čovjeku: udvajanja u predstavi Ex-pozicija Bacača sjenki' (Rejoining space and man: duplications in ex-pozicija by Shadow Casters), *Frakcija*, 47–48: 46–53.

Rogošić, Višnja (2011) 'Cheaper than a psychiatrist: Shadow Casters' explicit contents', *Slavic and East European Performance*, 31(1).

Shadow Casters
http://shadowcasters.blogspot.co.uk/2008/07/news-1.html

21 On courting the audience

David Bauwens, Alexander Devriendt and Joeri Smet (Ontroerend Goed)

When the Belgian collective Ontroerend Goed appeared for the first time at the Edinburgh Fringe in 2007 with a short run of its 20-minute interactive piece *The Smile Off Your Face*, it immediately scooped the coveted Fringe First, the Total Theatre Experimentation Award and a spate of glowing reviews from all major publications. *The Scotsman*'s Joyce McMillan called it 'an essay in intimacy, human warmth, and real emotional attention' and an 'unforgettable experience' (McMillan 2007). Lyn Gardner classified it simply as 'therapy' (Gardner 2007). By 2008, the word had spread, and their new show, made with a group of teenagers, *Once and For All We Are Going To Tell You Who We Are So Shut Up And Listen*, quickly sold out, adding another round of awards to their name. In 2009 and 2010, Ontroerend Goed returned with some more controversial versions of these two previous successes: *Internal* and *Teenage Riot*, respectively. Each of these shows divided the critics and the audience, but nevertheless caused a constant buzz. Matt Trueman reviewed *Internal* twice for his blog, revising his initial views (Trueman 2009). (He also saw *Teenage Riot* twice, before writing his review of this piece.)

A similar haunting effect was later experienced by Maddy Costa (2011) who documented her changing views of the company's work in her blog, following the publication of her feature about the company in *The Guardian*. In the comments section below her blog piece, Costa and her fellow *Guardian* critic Mark Fisher agreed that it is the inherent ability of the company's work to generate debate and long-term rumination that is its unique and distinguishing quality: 'debate makes it right no matter how wrong it feels' (Costa 2011).

The company's work seems to remain as slippery for the Belgian critics. Wouter Hilleart sees Ontroerend Goed as the children of Jan Fabre's generation 'who had only just claimed, during the 1980s, their right to focus entirely on themselves, instead of the collective visions of 1970s political theatre' (Hilleart 2010: 436). Comparing the company's work to that of

Fabre, Hilleart appears dissatisfied by an apparent foregrounding of 'pure experience industry' at the expense of political content, but at least he leaves the possibility open that Ontroerend Goed's work might be ushering in 'the future of theatre'.

One thing is certain, partly helped by their UK producer Richard Jordan, Ontroerend Goed have created an impressive international following in Europe, Australia and the US, thus becoming an ensemble for a globalised (st)age.

This interview with Artistic Director Alexander Devriendt, Dramaturg/Performer Joeri Smet and Producer David Bauwens took place in Edinburgh in 2010 during the run of *Teenage Riot*. The trilogy of interactive performance pieces, which subsequently became known as *The Personal Trilogy*, was completed in 2010 with *A Game of You* and shown as part of the One-on-One Festival at the Battersea Arts Centre. The company returned to Edinburgh in 2011 with another controversial show *Audience*, and in 2012, with a teenage two-hander *All That is Wrong*. In 2012 they also collaborated with Sydney Theatre Company on *A History of Everything*.

Interview

RADOSAVLJEVIĆ: I suggest that we start with the history of the company and how you met.

DEVRIENDT: 1993. 'Damberd' ('Chequers') – the name of the pub where all the alternative and arty people in Ghent went. I was 16. I was running a poetry magazine, I was looking for more poets and I went to the bar and said 'Is there a poet in here?'. And the guy behind the bar said 'Upstairs'. So I went upstairs and there was David, and in my memory there were four good-looking girls around him, and I thought 'Wow!'. I asked him 'Are you a poet?', and he said 'Yes, that's what we do'.

The magazine was called *Poëzieavonden* (*Evenings of Poetry*). We made some copies and we sold them to friends and people who liked what we were doing. And then Joeri heard about it.

SMET: Yes, like Alexander, I was looking for somebody to share my novel with. And somebody said 'That's the guy you have to give this to'. So I went up to David. I don't remember if he was surrounded by pretty girls.

DEVRIENDT: Probably in your memory by pretty boys.

(*Laughter*)

SMET: Yes. So I just put the novel on the table and I said 'Read this'. I was invited to the *Poetry Evenings*.

DEVRIENDT: At a certain point we felt that we wanted to bring the poems on the stage, because there was much to experiment with and because nobody did it. And we were really working on the performance, sometimes more than on the poems themselves.

SMET: We also drew in musicians and we looked for a graphic designer to design the bundle.

DEVRIENDT: My father works at a university design department and he saw that we were struggling, so he gave an assignment to his class to design this poetry bundle.

RADOSAVLJEVIĆ: When you say 'bundle', does that mean something that you hand out to the audience?

DEVRIENDT: You sell it. Once we sold 600 copies of one bundle, which is a lot for poetry. The best poet's bundle was 1,000 copies.

(They show me some bundles)

RADOSAVLJEVIĆ: Which year is this?

BAUWENS: 1997.

RADOSAVLJEVIĆ: So the name Ontroerend Goed was already in existence?

SMET: I think it was 1995 that the name first came.

RADOSAVLJEVIĆ: How did the name come about?

BAUWENS: We were looking for a name and we put a lot of names on a list. At the time I was studying Law. A friend of ours came round and I said to him 'Leave me alone now, I'm all absorbed by real estate and public domain'. And 'onroerend goed' without a 't' means 'real estate'. So I said I'm studying 'onroerend goed', and he said 'Well, ontroerend goed might be a good name'. Like: feel estate. And we put that name on the list and it came out as everybody's favourite choice.

DEVRIENDT: The translation can be 'real estate' or 'feel estate' – it's a pun.

SMET: The next bundle we presented was called *Terug naar de zolderkamer* (*Back to the Attic*), and that became a cabaret-like, stand up comedy-like . . .

DEVRIENDT: Freak show . . .

SMET: Freak show, which was called *Porror* . . .

DEVRIENDT: A mixture of porn, horror and poetry.

SMET: We did a try-out for mainly friends, people who knew our group for a long time, and they went 'What the fuck are they doing here? This is really good'.

DEVRIENDT: In the past when I said to people 'Thanks for coming', they would say 'You're welcome', and now it was different, when I said 'Thanks for coming' they would say 'No, thanks for the performance'.

It was the last time that poems were involved. But in retrospect I think that the live interaction and the sense of 'here and now' was something that we never lost. Or when we lost it, there was something wrong. That was really important.

RADOSAVLJEVIĆ: So there was *Porror 1*, and then there was *Porror 2*.

DEVRIENDT: *Porror 1* was an all male performance – even when they were dressed up as women, or dressed up as angels, like David was – and some people said it was about masculinity in all its aspects from machoism to gayism. Because it was so successful, and we felt we were onto something, we decided to make the second show, *Porror 2*, with a female group – The Wentelteefjes. They were a cabaret group, and because they had good voices we decided to go for an all cabaret performance. All of them were very good performers, and that brought us onto a higher level.

RADOSAVLJEVIĆ: Which years were these?

DEVRIENDT: *Porror 1* in 2001and *Porror 2* in 2002. We had all graduated by 2002, which is also important I think. Until then we could only work from May to September. So we made *Porror 2*, it was very successful, and we also toured that nationally.

BAUWENS: *Porror 2* was really the start of getting some touring experience. That's the first one that went around Flanders and even went to the Netherlands.

DEVRIENDT: We'd started as a collective: everybody is a poet, and everybody is on stage and everybody is director and artistic director. And we felt we were looking more for compatibility – but you don't do that consciously, it just happens. By the principle of compatibility, Sophie [de Somere] joined the group in 2001. By *Porror 2*, I became a director. I directed that one with difficulties – because it was my first directing job. Joeri was performing, and Joeri was lovesick. I didn't choose to direct, we were going to make it together but because he was so lovesick I had to do it on my own.

   By then I was also working with Stan. There were five big companies who worked as collectives in all of Belgium and The Netherlands at the time: Stan, Discordia, Dood Paard, Dito Dito and Hollandia.

SMET: You will find those in any history books of the late 1970s and 1980s Flemish and Dutch theatre.

DEVRIENDT: They represented a reaction to the ones before them such as Alain Platel, Jan Fabre, Anne-Teresa Keersmaeker – people who were creating their own performances without a school behind them, doing mixtures of dance and theatre, some really experimental performances. This second generation came out of theatre schools and their reaction was to bring back theatre based on plays.

SMET: They wanted to do classical texts but with a new fresh approach. Very important for them was the performer, here and now, doing the text.

DEVRIENDT: I was working with Stan as a sort of dramaturg and helping them out, and as a young guy, I was in awe. But in reaction to that, we wanted to do new work, devised work, not based on plays. Because we all did Literary Studies . . .

SMET: I also did an internship with Dito Dito. I think we could both see in these different groups how the collective worked, and we wanted to reflect on that and respond to it.

DEVRIENDT: I think so too – consciously or not, that was definitely happening. When I look back upon it I see that because they worked with existing text they didn't need one person to decide what the play was going to be about. The text did that. So in a way they could work more as a collective because they already had this backbone of content. Whereas if you make a newly devised piece and you do it with six, seven people, it's six, seven different stories.

So then we decided, one person was going to make choices, filter all the ideas, we didn't always do it so definitely, but it was already lingering in our minds.

SMET: With *Porror 3* we wanted to do the third part of the trilogy, but we were really interested in theatre by then.

DEVRIENDT: And the idea of performance – Forced Entertainment and all that stuff that we encountered somewhere, was even more interesting.

SMET: What we put on stage was four characters based on American stereotypes: an old cheerleader, a lonesome cowboy, a perverted television presenter, and an angry black woman. It was a crazy performance in the sense that there seemed to be no real storyline, it had a lot of reflexive moments, but at the same time it was also about – 'How far do you go to please an audience or to get attention on stage?'. So it had different layers, much more so than *Porror 1* or *Porror 2*.

DEVRIENDT: It was a dark show. You had to have some sarcasm in you to like it. But it was no cabaret show, and it totally flopped at the Ghent Festival.

Luckily, one guy, Don Verboven, who had already seen *Porror 1* and *Porror 2* said 'You should bring this to the Festival Theater aan Zee', which is the best festival for young theatre-makers in Belgium. He said 'I'll find the right environment for you', and he gave us this little room in the cellar of a jazz club, while all the other companies were doing it in more theatre-like environments. The jury was really open and looking for new stuff. They were programmers of arts centres – and programmers are always looking for the next new thing. They gave the prize to us. And to another girl who was from a theatre school, but also a maker.

SMET: That gave us money to develop a new play in the Arts Centre Stuk in Leuven.

BAUWENS: I could use that prize money as a base of certain income, which allowed me to ask for a grant. I had the minimum playing dates and the minimum income, I knew I was going to be at a festival the year after that. So I could actually turn that into 'working professionally' for the first time.

SMET: It made us question what we were doing actually. Because it all came into existence organically with a lot of messing around, and not really knowing what we wanted to do. We had this responsibility, having won the money. We had the attention, because we won this prize, so I think we wanted to return to the basics and think about what it means to create theatre. And that became *Exsimplicity*.

DEVRIENDT: I remember thinking 'OK, we have to make a play now', and then 'I want to make a play about a play – really go into metatheatre'. We were reading Peter Handke's *Offending the Audience*. And we thought of the girl who won the other prize at the festival: 'She also won the prize, let's work together!'. We gave her the job and we worked on this piece. What was good was that the audience also liked that. It could also have been a fucking disaster, but it worked.

BAUWENS: It did show one thing I think. It felt like we were putting our bet on this play *Exsimplicity*, but it wouldn't have worked without at the same time creating *A Smile Off Your Face*. We were starting to say yes to everything at that time, and we got this offer of doing something as part of an exhibition. We started to devise the idea that turned out to be *The Smile Off Your Face* – which basically was meant to be a one-time thing at a festival. But because of the weird structure of that play, it actually became more popular than the play we had devised with the money we got from the government. So for our next application we had two things to show for it. We've done pretty good in the theatre, but we've done something remarkable outside of it as well. And that worked in terms of continuing to get the grants.

DEVRIENDT: Joeri wanted to devise something himself, so he went for that museum commission, which became *The Smile Off Your Face*. On the opening day, the actors went on strike! It was a disaster really the first day. But everybody who saw it was 'There is something in this!', so we never dropped it.

SMET: The concept behind *The Smile Off Your Face* wasn't easy. It had to be tried out. It was made with very little money. And we were just experimenting.

DEVRIENDT: After the strike, Sophie started to help you out.

SMET: She was helping me out before as well, but that's where Sophie decided to take on the scenography. What we wanted to do was put people in a moving chair and let them experience something within the play on the stage. So it took quite some time before we came up with blindfolding them and tying them up and wheeling them around in the space – which was a very good solution.

BAUWENS: We also changed all the actors.

RADOSAVLJEVIĆ: After they went on strike?

BAUWENS: Yes. We fired them.

(Laughter)

SMET: That was also something that we developed: working with actors was also about counting on them as creators. *The Smile Off Your Face* is still pretty much like that.

DEVRIENDT: Seven actors were always working with Sophie and Joeri separately to devise an act, and after a while Sophie and Joeri . . .

SMET: Started editing the material. And started thinking: people are blindfolded, what is their experience, what do they need, what are the essential steps in this performance and what is actually redundant? So gradually it became more concentrated. It was really the essentials of the experience that remained.

DEVRIENDT: After three years it is in the form that it is now. But you couldn't compare the first premiere with the second one three months later. There is only one act still there from that second performance, there's nothing there from the first.

SMET: We designed this assembly line structure of people in, people out, 25 minutes per visitor.

RADOSAVLJEVIĆ: I remember you saying that this was about taking particular theatre conventions to their extreme.

SMET: Yes.

DEVRIENDT: In normal theatre you are immobile, so we made you mobile, in normal theatre you can see, so we took that away, and in normal theatre you could clap your hands, and we tied them together. Those were the basic conventions that Sophie and Joeri were creating for the piece.

SMET: Sometimes you have actors who are used to working with quite authoritarian directors who tell them what to do. And we find that difficult because we really like the actor to invest in it themselves and to be inventive and creative.

DEVRIENDT: But it's also because they have to play for six hours. If they don't feel ownership over it, they wouldn't do it. I wouldn't want to do something somebody told me, that I don't feel strongly about. And the same with *Once and For All*, if the kids didn't feel ownership,

they wouldn't do it 180 times. And that's what works for us as a collective. Everybody has some ownership over what they create. We
don't have a lot of money yet...

BAUWENS: Yet! But we will soon!

DEVRIENDT: Last year, I asked all these actors to work on *A Game of You*
without payment. They knew they were going to play it in several
places and when they did they'd get paid, but even then I felt: if they
don't have ownership over this, it's not worth it. There has to be
something in it for them.

SMET: Quite by chance, a guy from Morocco, a festival programmer, saw
The Smile Off Your Face and invited us to play in Chefchaouen
Festival. That was actually the first time we went out of Belgium, and
it gave us this sudden realisation – 'This thing works! Even in a totally
different culture'.

DEVRIENDT: We went to this city Oujda – and there was nothing there.
The whole factory was closed and there was one barber's shop, one gro-
cery store and one Western Union Money Transfer. Everybody in
the whole city lived on that Western Union Money Transfer. And the
people there, who hadn't seen any theatre at all before, really loved
the performance and came back again and again. Because of several
elements: Moroccan culture is also a social culture, so being in an individual performance, it was like 'I have some time on my own!'. They
could understand it without any knowledge of theatre, and that's something I find really important.

SMET: We are now in 2004.

DEVRIENDT: By then, we had a second round of project funding and we
made *Killusion*. We worked with two professional actors who graduated from the acting school and with Joeri – and the idea was: the
three people on stage say 'yes' to every fantasy. There was a lot of
celebration of fiction on stage.

BAUWENS: Quite contrary to *Exsimplicity*, which was a naked play, more
about the theoretical background of theatre itself. This was a play
that focused on the content, and actors saying yes to each other's
fantasies was moving the play along very fast – from one thing to
another. The stage objects kept changing...

SMET: It really celebrated the playfulness of theatre. Sometimes a bit silly,
but quite inventive all the time. We had toys and they could become
anything.

BAUWENS: Ping pong balls from one scene were the pearls in another scene.

DEVRIENDT: Mobile phones in one scene were midgets in another scene
and poodles in another. I think there were one hundred worlds in one
hour.

BAUWENS: Out of all the plays we've made in the past, this is the one I would most like to see Joeri and Alexander have another stab at.

RADOSAVLJEVIĆ: You say that it is really important that there is a concept that holds a piece together. Does this concept evolve in the process of making the piece, or do you think it up before you propose it?

DEVRIENDT: Gradually we realised that we had to have it beforehand. For instance, saying yes to each other's fantasies was something that evolved in the first week of working with each other; but that's also too open by comparison to 'blindfolded in a wheelchair'.

Each idea that was clear from the beginning was easier to work with. *A Game of You* was a good example. It was based on this very clear idea of me encountering five different versions of myself. I brought it to the table, and everybody was like 'OK, we wanna work on this'. And I mainly saw it as my job to filter all the ideas around the table. We increasingly realised that the more fixed the initial ideas, the more we would get out of improvisations.

SMET: For an actor it's really hard to 'just do something'. Whereas when you have the limits and the boundaries, you can give much more by doing something within that, and still feel like you have the freedom to do what you want. Finding the balance between that took us some time – but *Killusion* was risky, because we were still looking for it.

Killusion was a very successful play and gave us a chance to ask for a two-year grant for structural subsidy. We made an application for our most ambitious, biggest project ever. It was a theatre series called *Soap*, in five instalments. Five full-scale performances that premiered within one month. We took half a year or more to create that, and we wrote the scenarios – something that we never did before. To actually sit at a table, write things out and then go with this text to rehearsals. I think we wanted to make theatre in a serious way somehow. And we found out during that project that it's really not our way of working. Because the ownership for instance, wasn't really there.

DEVRIENDT: Two months before the premiere, we thought 'This is not our thing', but we still had to do it. We were working with famous Belgians and all this shit.

BAUWENS: Because of the whole idea of a soap, we actually engaged some people who were known from actual television soaps. I think those people actually, kind of liked doing it, because they were on stage, which didn't happen often for them, but for us it didn't really feel like we were enjoying ourselves.

SMET: So we had a premiere every week, and after the premiere, the next day we started working like hell on the next one, because we had so little time. And we were working, working, working, and by the last performance all the actors were pale and tired . . .

RADOSAVLJEVIĆ: You said before that the reason why *Soap* didn't work for you was because it had the fourth wall.

DEVRIENDT: And that's why we lost the fourth wall in the next one. We immediately went to work on the next project, *Hard to Get* – it wasn't our best show, but I still like it. It was loosely based on Julian Barnes' *Talking It Over* – not the text, but the idea. You had three people in a love triangle, and they invited the audience to go separately with them, so you had three groups, and the characters telling their side of the relationship, but you only heard two sides of a story. And your friend who was with you could hear two different sides.

It was too text-based still, but I remember that we felt 'OK, we've found ourselves again'. And by then David was calling me for *Internal*.

BAUWENS: I think it was about time that we started to look at performance again. After doing six shows in a row that were basically text-based theatre, it was high time.

RADOSAVLJEVIĆ: Did you say 'You have to make a performance now'?

SMET: David is very good as a producer, but especially as a visionary producer who can say to us 'I think we need this now'.

DEVRIENDT: That is great to have in the group. Joeri, Sophie and I are involved artistically, but David is somebody in the group who reflects on the group. And he can also think ahead. So while we were all doing *Soap* and not sleeping, David was thinking ahead already. David always sees all of our performances, and while seeing a performance for the 50th time, he's thinking about what we need next.

SMET: David also has the most contact with programmers and he always checks what these people like about us and how they see us, and he uses this.

BAUWENS: I don't see all the shows. We played almost 200 shows in 2009/10, I didn't see all of them, but I try to see enough. The thing is, when you watch one show after another, it creates a vibe of something that needs to finish that thread. When you are a spectator, and I try to see the company as a spectator sometimes, you feel like this is going somewhere, but it also needs to be finished somewhere. That's something that I felt most strongly about the trilogy that we have now.

The Smile off Your Face was a good starting point for something and we needed to do something like that again, because it was still our best work. We did seven or eight plays after *The Smile Off Your Face*, but *The Smile Off Your Face* was still the work people were calling me for and was still the work that was playing everywhere. So it became clear we needed to have another one of these.

I also saw that the way these pieces were devised wasn't the way that we were working at the time, which was: you work on something for a few months and then you have a premiere and you start playing. Because the audience was so important in this case, it needed to be tested much more. So I created a working period and a schedule in little blocks: we were going to work there, and at the end of that period we would have a showing – and we'd pull it out of each other with try-outs and avant-premieres, and then premieres that nobody would actually hear about, and then an actual premiere in a big city. And each time we felt we needed to reach a certain level of quality, it had to be finished then – but then there would be another chance to have it really finished.

DEVRIENDT: David talked about this and he said 'I have devised this whole working process, and we need a title'. And he also said 'It's important that we work together as a group again, and not with all the other actors'. And so I said 'Let's call it *Internal* then'. David was 'Ya, I like that title'. Joeri wrote the promo text, which was just mainly: 'David, we have to make this project work. And we don't have a clue what's going to happen. We are going to work maybe with two Moroccans to get special subsidy'. We used irony there, but the first day we sat down with the five people who were involved in *The Smile Off Your Face*, we were like 'What are we gonna do?'.

SMET: That blurb was also a starting point, because I thought: this is internal communication, but suddenly it's there as a promo text. It's something that shouldn't be read by the audience.

DEVRIENDT: That stayed there till the end. At first we had this horrible idea to put people – not in a wheelchair like *The Smile Off Your Face* – but on a stretcher.

BAUWENS: I remember seeing that and going 'What's happening now?!'.
(*Laughter*)

BAUWENS: That stretcher was stored for two years after that . . . We still have it.

SMET: But we were still discussing it very seriously and we even had a little fight over it, over how to push it around.

DEVRIENDT: We were still thinking within the frame of *The Smile Off Your Face*. The assembly line idea, the moving around; and then suddenly I had the idea of just using this personal relationship in a different structure. The internal information idea was still there, and I thought: what if five people came in and we put five actors before them? So don't think in terms of an assembly line, but in terms of a half an hour piece. And from that point on it was easier to fill it in.

SMET: We wanted to single out couples, and once we created the cubicles, we had another starting idea: you go into a cubicle – what happens there? You have the frame already, and then you have the freedom to fill it in. That's how the five cubicles came about. Everybody does something slightly different but essentially the same thing.

DEVRIENDT: Based on their character or their personality.

RADOSAVLJEVIĆ: And you decided the 'personalities' beforehand?

DEVRIENDT: We knew who was going to be in the play. We would say 'OK, we know you are interested in that, so talk about that'.

SMET: Alexander is good at charming people and making them feel comfortable, he could do that. I like to talk about the dark side, and dreams and negative feelings and problems, so 'Joeri, you do that' –

DEVRIENDT: Aurélie [Lannoy] is not really good at English, but she came out of the physical theatre school, she was tactile, so she went for the touching – we really based it on our own personalities. And that was very interesting for us. You play not a character, but a version of yourself.

SMET: We had lists of questions and at the beginning everybody did more or less the same questions, but we started to mould them to our own interests. And by now, in *Internal*, I notice that some people don't use the questions I use at all, or they use a different structure in the conversation. And actually we don't really know what each other are doing...

RADOSAVLJEVIĆ: You haven't done *Internal* with each other?

DEVRIENDT: No, no, no! At the beginning we did it, but then we said they had to have ownership of their own things so they made more and more changes. And I would hate to think that an actor was just going through the questions because you as a spectator would feel there's text involved, and that's the biggest danger of *Internal*. Thanks to David and this process, we could learn this.

In the first showcase we had a very strict scenario in the group that was more about us than about the spectators, and because of the process, we could change it.

SMET: As a trial we did the first version of *Internal* with test persons and they said 'It's not interesting when it's about the relationships between you, the actors, because I'm sitting here and it should be about me'. So then we adapted the whole scenario to the relationship between us and them.

RADOSAVLJEVIĆ: And what about the fantasy, when did that come in?

DEVRIENDT: That was there almost from the beginning. I loved the idea of somebody closing their eyes – immediately they start thinking about things – and I loved the idea that a spectator in the audience could be a creator – but so easily! So easily. You immediately go into it. I ask you to think about a landscape and people are open to doing that. That was so beautiful – that little piece of theatre in the theatre. It was already there in the beginning. And I remember my father at the first showcase in Ghent saying 'This is fucking dangerous!'. We were all shocked – 'What are you saying?!'. We didn't get it, and –

SMET: He was right.

DEVRIENDT: He was right. But we didn't realise that we were creating something on the edge. We were just looking for this possible reality, fictionally. And at the first showcase a couple broke up. And a girl fell in love with me.

SMET: I remember this first session – it was crazy . . . And my first partner had only one arm. So at the start we were all nervous, because this was something really challenging as a performance. And I was like 'OK, now, let's shake hands', and there was no hand! I mean it went wrong from the start.

DEVRIENDT: And Sophie had drunk a little too much vodka, and some guy said to her 'I don't have to click with you', and she was crying over it.

SMET: Sophie was in a bit of a difficult period and she took it as a serious rejection.

DEVRIENDT: And we were going 'Guys, do we really wanna do this?'. And then I got talking with the girl who broke up. She was an intelligent girl, and she said 'Look, you are not the reason, it could have been a book, it could have been a pub, we were bound to break up anyway, thanks to your performance we did'. And I said 'OK, I can live with that'. Because some books, some movies have changed the way I see things. And I love the idea of theatre being dangerous.

BAUWENS: I think it's also part of an evolution. Lots of the shows that we did in the early years came out of some organic process, that you felt like you couldn't do that three times in a row, because you'd probably end up in a very similar situation. So if we wanted to evolve we had to think about what we were actually doing. And then you make a stronger choice of the actual concept you are going to work on. That happened, I think, for the first time in *Internal* – there was some thought being put into what the show needs to be before it started to be created. And that made it easier for a show like *A Game of You* to appear.

DEVRIENDT: In 2008, we had the showcase of *Once and For All* here in Edinburgh. I felt that as a director I needed to see what I want and what I'm good at, and working with youngsters gave me the freedom – it was a sort of playground.

SMET: Also after the *Soap* episode you really needed to get back to basics.

RADOSAVLJEVIĆ: How did it come about?

DEVRIENDT: I remember seeing my younger brother in one of the performances of *Kopergietery*, and seeing that he was having no fun at all. I looked back on the time when I was there as a kid myself and I remembered that I loved the bus trips and everything, but not the actual performing. So I decided to work with this group of people. There were 13 kids. And we worked with a little bit of metatheatre: 'How does an adolescent play adolescence on stage, a cliché version of adolescent?'. They are bright kids, and they loved doing that. I showcased it to Sophie and she found it really interesting, but at the same time I thought it was too 'devised', too intellectual. So I still wasn't happy.

I was also working with them on what happens 'here and now': 'How do you get to the point that you can be yourself as an adolescent?'. And one Sunday afternoon when I had a bit of a hangover after a party, I said to them 'Just sit down on this row of chairs and just leave me alone for a moment', because they were really getting on my nerves – I was watching them, and they were messing around again in no time. I remember one of them dripping saliva out of his mouth and five others underneath trying to catch it. And when I went home, I immediately had the idea – what if they could copy exactly this, and then I would have the paradox of adolescence: that it seems like you are very free as a child, but at the same time you are very self-conscious. Because I constantly felt while they were dong it, that they were doing it for me, even though they acted like they were ignoring me. But I felt they wouldn't have done it if I hadn't been there. Or at least not in the line of chairs.

From that point on I was talking about it with Sophie, although Sophie still had some doubts about it. I said 'But then they could do a hip hop version, followed by a wild version'. And Sophie said 'Isn't that going to be boring?'. And I said 'No, no, no.' We showcased it and everybody felt 'OK, there's a play in this', so we started working on it. We had a really clear concept. I had nine months of work, which is good with the kids. And for the first few months I just created this free space. They could do anything. We went to a second-hand shop, they could buy anything. And they all had ownership of their own performance, even in the devised performance afterwards. Everything they do, they came up with themselves. They didn't have to do anything I told them to. And I did tell them to, if I saw something interesting about them somewhere, even outside rehearsals.

RADOSAVLJEVIĆ: How is *Teenage Riot* similar or different to that?

DEVRIENDT: In *Once and For All* you had 13 kids on stage and they didn't care about what the audience thought. There was so much to do between them. We played it ourselves once – you are so busy, you don't really care whether the audience is sitting there. So it feels truthful.

In *Teenage Riot* – I also want to protect them. They are kids, they are not professional performers. They are inside a box on stage and they are cameramen, actors and directors themselves inside the box. By being put within confinement and being allowed not to care about the audience outside, they have the same kind of freedom. But what is different in *Teenage Riot* is that I also devised the content more with them. They'd all seen *Once and For All*. I knew them already – some I knew for five years. So in this performance I was more of a filter for their feelings. But this was also working with eight people, so it's easier to work with personalities then.

RADOSAVLJEVIĆ: What I liked about *Teenage Riot* is that the use of the camera takes the audience's focus onto something that's very specific and cuts out all the potential incompetences of the young performers. So it becomes about something else other than young people performing.

DEVRIENDT: Young people behaving! Because you can choose with your camera where you fix it. Which they devised. But like a Youtube movie you don't know if it's real or not.

RADOSAVLJEVIĆ: Yes, Youtube is a very useful point of reference.

DEVRIENDT: If somebody says in their Youtube movie 'I wanna kill everybody in my school' – there are Youtube movies like that – I don't know if it's real or not. And I like it if you can have the same feeling on stage.

SMET: I think we were always a little bit allergic to having to count on suspension of disbelief in the audience.

RADOSAVLJEVIĆ: And in dealing with those realities, how was it doing *Internal* six, seven times a day last year in Edinburgh?

SMET: If you do it for such a long time, it really is your job talking to people. Doing it at a festival is problematic because you see people who have been to the performance everywhere: in the festival bar, and you get more confrontations, and there is the buzz at the festival – you see various Facebook references. What was special about Edinburgh was that there were ethical concerns about it, when people were looking at the performers too personally – too upset or too much in love. So that was quiet challenging – to feel the boundaries of what you do as a performer and how real the fiction can get.

There was also the impact of the controversy around it. And you'd be wondering 'What am I actually doing here? Am I really fucking people up or not?'. You'd start to question that. But afterwards we performed it in other countries and I didn't have that feeling any more.

RADOSAVLJEVIĆ: Oh, really?!

SMET: Like in Italy, it felt quite relaxed. And people reacted differently. In a kinder way, somehow, or in a more distanced way. I remember thinking after that, 'Edinburgh was extremely hard'.

We really noticed in Italy that having flirtatious conversations was something that happens on a daily basis with strangers. So they took to that very easily: 'Oh, yes, we are doing that, go ahead!'. Here you had all this 'Is she really flirting? Is this really a relationship? Is she really into me?', thinking about it all, taking it very seriously. I think these performances also reveal certain cultural patterns.

RADOSAVLJEVIĆ: You had people coming back, people who wanted to see it again. How was that to deal with?

SMET: I remember this one girl disguising herself to get in again, and actually moving herself in the line up to be with me again. She was quite well disguised because I didn't recognise her until we were in the cubicle.

BAUWENS: Yes, that happened several times.

SMET: In the cubicle she took off her glasses and her wig. And I was like 'Oh, my God, it's you again!'. The first time I already found her a little bit freaky, so the second time I was thinking 'I've got a stalker here'.

RADOSAVLJEVIĆ: You were the one who was asking the questions in the circle of the person who went into the corner. Knowing that you are the company dramaturg, I was thinking about the way in which the dramaturgy of the piece is actually performed as part of it.

SMET: I must say we came up with the name dramaturg to find a clear way of communicating. But it shifts, sometimes I am the writer, sometimes I'm the performer.

DEVRIENDT: We always look for the compatibilities within the collective, more so than looking for the equal communist democratic way. That's an evolution that hasn't finished yet.

We all help to devise the piece. And I work well with Joeri because he really understands what I'm doing. For instance, in *Once and For All* he wrote some text, whereas in *Teenage Riot* it was less writing text and more 'I want to help you tell this story'. That's two kinds of working as a dramaturg.

SMET: It's also looking for: 'What does this piece need?'. In *Teenage Riot*, most of the text was already there, but there was a question of 'How are we gonna put all this together into a good structure?'.

DEVRIENDT: What helps in a working process like that is one question that I could always have at the back of my mind. With *Internal*: 'How fast can you build a valuable relationship with one person?'. And with *A Game of You*: 'How do you create your viewpoint of a personality?'. *Teenage Riot*: 'Is a riot still possible?'. And with *Once and For All* it's

'A celebration of teenage of destructiveness'. There is always one sentence that helps me test if the piece is still saying this.

RADOSAVLJEVIĆ: I really like that definition of ensemble in terms of 'compatibility' rather than 'democracy'.

DEVRIENDT: I really have that feeling, because each of us can discover what we are good at. It's a joy that that is possible.

SMET: But it's also a luxury, I think. Because the last time I was on stage, in *Soap*, I didn't feel like acting anymore. If I had been exclusively an actor, I would have been in big trouble. Within the company, I can suddenly feel again the urge 'I really would like to be on stage again'. And there is space for that.

References

Costa, Maddy (2011) 'Scratching at the surface of Ontroerend Goed', *States of Delinquence Blog*, 9 December, http://statesofdeliquescence.blogspot.com/2011/12/scratching-at-surface-of-ontroerend.html (accessed 19 December 2012).

Gardner, Lyn (2007) '*The Smile Off Your Face* is more therapy than theatre', *The Guardian Blog*, 17 August, http://www.guardian.co.uk/stage/theatreblog/2007/aug/17/thesmileoffyourfaceismor (accessed 19 December 2012).

Hillaert, Wouter (2010) '(Long) live the experience: reflections on performance, pleasure and perversion', *Contemporary Theatre Review*, 20(4): 432–6.

McMillan, Joyce (2007) 'The Smile Off Your Face', 17 August, http://joycemcmillan.wordpress.com/2007/08/17/smile-off-your-face/ (accessed 19 December 2012).

Trueman, Matt (2009) 'Going back inside: *Internal* revisited', 6 September, http://carouseloffantasies.blogspot.com/2009/09/going-back-inside-internal-revisited.hrml (accessed 19 December 2012).

Ontroerend Goed
http://www.ontroerendgoed.be/projects.php

22 Towards a global ensemble

Richard Jordan (Richard Jordan Productions)

Having seen Cameron Macintosh in a TV interview, Richard Jordan, then aged 11, wrote him a letter to ask how one becomes a theatre producer. Macintosh replied with the advice to see as much theatre as possible, and four years later he offered him a work experience on *Cats*. Jordan's career started at the age of 16, working as assistant to Peter Wilson, a London-based producer who entrusted him with looking after the Edinburgh run of *Dylan Thomas: Return Journey*, directed by Anthony Hopkins.

Following his original inspiration, Jordan picked the Oxford School of Drama to train as a stage manager because of its links with the 'Cameron Macintosh Chair in Drama' at Oxford University. That year the Chair was held by Alan Ayckbourn and producer Michael Codron. A firm believer in networking, Jordan kept in touch and eventually worked with both of those men. After a stint as the manager of the Cottesloe at the Royal National Theatre, Richard Jordan founded his own production company in 1998.

Richard Jordan became the main producer of Conor McPhereson's early plays in the UK and also took some of the playwright's work to New York and to Sao Paolo. In 2000 he produced and directed a site-specific anniversary production of Stephen Sondheim's *Sweeny Todd*. In the same year, he won the TIF/Society of London Theatre Producers Award, and in 2004 he was featured for the first time as one of the top 100 UK theatre professionals in *The Stage* newspaper. Since 2005 Jordan has been a regular contributor for *The Stage* and he has also appeared as a guest speaker at numerous panels and training institutions in the UK and internationally.

Based in London, Jordan continues to produce internationally and at the Edinburgh Festival Fringe. He has produced over 160 productions in the UK and 16 other countries. His productions have won a variety of awards and received nominations for both the Tony and Olivier awards. Recent hits have included the South African monologue *Itsoseng* by Omphile Molusi, Cora Bissett and Stef Smith's *Roadkill*, and the UK runs

of the Belgian company Ontroerend Goed. As part of the Cultural
Olympiad in 2012, Jordan brought to London the Australian company
One Step at a Time Like This with their site-specific piece *en route*, and
the Chicago-based ensemble The Q Brothers with their hip hop version
of *Othello* as part of the Globe to Globe World Shakespeare season.

   This interview took place in October 2011 in Ghent, Belgium.

Interview

JORDAN: The West End has never been the most exciting place for me –
the West End is where you may end up with something. Far more
exciting theatre happens elsewhere. The West End, like Broadway, is
a commodity – you need it because it also fuels a theatrical economy.
The two need to work hand in hand – you can't have one without the
other in many ways. I actually think that the gulf is not as big as people claim it to be, and the art of producing is to find work that is both
artistic and commercial or populist. There's a great stigma attached to
what people believe are commercial producers. I call myself a 'creative
producer' because if you look at some of the work I produce you'd say
'This is completely uncommercial'. But I also have to be realistic – I
don't receive grants to do my work. I have to run my company as a
business: pay the staff who work for me and the bills and, although it's
now become synonymous with the tap dancing feet of Broadway, I
work in a business that is called 'show business'.

RADOSAVLJEVIĆ: Would you see your work as developing in ways that are
groundbreaking?

JORDAN: Nearly everything that happens in theatre has been done
before – it's the same with almost anything. You are only as good as
your last show. I would say that the most interesting and important
thing is to have your own identity. Even if only you know what that
is and no one else does. I know exactly every reason why I do a show,
the passion behind it and what interests me.

   The art of producing is basically to be able to link all the collaborative talents together, help to guide that process and make it happen.
The worst type of producing is the one where the producer doesn't
work as part of a team, where they feel that they have to do it all
themselves to seek some sort of personal accolade. That usually turns
into a complete shambles because the producer is usually running
around very stressed and doing the polar opposite of inspiring any
kind of confidence or leadership. I trust absolutely everyone that I
work with, that's why I work with a lot of the same people regularly,
but you have to have artistic faith in what you're doing and who you

are working with. You've got to also have the courage to fail and be adaptable, because things don't always work in the way that you think they will. Theatre requires fluidity and a vision, which is also what makes it exciting.

RADOSAVLJEVIĆ: You work with several ensembles – Ontroerend Goed, The Q Brothers, and One Step at a Time Like This. What makes this interesting is that one is a Belgian ensemble, one is an American ensemble and one is an Australian ensemble, so there is this notion that you facilitate the ensemble way of working in a global way. It also seems to me that you've got a lot more international work developing than has been the case up until your generation?

JORDAN: Yes, I think that's true. The world has got a lot, lot smaller through the Internet and travel. I can actually watch the first day of rehearsals in a rehearsal room in New York or in Chicago, or in Brazil, on a webcam in my office in London. Twenty years ago you couldn't do that! That's made the global theatre economy become much smaller because technology has allowed that to happen, which means that we can become much more aware of what's happening in Belgium, or what's happening in India – because there's much more awareness on the Internet. That's allowed a lot of my generation to become international producers on a bigger scale.

Another element of producing is: you've got to understand the culture, you've got to understand people, you've got to understand how it works – and that's where the element of teamwork comes together. You have to command a level of respect, and producing is terribly lonely, because when it's all going wrong, you've also still got to be able to lead that team with confidence. If you have terrible reviews for a show, you've got to be able to walk in the next day and still motivate a team of people however much your heart might be breaking. As an actor, director, and designer, if a show closes or a company folds then OK, it's tragic and heartbreaking, but you can walk away and probably go on and eventually find another acting, designing or directing job. But for a producer, if you get it wrong, you could lose everything and that's then the end of your career.

Closing a show is as important as how you open it. When and where we put on Ontroerend Goed is incredibly important – the strategy is one of careful placement that can be adapted and moulded to the fundamental success of every production wherever they play. Placing any show is about what instinctively and aesthetically you feel is right for the show, and it is of critical importance for you as a producer to serve the work to the best of your ability. Plymouth Drum Theatre have been a key player with us in driving forward the success of Ontroerend Goed through a shared belief, trust and relationship we have built over several years of happily working together.

From an international perspective, these relationships and collaborations only come from getting out around the world and taking the time to understand those economies. If you want to get work in China – which of course is going to be a huge market in coming years – you have to allow yourself a good number of weeks to actually be there, meet those people, almost become part of that family community, and understand the way that their theatre economy works. The worst thing is to think that we UK theatre producers, directors or artists can stride into various countries and arrogantly tell them what to do. I mean, many of these countries already have their own healthy theatre economy that we can enhance and add to, and share knowledge about.

RADOSAVLJEVIĆ: Was Ontroerend Goed a risk in any way when you first discovered them?

JORDAN: Ontroerend Goed was a bit unusual in the way I discovered them because I gate-crashed their show *The Smile Off Your Face* – as it had completely sold out in Edinburgh. I got tipped off by the theatre critic Philip Fisher who said to me 'Richard, I've just been to this great show, you get tied up and blindfolded in a wheelchair and you get talked to by a beautiful girl on a bed – it's a true Edinburgh Fringe experience'. I hurtled down to C Venues only to discover that this was its last day. When I arrived, there was complete chaos because they had won the Fringe First the day before and the box office had oversold the performance. David [Bauwens], Ontroerend Goed's General Manager, was in the foyer trying unsuccessfully to pacify audience members with tickets to see the Oxford University Dramatic Society's production of *Company* instead. Myself and another lady called Christie Anthoney, the director of the Adelaide Fringe, who also wanted to see it, bumped into each other at the venue and we decided that if we sat round a corner, no one would notice if we were just to sneak in. So, in the muddle we just sat on these two chairs by the door to the venue and became the last two people to go in and do the show in Edinburgh. Alexander [Devriendt] was the actor at the end of *The Smile Off Your Face* who cried for me in the performance, and Christie and I both walked out at the end of the performance and said 'This is the most extraordinary experience we've both ever had in Edinburgh'. As we stood talking in the foyer, members of the company started coming out and Christie said to me 'What do you think? Shall I take it to Adelaide?', and I said 'You have to take this show to Adelaide', and at that point Alexander came out and we started a conversation. I didn't know at the time that he was the artistic director of Ontroerend Goed, but that conversation led on to a relationship where we hit it off, and we then re-connected again in Adelaide because the show did go there.

In Adelaide, Alexander started to tell me about *Once and for All*, the show he had started to work on with kids. Then, out of the blue, the Traverse – who I have a long relationship with – suddenly phoned me up and said 'We're delighted to hear that you are producing Ontroerend Goed in Edinburgh!'. I said 'Really?', and they said 'Yes, we're absolutely thrilled to hear, because we were worried about these crazy Belgians we had heard about – and now we know there's a grown up doing this!'. (I can testify they really are not that crazy, only when they are performing their shows!) Consequently that became a co-production, and since then *Smile, Internal, Teenage Riot*.

The thing that I needed to do after getting involved was work out how you move a small company from Ghent and build with them on their success. We had been fortunate that the Battersea Arts Centre had been a key ally and a supporter in the development of the shows. *Smile* is an important show because it is what I call a 'door opener show'. Every talented small company really benefits from having one in their stable. *en route* is the same with One Step at a Time Like This, *Roadkill* is the same for Cora Bissett – these shows can make a strong impression and prove to be very popular. With a small capacity, they quickly become hot tickets and take on a great reputation; people can get very excited and inspired by what they're watching, and out of these you can hopefully engender conversation for the next show. The fact that Sydney Theatre Company got to see *Smile* at the Sydney Festival led to *Once and For All* touring Australia with them, and three or four years later that led to a co-production with us all on *A History of Everything*. With any show, none of this is going to happen overnight; it begins with putting on a good show and then building relationships.

RADOSAVLJEVIĆ: You have already spoken about the importance of art meeting business in what you do, but what about a show like *Internal*, which is just for five audience members at a time, where you can't sell as many tickets as you would if you were doing a conventional proscenium arch piece? How do you as a producer take that financial risk?

JORDAN: With great care. *Smile* and *Internal* are almost always festival shows, they do those seasons because they suit that context well and there is a different funding structure where they can play a run. Nonetheless, with shows like these everyone has to be sensible and realistic about the budget. I view these styles of intimate or indeed site-specific shows as great platforms for a company, writer or artist, and it is from the success of these often early works that get discovered, that you can build upon the interest in the work. You are still not producing or presenting these out of blind love – we are all working to make them be affordable and try to cover their costs. To this end, some of these theatres where we have toured have also been quite clever – they've treated it like this is a massively exclusive event, this show is completely sold out. So they'll do a benefit performance where they're selling tickets at a much higher ticket price – because it becomes a show that people want to come and see. If the show is successful or has a vital message or role in raising particular awareness of an issue, you want it to reach as many people as possible. Depending on the nature of the work, one such way for a smaller capacity show such as *Roadkill* is through international licence. For example, it may not be affordable to take *Roadkill* to some of the Northern European countries where we want to take it – and where the issue of sex trafficking and raising greater awareness surrounding the issue is very relevant – but we could do a translation and Cora Bissett, who conceived and directed the play, could come out and direct it, working with a team of people in that country, which also means that it could thereafter stay in the repertoire.

RADOSAVLJEVIĆ: You started building your career around text-based theatre and then ventured into this more performance-like work that's scripted in a different way. How did that occur for you?

JORDAN: I've seen a lot of work in Edinburgh. While it may not be obvious what I choose to produce and develop, as I have an interest in a lot of different areas of theatre, I make choices for very specific reasons, the biggest being that it is something I connect with and feel passionate about working on. I have always been interested in theatre in other countries and ideas, whether that is coming from text-based drama or an interactive piece of theatre.

The thing that most drives me crazy in the arts is the way people are so quick to dismiss things in a generalised and sometimes arrogant and pompous way. For example, people saying 'I hate musicals but I like Stephen Sondheim', or 'I hate ballet but I like Matthew Bourne'. These sorts of remarks I find ridiculously condescending. By all means don't like something, but don't generalise an entire art form – at least afford it with a deserved respect.

I like the fact that everyone has their own opinion. If theatre can make you feel something, even if it can make you hate a piece of work, it still is provoking something that another genre cannot necessarily do as successfully. When I produced Ontroend Goed's *Audience* in Edinburgh, it provoked strong reactions, but the people in Edinburgh who hated *Audience* still wrote quite a lot of stuff about how much they disliked it. Elsewhere we have played, several people proceeded to get cross towards those who were liking or defending it. Ultimately, no one is ever going to please everyone all of the time, so it's not worth beating yourself up about it. But just getting up and creating work takes incredible courage and therefore, as an industry, we should try to be generous in respecting this.

RADOSAVLJEVIĆ: Let's talk a little bit about this notion of you as a producer connecting people with places – you are working with up to maybe a dozen different companies, writers, festivals and theatres around the world, often all at the same time. You're taking different kinds of works to different kinds of places, and you said something yesterday about the particular cultural contexts that generate particular kinds of works –

JORDAN: This isn't exclusively just the way I think – a lot of people think like this around the world. To me, theatre works in different cities in very specific ways. Ontroerend Goed works in Ghent for many, many reasons, but one of them is linked to the question: 'What is the DNA that makes a creative city?'. If you look at Edinburgh – long before the festival existed, it was a creative city that was inhabited by writers, so the festival really is a logical extension of that. But what makes a city become creative? In Ghent, the urban, young population is growing by five per cent each year – there's a lively university student feel. That's very significant towards the makings of a creative city. If you look around the world, those cities that have a creative growth within them have an expansion of urban youth running parallel with it, often from university students staying on in that city. If you have that, then what you find is that your exposure to culture is completely different: if you've got public art, you've got theatre, you've got street entertainers – all of those will be contributing to the creative growth and awareness of a city and its inhabitants both visibly and psychologically. Those people who also grow up in these cities are being exposed to that culture at a very young age. If you take Edinburgh again, many of those kids who are growing up in Edinburgh are exposed to culture because of the festival at a very young age, so it actually becomes part of their soul, it becomes part of their own DNA make up. So culture just feels accessible, a part of their lifestyle and, more importantly, throughout their lives it will be part of the choices they make in where they choose to live.

If you put alongside this the component of the geographical location of a city, what makes a theatre, or a cultural, artistic city survive or succeed is its geographical layout. And by that I mean the urban density. If you have mass urban density in a city 10 minutes' walk away from the centre, you will find that you are thus encouraging people to walk, to take public transport, to sit and drink in a café, and actually with that you breed conversation, you breed creative collision. Sooner or later someone is going to sit down with someone in a café and have a conversation about something. Someone's going to overhear a street conversation, you're going to hear something on a bus. And if you've got that collision happening on the streets close to the heart of the city centre, where people are moving around and walking, I think you'll find art starting to breed.

We were talking earlier about how easy it is to be able to connect in today's world with people from so many different countries. We also have with the Internet an ability to connect in ways with others that we never before imagined; however, as a result, digital contact has actually regularly taken the direct personal face-to-face interaction out of the process. We can go on the Internet, on Twitter, or Facebook – we can be talking to someone somewhere, who we'll never actually meet in our lives. But when you go into an environment where there is a café culture and mass density of population and transportation and collisions on the streets, you begin to connect all over again. Out of that, you help breed a living creative and cultural economy.

If you put all those things together, then eventually out of that is going to stem at some point, somewhere, some sort of artistic collaboration. Take Ontroerend Goed in Ghent – a bunch of artists, poets and friends, all from different parts of the city and region, who collide in a cultural hub via the streets, cafes and bars of Ghent. One Step at a Time in Australia – they're all friends that collide, they've got similar interests because they meet each other through the community they work in and the big café culture of Melbourne. The Q Brothers collective – slightly different, but Chicago has a very urban, very kinetic vibe, because it is an American city where people walk. If you look in LA you don't find the same collectives because people are driving often on their own in the car.

This is why *Once and For All* worked in Ghent with its teenage cast, but it may not have worked if you created it in another city even in Belgium. It's the fact that those youngsters from Ghent are exposed to culture from a very young age just as their parents were, but they also have a direct and visible cultural exchange going with where they and their friends all connect together.

RADOSAVLJEVIĆ: What's the actual professional background of the people of One Step at a Time and The Q Brothers?

JORDAN: One Step at a Time were artists and actors. Julian [Rickert] was very interested in digital, technical media, and they were free thinking theatre artists in the way in which you fuse different art forms together – they all met through various projects and conversations finding they shared the same passion and interest. In the case of The Q Brothers it was two brothers and a group of individuals who came together and became friends through a shared interest in hip hop, whose artists respect the art of language and verse. When some of them stumbled upon Shakespeare they all believed that if he was alive today he'd be Eminem! The Q's first show *Bombitty of Errors* came out of necessity to make a work that could couple these interests together.

RADOSAVLJEVIĆ: In Europe there are creative processes that tend to last over a number of months, as opposed to a three or four week rehearsal period in the UK. How do you negotiate around the challenges of that?

JORDAN: That was quite a big challenge for Sydney Theatre Company with *The History of Everything*. Because here suddenly there was a significantly longer rehearsal period than they've ever been used to. With Sydney we said 'That's the way that Ontroerend Goed work. So if you want the show, that's what you're signing on to do'.

RADOSAVLJEVIĆ: How many of the Australians are involved?

JORDAN: There are three Australian actors that are doing the show. So it's half Belgian from the Ontroerend Goed ensemble and half Australian from the Sydney Theatre Company ensemble. This makes it a really interesting collaboration where we all share and learn from each other, and a vast range of valuable knowledge and skills that get brought to the production.

RADOSAVLJEVIĆ: Does that mean that you would have to invest more than you would with a British theatre company?

JORDAN: Yes, to the extent that you are rehearsing a production like this for a longer period of time, but I think that this is another interesting point about the rise of international work. With people linking together and partnering much more, they begin to understand the nature of how these different countries work and make art. People have started to develop a respect and understanding that if you work and want to work with a particular country, then they create in this way. The more you see this represented in various collaborations, the more it is understood and respected. An example could be Robert Lepage, who creates a show over two or three years, developing it in runs in different places. There was a time when people would say 'Well, why do they need this sort of time?', but the fact is: good art takes time however you want to do it. Of course, here we are dealing with work that is being created from scratch; we're not necessarily picking up a play which already exists and provides some template to work from. It's something that makes some people in some organisations nervous when they first get told this is what will be needed, and I greatly admire them when they recognise this is the model these artists work with and then continue to have the courage to support this process. Thanks to those people like BITE at the Barbican and many other organisations, these working models have become accessible forms of creation both in an international artists' home country and on the global map. Peter Daubeny used to bring a lot of amazing world stage companies to the World Theatre Season in the 1960s and 1970s at the Aldwych.[1] But they were always seen as the two-week visit of this particular state company. They weren't being integrated in the way that companies can do now – where we can have Sydney Theatre Company collaborating with Ontroerend Goed and us and Theatre Royal Plymouth and City Theatre of Amsterdam and Vooruit in Belgium.

RADOSAVLJEVIĆ: I can see that there is more understanding, but what impact does it have simply on the notion of business?

JORDAN: It has an impact because people are often rehearsing over a long period of time. But it's a very difficult question to answer because it would depend on what the budget of that show is. If you've got a show that's got 20 people in it, then the impact is going to be a lot higher than if you've got a one-actor play. And also rehearsals are not always happening consistently through the six, eight or nine months in which the production is created. It might be that there is a period of work that is done and then people go away and then come back again. With *A History of Everything*, we did a month's development in Sydney during November 2010. It's still hard for some theatres to understand and sign on to this production model. But if you are going to work with some of these companies, that's the deal. I would hope that anybody who wants to come in to work with or produce a particular theatre company or artist is going to want to do it because they've got a particular awareness of their work. If they're just coming because they've heard 'Oh, this company is really trendy', it is not the right reason to work together.

RADOSAVLJEVIĆ: How would you summarise what's necessary for good collaboration?

JORDAN: You've got to get on with everyone and become part of that gang or team. You've got to have a sense of humour. You've got to understand that people work very differently, and that's why you have to spend time with them and understand how they work and why it works. You need to understand the vision of the company and contribute to that growth and development. In working with a playwright on the development of a play and its many drafts, you need to understand writers and be approaching this from a good background knowledge. In both cases it is all about trust and mutual respect, but also nothing is more important than the show, and all of you are the engine that's making the thing happen. Having a big star in a show is a great component, but the most important thing is having what you believe is a good piece of work to begin with.

What makes any collaboration a good one? I think it's understanding each other's shorthand and having the courage to fail. When I work with people like Ontroerend Goed, we are all beside each other through good times and bad times. I'm interested in long runs, my career being one of them, but equally you have to understand that people can't be marvellous or geniuses every day of the week. Everyone in a theatre show makes an enormous act of faith and trust when they decide to work with each other.

Theatre and producing is probably 99 per cent luck and one per cent very good luck, but it also does require a modicum of skill and common sense. The thing that it does require most is knowledge drawn from experience, but that's the same with running any company.

Note

1 These were seven-week long seasons of world theatre sponsored by the RSC and the Arts Council taking place annually between 1964 and 1975 (http://www.thisistheatre.com/londontheatre/aldwychtheatre.html).

Bibliography

Inverne, James (2000) *The Impresarios*, London: Oberon Books.
Smith, Alistair (2008) 'Producer Richard Jordan recognised as British young business leader', *The Stage*, 1 April, available online at http://www.thestage.co.uk/news/2008/04/producer-richard-jordan-recognised-as-british-young-business-leader/ (accessed 19 December 2012).

Richard Jordan
http://www.bbc.co.uk/norfolk/content/articles/2009/02/06/richard_jordan_baftas_20090206_feature.shtml.

Index

Note: Plays by single authors are listed under their names; other plays and productions under their titles.